QABALISTIC
CONCEPTS

QABALISTIC CONCEPTS

LIVING THE TREE

William G. Gray

WEISER BOOKS
Boston, MA/York Beach, ME

First published in 1997 by
Red Wheel/Weiser, LLC
York Beach, ME
With editorial offices at:
368 Congress Street
Boston, MA 02210
www.redwheelweiser.com

Library of Congress Cataloging-in-Publication Data

Gray, William G.
    Qabalistic concepts : living the tree / William G. Gray.
        p.   cm.
    Rev. ed. of: Concepts of Qabalah. 1984.
    Includes index.
    ISBN 1-57863-000-2 (pbk. : alk. paper)
    1. Cabala—Miscellanea. 2. Sangreal Sodality (Society).
   I. Gray, William G. Concepts of Qabalah. II. Title.
   BP605.S116G72   1997
   135'.47—dc21   96-47895
                                       CIP

BJ

Printed in the United States of America

08 07 06 05 04
11 10 9 8 7 6 5 4

The paper used in this publication meets the minimum require-
ments of the American National Standard for Information
Sciences—Permanence of Paper for Printed Library Materials
Z39.48-1984.

Contents

KEEP QUESTING!

Also by Wm. G. Gray

Introduction

When most people hear the mysterious word "Qabalah" (or Cabala, or Kabbalah), they may have vague ideas that it is something extremely abstruse and probably Jewish. If so, they would be only partly correct. The word itself does derive from the Hebrew root QBL, signifying to meet or embrace instruction, admit or allow a law, receive or obtain. By implication it points to a "secret tradition" known only to a few select scholars and imparted by them directly to carefully chosen disciples down the ages. In early days it was entirely an oral teaching, like that of the Druids. It did not reach a literary public until the late Middle Ages, and remained an obscure topic of interest only to the most eclectic students of esoterica until the nineteenth century. It did not become freely available until this century, mostly since World War II. Even now, although many have heard of it, relatively few could give a good description of what it is and of what use it might be in a modern world.

The fundamentals of Qabalah are really very simple. It is essentially a search for "God," "ultimate identity," or however a human life quest might be termed, by using a system of mathematically relatable concepts acceptable to a consciousness activated by rationality and logic, as well as romantic idealism and imagination. Civilization depends on the human qualities of literacy and numeracy—thinking with both words and figures—which, though obviously connected, are distinct capabilities. People who are "good with figures" are often deficient in literary ability and vice versa. It may also be noted that mathematics and music (which really consists of sonic values) frequently "go together." Ever since man learned to count and calculate, we have had a kind of Qabalah in this world.

The particular arrangement of Qabalah which survives among Western culture today is based on Hebraic principles from sources related to those which produced the Bible, and which have had such a marked effect on trading, commerce, and finance throughout our history. Other cultures have evolved their systems, such as the Chinese I Ching, the almost universal practice of astrology, the Pythagorean spiritual system of numbers, or the arcane teachings in triadic form of the Druids. The Qabalah we know and study now is far from being exclusively Hebrew. It has Hebrew as its language base because it derives from documents and legends recorded in that language by Semitic scholars principally for their own purposes, phrased in their own idioms and couched in obscure allusions which are difficult for others to grasp. To compound the confusion, early translators produced their versions mainly in classical Latin which only a minority of educated people could read. When some of this was converted into European languages it was usually in the stilted and torturous phraseology of the times, complicated by literal interpretations of figurative or allegorical terminology. It is scarcely surprising the word "Qabalistic" became synonymous with "incomprehensible."

Nevertheless, all these non-Hebrew scholars and specialists through centuries of Western culture had been struggling with the metaphysical concepts involved, and in one way or another were converting their systematic presentation into forms acceptable to our ideology in particular. Mathematics are of themselves a pure "language of the mind" applicable to all human cultures alike, and it was eventually realized that Qabalah was supposed to be a "language of the soul" understandable to anyone with beliefs in its primal principles. Hence, exponents of this westernized Qabalah have steadily improved its image and expanded its techniques. In the post-war era, Qabalah has been properly modernized and has become an integral part of Western esotericism. Anyone of average intelligence should be able to comprehend and appreciate it as a valid and practical philosophy of spiritual life values.

The concepts of Qabalah which you are being asked to follow in this book are a straightforward 1-2-3 set of studies based on the latest developments in this century which align the old principles with our modern alphabet and current outlook. So much of our present living is numerate. Our lives are bounded by times, prices, amounts, calculations, percentages, and proportions. If only we might work this on a spiritual rather than a purely material basis, we might become better humans than we generally are. Let us face it: this world greatly needs improvement in overall human characteristics if we are to survive into the next century.

A better world is impossible without better people, and that calls for changes in human nature itself. An alteration of attitude from materialism to spirituality is needed if we are ever to evolve beyond the limits of mortal embodiment on this earth. This can only be accomplished by making spiritual values and considerations the main motivations of our conduct. For many millennia, religions of all kinds have been trying to reach human hearts deeply enough to accomplish such a miraculous transformation, yet they have not shown any worldwide signs of success, largely because humanity is inherently unable to recognize or relate satisfactorily with a "God" we are unable to find in ourselves.

Qabalah is not in itself any form of religion. It is more of a "way of working" with the inner principles of life, the "powers that be" behind Being, so that it relates most directly and intimately with our natures, not through any sense of the supernatural, but in terms of pure values applied to everyday awareness. In using Qabalah, we encounter spiritual principles with absolutely everything we evaluate. Practicing Qabalists are not merely reminded of spiritual values every time we think in evaluative terms, we actually *experience* them to the depth or degree invoked. Though this might be slight on each separate occasion, the total built up during a lifetime produces a considerable effect. That is a major use of Qabalah in the modern world.

There is, of course, a literary side to Qabalah as well. Every numeration or value-combination has a definite archetypal quality connected with it, but this is regarded as an effect rather than a cause. For instance, the quality of *mercy* is an outcome of quarternity and not the other way around. Be quarternal in order to be merciful. Just as you use a number-code to telephone someone, so would a Qabalist use a number sequence to contact specific classes of spiritual consciousness. Perhaps it might seem odd to say that Qabalah is a matter of knowing the cosmic directory of "God departments" but that could be a modern analogy.

In order to make any mind work most effectively, its owner must be able to classify, marshal, and direct all its available consciousness at will. Just as a musician has to know which notes to combine in what manner before a melody can be meaningful, so must a thinker know how to choose and connect every item within his range in order to make maximum sense out of everything. It is the aim of Qabalah to formulate and use a "master code" which automatically selects the most effective currents of consciousness available. Theoretically, that should be as simple as dialing a phone and waiting for a response. Everything depends on how practiced in the application of its primal principles the Qabalist becomes, and that is something each must determine.

In this book which embodies the concepts of Qabalah, you will find the learning system laid out like an instruction course, with test questions at the end of each Chapter/Lesson. If you want to obtain maximum value for your money and effort, you should practice the recommended exercises to the best of your ability and answer the questions only after spending not less than two weeks on each Chapter. For a full description of how you should treat this material, see the Introduction of my previous book, *Western Inner Workings*, and follow the general outlines given there.

Whatever you do, don't be tempted to think, "Oh, this is old stuff, I've read all about the Tree of Life before. It can't teach me anything I don't know already." That would be a bad mistake which could cost you a lot in terms of lost learning. Qabalah itself *is* old, very old. Approaches to it and methods of use, however, are constantly changing to keep pace with current consciousness. In these pages you will encounter such new changes. Another century will make them out of date too, but those wanting to comprehend future changes will have to find out how they happened through studying present developments. This is why my material is presented in this particular way.

You might wonder why the art of Qabalah should be connected with the Sangreal concept which concerns the spiritual quest of Western souls for their own particular inner inheritance. No literate inner tradition could really be considered as complete in itself without a corresponding numerate tradition to accompany it. Imagine a culture without any form of mathematical computation whatsoever, or the slightest conception of what values meant. Attempts to do this might boggle the best imagination, an only certainty being that such a culture must necessarily be unstable and altogether unpredictable. An equal imbalance would be a numerate culture without a literate one. In this world, the system known as Qabalah is the only coherent, workable, and dependable scheme relating computable values with spiritual realities. There are therefore no reasonable alternatives; it is utterly unique. So either we accept it as a workable hypothesis for a concept which it adequately supports in practice, or we have nothing more to offer than idealistic mysticism en masse.

The majority of spiritual and religious systems do not openly proclaim or emphasize any particular connection between their doctrine and a sense of numeracy. This leaves a great gap between human beliefs in fundamental life principles and a working relationship with life by evaluation of our experiences with it.

By not attaching any special spiritual significance to our conscious numeration code, we deprive ourselves of a primary mystical faculty for directly connecting ourselves with the life power considered as Deity by so many humans.

Early Semitic scholars believed in getting away from basics as soon as they could and involved themselves in one complication after another until they lost themselves in a mystical maze of their own meanderings. This was not unlike the tales of the Arabian Nights wherein one character began to tell a story which contained another character commencing a different account, and so on until a reader or listener became too bewildered to follow any further and just listened in a half-hypnotized state of suspended interest for the sake of *dolce far niente.*

We of the West believe more in pursuit of purpose until consciousness clarifies our minds enough to continue the quest along other lines. Some of us might be like the strange Questing Beast of the old Grail story. This was a smallish white female animal of an appealing nature which had twelve hounds inside her. These emerged when she reached a blood-colored cross and they tore her to pieces, though they did not devour the fragments, but left them to be collected by a knight in white and gold clothing bearing a gold vessel. His companion was a young woman in similar attire. These two took the flesh and blood of the slaughtered Beast, and removed them into the Lonely Forest.

This lovely little legend tells the story of how a soul (animal) in search of true faith (the Crux) may still be torn to pieces by the dogs of doubt and dissension within it. Nevertheless, if contact has been made with the Sacred Blood, nothing may be lost of the sacrifice. Remnants will be reverently removed by the guardians of the Grail and borne by them into secrecy and silence. The untold, but implied, part of the tale is that, having consumed their portions of flesh and blood, the twain will mate and invite the soul into incarnation once more through a noble line of life. Moral: If you lose your physical body while searching for a spiritual truth, you may be assured the inner guardians of that truth will care for your continuation.

The exegesis of Qabalah into a considerable mass of myth and spiritual speculations is a natural result of inquiries and interested commentaries made during the centuries it has attracted the attention of intelligent and inquisitive students (probably more in this century than in any previous one). In past times studies tended to be more or less confined within circles which held such reverence for and deference to earlier protagonists that they were afraid of making any advances on their own accounts or of differing in the slightest from what were taken to be definitive and unalterable doctrines. This attitude made it impossible for them to distinguish between firm fundamentals and alterable angles of approach to these doctrines. Consequently, investigative progress slowed to a snail's pace on most Qabalistic fronts. Jews, principally in Poland and Lithuania "sat on their secrets" without daring to disturb them for fear of inviting divine wrath on their already precarious positions in other peoples' lands. Their God was an easily provoked one at the best of times and to annoy Him into actual anger by taking liberties with His Name and precious "secrets" seemed a reckless risk to their entire race. So they left well enough alone and, as we say nowadays, kept a low profile.

Thus it was mainly Gentiles who opened up Qabalah for "Wesoterics" of all kinds and adapted its principles to our spiritual styles. Let no one argue that this was an unjustified interference with some God-given set of infallible instructions properly preserved by a few faithful for the benefit of an initiated minority alone. New outlooks on old discoveries had to come with an expanding consciousness and enlarging viewpoints largely in the West due to both educational and evolutionary developments which caused changes in our cultural atmosphere. In the East, cultures had been more or less at a standstill for centuries, while in the West, waves made by the Renaissance and later the Reformation, were still stirring awakening minds and souls to look around and readjust with an altering world.

Instead of accepting blind beliefs without arguments, awakeners on inner fronts were asking questions. They did not expect

instant answers but hoped the answers would arrive from somewhere as an eventual result of whatever streams of consciousness
they had stirred up. In doing this, of course, they were using the
Qabalistic principle of asking the Eternal Question of God in the
hope He might reply through the mouth of man. Western humanity was no longer content to lie down meekly and take whatever the
Lord saw fit to send it. Questioning everything, man questioned
God most of all, and divided (like the poor Questing Beast) into
many different parts on that point alone. Maybe the Grail Knight
and his Maiden are still trying to unite the bits together into something more beautiful.

It may be well to remember that change for the sake of
change alone is futile and anti-progressive. There are many things
in this world which have not altered fundamentally for millennia
and are still serving very useful purposes. For instance, knives, chis-
els, hammers, craft tools, nails, string, and a long list of items in
common use today are much what they were in prehistoric times.
Our materials and manufacturing processes have improved vastly,
but the article per se has not altered in purpose because that is its
value for humans. The same is true of non-physical utilities. Ten
thousand years ago, 2 was still the same as 2 now, even if we do signify it a different way. 1% in our time will be 1% in a million more
years—if we last that long in this world, and even if we do not, the
concept of 1% is indestructible in the consciousness of existence
itself.

Therefore, there is no need to feel that you must necessarily disagree with what follows in this volume purely because it has
been collected and assembled by other minds than your own. Nor
do you have to accept it for the same reason. All you are being asked
to do is *study* it without rejecting anything until you discover, *by
your own efforts and researches*, something better to put in its place.
That should be the aim of all study, if possible: to use contributions
of consciousness from each generation so as to enhance them for
the next. If you cannot see genuine reason for altering something,
leave it alone and pass it on to newcomers as it is, enjoining them

to treat it accordingly. Eventually someone will make something better out of it. That should be how any tradition works.

So although the fundamentals of Qabalah cannot be changed any more than enumeration can be eradicated, here is one of the most recent rearrangements of its essentials for your consideration and, it is hoped, practical usage in the art of living as a conscious entity within this world. Remember that Qabalah is not an end in itself but only one quite helpful means towards the same end we should all hope for—ourselves in and as infinite identity. Neither Qabalah nor anything else will get you all the way there on its own, but at least it could give you a very strong push in the right direction.

QABALISTIC
CONCEPTS

· Part I ·

Qabalah Perceptions

· 1 ·

Begin at the Beginning

There is only one way to start anything—at its beginning. How did you start this incarnation? Like the rest of us, as an egg in your mother's body which became active and fertilized by a single sperm, one amongst millions, proceeding from your father. That is what you are, one among millions. You might have been anybody else, but you aren't, and never will be. You will always be you, no matter how many bodies you have from one incarnation to another, or how often you change your personality with each. "One is one and all alone, and evermore will *be* so" as the old folk-song tells us. But what is the *real* you behind yourself "which was in the beginning, is now, and ever will be, amen"? Because we cannot very well name the unnameable, most mystics agree to term it *nothing*. No thing. Zero. The cypher of infinity. 0.

Let us think about this for a bit. Ideas of *nothing* frighten most ordinary Westerners. All they can think of is death, destruction, ruin, poverty, and the absolute worst of everything they can imagine. For the average materially-minded Westerner, "things" mean wealth, possessions, power, prosperity, all he wants out of life, while "no-thing" means exactly the reverse. He finds it almost impossible to face the fact that physical death deprives him of all his "things" in a split second. He knows this well enough deep inside himself, but he would rather not confront it consciously. The last thing he wants to admit is that his "things" will only last a lifetime, whereas his "nothing" is going to last forever.

The mystic, on the other hand, takes an opposite view. He is interested in whatever exists eternally because he realizes it must be far more important than temporary and transient things, however fascinating they may be in the moment. If "nothing" or 0 is the symbol for what he consider to be true "spiritual solidity," then he means to make relationships with this, and if possible, discover his own immortal identity therein. Something "deeper than deep" in himself tells him to do so, even though he may not know the whys and hows on the surface of his consciousness. That is the condition called faith, trust, or belief. It transcends logic, reason, or any of the purely intellectual faculties humans have developed.

Without the faculty of faith, we cannot do very much. It is the prerequisite of all action. Strange to say, the greatest faith attainable is to believe so firmly in *nothing* that anything becomes possible. That is the sort of faith we need at the start of a mystical journey through our Western Inner Tradition. Our western inner beliefs are grounded on this ultimate. Sometimes we call it "Nothing," sometimes "God," but probably the most acceptable definition so far is the old Rosicrucian one of Perfect Peace Profound (P.P.P.). That is what Western mystics and magicians mean when they think of *nothing*, a state of perfection, of peace and of profundity utterly beyond any human comprehension. It is the *nil* or nothing from which comes *all*. *Ex Nihil, omnes est,* says the Latin phrase. To coin a useful word, we can combine the Latin words and make *omnil* (All-Nothing) to signify the basis of our magical beliefs. It might be well to point out that a mystic is one who is contemplative, and inward thinking while a magician is of like philosophy but is dynamic and outgoing.

So the start of everything in Western esotericism is to achieve a state of positive faith in an ultimate negative. Even modern schoolboys should know that you have to connect positive with negative in accordance with the laws of electro-mechanics before any action will happen. It is the same with metaphysics as with ordinary physics. We have to connect our maximum potentials with the greatest negative of all, before we can expect even the slightest spiritual activity. What is more, we have to connect ourselves correctly into proper circuits if we want the right kind of responses. Otherwise we might just "short circuit" ourselves like an overloaded fuse. We not only have to know what to do, but also how to do it. All this is part and parcel of the groundwork to be covered in any practical course of instruction dealing with our Inner Tradition.

Clearly, the first thing is to find out what mental blockages you may have concerning the idea of *nothing* or *omnil* and negate them, or put them back into the nothing they came from. Get a piece of paper and pencil and write down everything the term *nothing* evokes in you. It is important that you write down exactly what you think as it appears to you. There is no use trying to conceal your own feelings or ideas from yourself. You are not writing for anyone else to see, and you can destroy the paper afterwards if you want to. Do this until you have exhausted your imagination or vocabulary concerning what *nothing* means to you personally. Do not list other people's concepts, only your own thoughts about *nothing*. Record new thoughts by all means, if they come to you, as long as you have discovered them for yourself. If necessary, leave the list partly finished and come back to it again with a fresh mind. Let's call this our "Nothing List."

One useful experiment here is to start the list before going to bed, then pick it up again in the morning and see if anything else has come out of the unconscious during sleep. Most of our "inner wisdom" reaches us this way, while our bodies sleep and our real, deep awareness makes contact with much higher "Intelligences" than humans can normally communicate with. Anyway, work with the "Nothing List" for a few days, and notice if it begins to build and develop in breadth and meaning. Try reading it through, reaching into your mind for anything fresh, noting this briefly, then putting the list away again. It is a good idea to start keeping such lists or written ideas in a special file and always keep this in one location, preferably where it is easily accessible, yet not likely to be read by anyone else. When you begin filling up a "Magical Diary" or daily account of inner experiences, you will need to make a habit of guarding your writings, so it is best to begin the way you mean to continue.

When you feel that your "Nothing List" is just about complete, find some occasion when you are unlikely to be disturbed, and go over the list carefully, thinking about every single word. Ask yourself, for instance: "Why did I write that?" or "What made me use that word instead of another one? *Is* there another word I could have used and, if so, what is it? Let me get a dictionary and look up its full meaning," or any other thoughts which seem relevant. Make a little ritual out of this if you like. Prop the list up where it can be read easily, spotlight it with a desk lamp while the rest of the room is in darkness, burn some pleasant incense. Silence is best here, but very quiet music may be used to cover some irritating background noise should this distract concentration.

Now really give your full attention to your "Nothing List" and go back and forth over it a number of times. By this time you should have come to a few definite conclusions. Take a new sheet of paper and write all your altered ideas down. For instance, are you afraid of *nothing* because it will strip you of every earthly possession? If so, why? Might it not make you independent of all possessions so that you would be better off rather than worse? Do you want to be the same personality forever? Wouldn't you rather be somebody with far greater ability and prospects? If the idea of death frightens you, why aren't you scared by what happened before you were born? Do you really believe that once your body dies, that will be the absolute end of *you*? Is your body *all* you are? Are you confusing your *real* Self with the personality you have been developing during your lifetime? Very many people do, and get sadly discontented with what they think are themselves. Surely you intend to learn better than that in the course of your spiritual studies?

Have a good look at what you have been thinking of as *nothing,* and see how wrong you have been. Begin getting used to the realization that *nil* is the "pre-principle" of life itself, without which there would be no life at all. It is also the "post-principle" of life which absorbs us all as entities and eventually re-issues us into other states of existence. There is no point speculating on details at this stage. It is enough just to grasp a few broad outlines. For instance, it would be impossible to postulate the figure one unless there were a zero to start counting from. It is equally impossible to *be* anyone or anything unless there were a *nil*-state to emerge from. Non-being and being chase each other eternally round the Cosmic Circle of existence. When Hamlet said: "To be, or not to be, *that* is the question," he was stating a far greater occult truth than any audience recognized.

Now draw a fairly large sized 0 on the paper and examine it carefully. It is the cypher, symbol of Nothing. Think of it as the outline of a conjuror's hat, out of which all sorts of things can be produced by the wave of a wand. Draw a wand across the hat. ⏀ One out of Nothing. Or one and zero mean ten somethings. Draw another wand across at right angles, and we have the Circle Cross of Cosmos ⊕ . The symbol of a Rod in magic means especially an application of will. So we have illustrated by a few lines the principle of Cosmos emerging from Nothing by means of Will.

Draw the Rod by itself. 1. Now put *nothing* beside it. 10. Then 10 *nothings*. 1 0000000000. Why is it that the more *nothings* we keep adding, the greater the value of that single one becomes? If we add *nothings* to the other side of the single one, it suddenly becomes more remote from us. Play with this idea and see what comes out of it. This might alter conceptions of *nothing* quite a lot.

The whole object of these exercises is to change the ordinary concept of *nothing* from a viewpoint of avoidance to enthusiastic acceptance. Most modern people of the West look at *nothing* through the wrong end of their mental telescopes. Far from being insignificant or valueless, *nil* is really the most important concept of all. Until we learn to see it in that light, we shall never make progress with our Inner Tradition. Only an empty cup can be filled, only a cleared consciousness can be instructed, and none but the "pure in heart" (those of clarified minds and souls) shall "see God," that is, realize divinity in themselves and all else in existence.

This does not mean we have to reject everything we have ever believed or depart from anything we have accepted as being true and worth basing our lives on. It does mean that we are going to begin a new journey in life which starts and ends with the infinite *nil* behind all. *Omnil.* Now we know very well that we cannot literally put ourselves into a state of *nil* as we are at the moment, but we *can* symbolize it. Magic, like mathematics, is very largely a matter of symbology, and the sooner we start working with magical symbology the better.

Symbolization of *nil* is mainly a matter of stillness, silence, darkness, and "empty-mindedness," simulation of pre-birth and death-like consciousness. The stillness, darkness and silence are relatively easy to symbolize by means of a hooded cloak and a comfortable seat in a darkened room. This is the principle reason why the hooded cloak has been adopted by most Western esoteric workers. It is an assumed symbol of the ultimate *omnil* they all hope to attain, a portable inner temple in which they can become their beliefs. Even if not actually worn, it is usually visualized or mentally accepted as being there during meditational practices.

The empty-mindedness is the hardest part of the exercise. This means conscious control of the objective awareness so that we do not think of *things,* or people, or anything else that is perceivable to our ordinary senses. On the other hand, we have to become *intensely aware* of the *pure energy* which lies behind all life and being. That is *omnil.* It is the energy of existence, nothing and everything in one. It cannot be explained, only *accepted.* It is all we ever were, and all we ever shall be. We have no name for it, but if it helps to call it "God" until clearer consciousness improves relationships with it, then this may be done, because "God" is not a name, but a generic term for anyone's belief in an ultimate.

If you have a full hooded cloak, put it on. If not, then imagine one around you. Arrange a straight-backed chair where you can sit comfortably with thighs parallel to the ground, hands with palms relaxed and resting quite lightly on each knee. The spine should be kept straight, though the head may be slightly inclined forward. Feet should be a natural distance apart, but level with each other. Eyes gently closed. This is the normal Western meditation posture, and there should be no sense of muscular strain in holding it. In no circumstances should a low, or armchair type of seating be adopted. The seat should be solid, but may be cushioned suitably. For those who like fine details, it is normally best to set the chair so that it faces West. This positions the body in line with the Earth's lines of magnetic force in the direction of maximum light intensity.

To improve the symbology further, trace a real or imaginary circle on the floor around the chair. In old days this would have been done with common chalk or colored sand. Nowadays, the most practical means is by laying out (clockwise) a piece of colored string or cord around oneself so that it makes the magical circle of containment. Traditionally, this should be a nine foot diameter circle, but the diameter is not vitally important so long as it can be conveniently traced around the chair before sitting down. The control switch for the lights will obviously have to be within reach of the chair, unless a candle on a tall holder is chosen, in which case the flame is simply blown out. (Remember to have re-kindling means at hand). The candle makes for better symbology.

Such a setting illustrates the important adage: "God is a circle, the circumference of which is nowhere, and the center everywhere." Here we have a human being seeking contact with its own infinite immortality, and symbolizing this by his surroundings. The circle is the zero of *nil*. The solitary flame signifies the Divine Spark which is the "real self" in each one of us. Blowing out the flame means returning our separated selves into the Eternal Entity in which we truly belong. "Giving ourselves back to God" as a Christian might put it. Uniting with the whole, of which we are infinitesimal parts. All this and much more is illustrated by the simple psychodrama enacted in this elementary practice.

So, wearing a real or imagined robe, arrange the seating, trace the circle around it, place the lighted candle on a small stand to one side if no proper holder is available, be seated, take a deep breath while thinking about filling yourself with the Holy Spirit, then blow out the candle while considering your own return to that Spirit. If you like, you can verbalize this part by saying: "I take from God all He wills" as the breath is inhaled, then: "I give to God all I am," while breath is exhaled and the flame blown out. No other verbal formularies should be made at this stage of the exercise. The final settling down is then done with a minimum of movement, and the working meditational posture assumed. If ordinary electric lighting is used, then it is no more than a matter of switching off and settling.

Questions are often asked about the use of incense as a background here. However much people might be tempted to use it, it is symbolically inappropriate at this particular point. There should be no definite sense of any smell or other sensual stimulus demanding conscious attention here. It is essential that all sense stimuli be kept to an absolute minimum, and preferably eliminated where possible. Later on, with development of expertise, minor distractions can be overridden or ignored, but at first the best possible conditions are a positive necessity. It would be useless, for instance, trying this exercise for the first time with a TV screaming its head off in a room overhead, and a pneumatic drill going in the street outside. Somehow or other, the requisites for this exercise have to be brought together before it will work. Obtaining them may be simple for some, and greatly difficult for others. Overcoming such difficulties can be a major problem demanding very ingenious solutions calling for almost magical skill from people. It also calls for a lot of specialized study to be dealt with elsewhere. For the moment, let us assume that conditions for this exercise are reasonably favorable, and our beginner is actually confronting his inner identity in quiet darkness.

This is where it becomes impossible to lay down any hard and fast guidelines which have to be followed. Every single soul has to face its own God in its own way and come to its own conclusions thereby. There are a few helpful aids which may be noted however, most of which come from practical experience and experimentation by quite a number of people over several centuries.

Seeking the *nothing* means just the opposite of going to sleep or letting oneself drift aimlessly into unconsciousness. On the contrary, intense concentration is needed, yet without arousing physical tension. If muscles begin to tense up to a point where they become noticeable, they must be allowed to relax without losing a hold on the point of consciousness. This may take some practice before it becomes a usefully controlled ability, but nevertheless it is more of a "knack" than a mysterious gift, and most people should be able to do it with a certain amount of applied attention.

It is important not to think of people, places, or things, or for that matter anything with connections of "otherness" to oneself. In other words, cease objective thinking. Do not think in terms of words, colors, sounds, or any observable phenomena at all. This means much more than merely "making the mind a blank." It means transcending (or "going above") all ordinary commonplace limitations of consciousness and reaching a level of awareness which is beyond normal human range, though by no means beyond the range of normal humans if they really mean to extend themselves by intentional efforts.

Our objective thinking and thoughts are *effects*. The cause of them lies in fluctuations of our consciousness itself. Stop these at source, so to speak, and all thoughts cease, while the actual faculty of consciousness remains unaffected. We shall really be doing no more than turning off a tap or a switch controlling supply. Why do this at all? Because our ordinary everyday thinking, interesting though it may be, forms a barrier or screen which obscures our deep perception of the inner realities we need to consciously seek if we intend to make spiritual progress. Therefore we must learn how to handle this difficulty before we may expect any inner development.

Look at it this way: Suppose you are in a room where a radio or TV is blaring away full volume. The telephone rings. The call is for you, from some very valued friend whose every word means a great deal. The line is poor and your friend's voice barely audible. What do you do? Either turn the noise off, or yell for someone else to do it. That is exactly the position you are in when you try to listen to the "Voice of Silence" inside yourself, and no one but you can turn off the "noise" which prevents closer contact with Perfect Peace Profound.

Although verbalization is not encouraged for this initial exercise, it may prove necessary for controlling some seemingly uncontrollable thoughts. The thing to do is look at these thoughts racing through your mind, and try to take a step back from them.

From this standpoint give the mental command very firmly and steadily: *Be still. And know. That I. Am God.* Try commanding this in rhythm with slow breathing this way: *Be* (inhale) *still,* (exhale) *and* (inhale) *know,* (exhale) *that* (inhale) *I* (exhale) *am* (inhale) *God* (exhale). If visualization must be made, keep nothing but a zero-circle in view as a ring of light against a totally dark background. Maintain this a while, then let the words sink into silence and the vision into *nil,* yet keep their meaning going mentally as a force after their forms have faded.

It is important to understand when using that formula that the "I" therein does *not* mean your human self. As such, you are not God, nor can you ever be. As an infinitesimal fraction of that God, you have both the right and the obligation to call consciously upon your share of God, and that is what you mean when you use this invocation. What you are trying to obtain here is even a momentary experience of existing as nothing but pure energy, without body, mind, thinking, or *anything.* Granted this will be a symbolic experience rather than an actual one, but that is as much as we can expect for the present. It will be enough to accomplish for the first few sessions.

That is all to be done during this initial training period. There is no point in prolonging a session unduly, a quarter of an hour will be ample at first. In any case, once it is felt that an awareness in and of *omnil* has been achieved to some degree, consciousness can return again to normal levels. After a comfortable pause the light may be turned on again and the circle-cord gathered up in reverse winding from right to left. If a hooded cloak has been worn, the hood should be first pushed from the face with both hands in a gesture of "awakening" as if rubbing sleep from the eyes. Then everything has to be restored to place, and brief notes made of the experience in accordance with specified requirements.

It should be particularly stressed that it is useless and counter-productive to lengthen this exercise until boredom or indifference takes place because of inaction. Sitting aimlessly waiting for something spiritual to happen is no more than a waste of existence. Simply set the symbolic stage, settle your body thereon, clear your consciousness as far as you can from objective thinking, make a real effort in yourself to feel even the slightest connection between your consciousness and the infinity from whence you originated, then come back to earth and carry on with your ordinary living. Since all (including yourself) came from *nil,* you are doing no more than seeking contact with your own origins.

For the first week, do this exercise no more than three times, choosing the best opportunities for yourself, and continuing with the routine daily. For the second week, increase the *omnil* practice to four times. Finally, these simple suggestions should prove valuable:

1. Do not tackle any mystical exercises on a full stomach, under noticeable alcoholic influence, or that of unprescribed drugs.
2. Remember also such commonsense matters of attending to bladder and bowels needs if likely, silencing, telephones, and doing everything possible to avoid interruptions.
3. Common sense is always needed to attain a cosmic sense. For example, do not attempt occult exercises if you are feeling ill or seriously disturbed mentally or emotionally.
4. Calm yourself first.
5. Do not attempt to "obtain messages," hear mystic voices, or seek any kind of phenomenal responses. Should you think anything of the sort is happening, refuse firmly to be distracted by it, and strive for closer contact with infinity. Even if you cannot quite manage this, your act of intention to transcend distractions is of considerable spiritual value in itself.
6. Maintain this discipline daily and make a daily entry in your Magical Diary.
7. Do not attempt to give a false impression of your abilities. You would be cheating nobody.

Questions

1. What does *omnil* mean to you?
2. What do you understand by the phrase "energy of existence?"
3. Does the idea of *nothing* frighten or bother you? If so, why?

4. How do you define "faith" and why is it necessary?

5. Why should the addition of zeros to any figure increase its value ten times for each zero added?

6. How does it feel sitting or standing in your Magical Circle?

7. What is your major difficulty in trying to "think of nothing," and how would you propose to deal with it, if you could?

8. Choose what you think are the nine most important sentences in this chapter.

9. What is your concept of "God?"

10. What is your own concept of yourself?

·2·

The Value of Nothing

There is a rate of spiritual progress which average humans may safely make during their earth lifetimes. Though this rate tends to speed up over the centuries, to exceed the average rate of progress may be dangerous. In earlier times, Mystery Schools worked very slowly but with extreme thoroughness and attention to minute details. They might spend a whole incarnation attempting what we are trying to cover in a matter of months. Their approach to the zero-nil concept was one of total commitment. Initiates would isolate themselves indefinitely in search of it. Others, seeking to shorten the process somewhat would spend the traditional three days in the "tomb-womb," mostly in a condition of trance or semi-trance, often in a cave partly buried in warm sand or otherwise cocooned until aroused by their Initiator to a "new life" as a member of the Holy Mysteries. That was why they became known as "twice-born." The first birth was their human, physical birth; the second was a spiritual birth symbolized by the burial ordeal. That practice remains today in rituals such as Christian baptism in which immersion in water substitutes for the older burial in earth. Modern experimental psychology simulates this condition in various laboratory techniques to induce what is called "sense deprivation."

Here, we are using conventional magical psychodramas or summative rituals in order to simulate a pre-birth condition of *nil* potential wherein we achieve some sense of contact with the energy behind life. When we have gained a minimum of this unique experience, we shall attempt the symbology of "being born again" to our new (or renewed) spiritual outlook on life. Since we intend to enter this spiritual life by way of the Western Inner Tradition, we had better have a preview of its general pattern.

Everything in existence has some kind of basic pattern, and our Inner Tradition is no exception. Its basis is very simple, being the Cosmic or Solar Circle Cross; a circle containing an equilateral cross (see Figure 1.1). The *nil* creating *all* within it. *Omnil* again.

This was probably our earliest symbol of companionship with Cosmos. It is our recognition sign of Divine Order behind the universe, and our acceptance of Its authority over ourselves and our living. As we evolved and began to understand a little more about the complex spiritual structure of creation, our simple Circle Cross became extended into the sophisticated "Tree of Life" design which we shall study later on. For the time being it is best to stay with the fundamentals. So far as we in the West are concerned, the Cosmic Circle Cross holds our primal allegiance. It is still sometimes referred to as the Celtic Cross because our ancestors bore it with them westwards as a symbol of their faith in creation and its

---

Figure 1.1. The Cosmic or Solar Cross

Creator. It is much older than official Christianity, being a representation of the Sun and the quarternal cycle of the seasons. We assign the quarters (West, North, East and South) to the circle.

Our immediate task is to start aligning ourselves with the basic pattern of the Circle Cross. That means making a magical relationship with it which will link our normal consciousness with the roots from whence our tradition arises. In many cases it will do more. Those who belong to the western inner way by birth, blood, or genetic inheritance of any sort, physical and/or spiritual, may not be aware of this with ordinary consciousness until an awakening happens through close contact with our special esoteric symbolism. Deep in every evolving soul there are "far memories" of past incarnations continuing back to our Cosmic origins. These memories normally do not come to the surface of our consciousness. Nevertheless a sense of their actuality does help in our search for immortal identity. Once we realize that we are indeed souls that have come a long way already in search of our true selves, this gives great impetus to our present travelling in that direction.

Confront anyone with some particular symbolism which has meant a great deal to them in previous existences, and they are most likely to experience some kind of spiritual reaction as this activates energies usually dormant in the depths of human souls. If Western magical symbolism arouses interest, curiosity, or a strange sense of familiarity in those confronted with it, the chances are they already belong within the tradition which has passed it down the generations of mankind, and are seeking conscious re-connection therewith in their present incarnations.

At one time, this re-awakening or "second birth" would most likely have been arranged under special conditions in a Mystery Temple or Lodge. The neophyte, having been properly prepared by long training and instruction by his sponsors, would be introduced into the Temple while in a psychological state of anticipation which would produce the maximum impact from spiritual symbolism at the moment of contact. That was why candidates were bound, blindfolded, and otherwise sense-deprived so that an element of sheer surprise would add needed force to whatever revelations might meet their suddenly restored senses. When they actually "came to light" among all the psychodramatic surroundings of a Mystery Temple and its assembled members, the spiritual significance behind such a "birth-shock" was usually driven home in that candidate's soul in a memorable way which influenced the rest of his earth-life most profoundly.

Although this is still carried out today here and there, the practice is becoming obsolete and very largely unnecessary because of recent advances in general intelligence and a raising of cultural levels among Western peoples as a whole. Our reactions are becoming markedly different from those of even our grandparents' days. Two appalling world wars have altered human genetics more than may be realized. You who are reading this may suppose those long ago happenings have nothing to do with you, but they *have*. What to you is "nothing" because it all occurred before you were born, is a part of your genetics, influencing you imperceptibly the whole of your lifetime. You are the living product of your own past extending to unknown origins which are determining your present and future to a considerable degree. That is why we need to concern ourselves with the *nil* concept here, and discover if possible how we may adapt and alter its present effects on us for best future results.

So even though it may no longer be obligatory to undergo ceremonial initiations in formal Lodges or Temples, the underlying principles still apply for those intending to follow our Western Inner Way. It is simply a question of method. What once had to be done for you by others, you are now meant to do for yourself. We grow up in spiritual dimensions as well as physical ones, and many more of us are becoming "adult" than in former times. Just as a child's toys are replaced by an adult's tools and equipment, so must our erstwhile "child-style" symbology become meaningful in more up-to-date ways as we advance.

Now we will expand our omnil exercise with a few additions. This time try to arrange things so that the candle is on a stand in front of you where it will be within reach and about eye level or slightly below. Make absolutely sure that the candle in its holder is secure and unlikely to be knocked over. For instance, do not prop it on piles of books or anything like that. Make sure nothing inflammable is within range. The best thing, of course, is a candle-holder of the right height with a wide, heavy base such as seen in churches. Since this is not an item of normal household use, a substitute must be employed, and care must be taken that it is a satisfactory one. This may sound like a lot of fuss about trivia, but there is a good reason. In earlier times the most meticulous attention in magical practices was directed to minute and apparently pointless details. This was not so much for the sake of the thing itself, as for arousing the necessary interest and concentration called for to accomplish the real purpose of the rite. A clever psychological device to condition consciousness.

Prepare to be seated in the dark silence, facing West, with a match and a striking surface ready. It makes a nice symbolic gesture if the match (non-safety kind) is held in the right hand and the flat striking surface is held in the left. Thus it symbolizes the male (match) impacting with the female (surface) and so bringing forth Light between them. To refine the symbolism still further, the friction surface could be a suitably shaped stone from some spot considered sacred or special by yourself. At any rate, have the match and means of friction handy and settle down in the dark.

Let breathing become calm, slow, and regular. Let your eyes turn up and in naturally so that attention is fixed just above the root of the nose, eyelids closed. Intend to "not-be" without any words, and bear in mind the introduction to Genesis: "And the Spirit of God moved upon the face of the waters." The original word for "moved" implies brooding or hovering. There is a connection which suggests the hovering of an eagle protectively over its nest where eggs or fledglings may be present. That is exactly what you have to do here. Hover.

You are no-thing, and no-body. Unexpressed energy. Uncondensed consciousness. Everywhere and nowhere. Timeless. Spaceless. Eventless. You are above thinking, feeling, or being. Those are all limitations which you may or may not accept if you will. *If you will.* Intention. *Intention.* An interesting word. It means to extend oneself, exertion, to design, and to apply. That is what must happen if you intend becoming a creator of your own Cosmos. You may *be* or *not-be,* as you will, or hover neutrally between both. Yes, No, and Maybe. Later these will develop the Three Pillars of the Tree of Life or the Three Paths of Progresson—Orphic, Hermetic, and Mystic. At the moment you are hovering on the extreme edge of existence. Once committed to a course of action, you cannot return except through a complete cycle of Cosmos. When will becomes word, that word must be fulfilled to its last letter. Hover and nurture. Brood.

Eventually, the will-to-be must surely arise in you. Only you can determine exactly the presence of this change within your consciousness. It commences imperceptibly as a circulating current which slowly becomes more evident in the energy you consist of. If you were "thinking back" at it from another viewpoint you might be reminded of a most remote and scarcely existing nebula. But you do not perceive it; it is no more than a behavior of your being. Your being? But you are *not*-being. No, you are not! Then you *are* being. Are you being, or not-being? Energy is now beginning to circulate more strongly and pulse with a steady beat. Nothing but your will can stop it or continue it. Make your divine decision; become yourself. Utter the word which condenses your consciousness into creative kinesis. Call life into existence as *Light!*

All this, of course, should be worked wordlessly within yourself. It is just meant as a general guide by which to steer your consciousness. There is no reason why you should not write another script if you prefer, providing you do not verbalize the ideas in your head. The moment for words arrives when you come to the point of actual creation. At that instant, find the match and friction-stone, arise, and *breathe* the formula:

O. I. AM.

Do it this way. Taking a full breath as you rise in the darkness, release it as a drawn out *OH.* Take in a breath while making movements of the lip and throat muscles to form an *I* (ai) sonic. During this, strike the match. Light the candle while outbreathing *am* with the accent on the *m.* Then utter a symbol for the Divine

Name to the four quarters of the circle, like this: Raise both forearms level with the shoulders, arms to the side, fingers together and palms up and flat. This is the normal priestly "altar-approach" attitude. Open the mouth something like an O. Then, simply inhale and exhale so that the breath makes a low sound. Do not attempt to articulate anything definite. Turn a quarter so that you face where your right hand was, and repeat the action. Then do the same at the last two quarters. Come back to the original position, pause and sit down. Think out this symbology.

What, in fact, have you done? For a start you have made your consciousness simulate the story of your own creation as an entity within existence. Not the person attached to a human body who is now reading these words and will eventually die, this is the *you* behind that personality which normally projects only the merest fraction of itself into personification. Sometimes it is called the Real Self, or True Self, or innermost identity. However termed, it remains the *you* intended or willed by the creative spirit of life at your origin, the being you were meant to become. As a human being you are obviously very far from the point of perfection. Otherwise you would not be here as an incarnate creature. The "Great Work" it is hoped you will attempt during this incarnation is directing the energies available to you now so as to become nearer to a state of spiritual perfection. In other words, your life mission is looking for your own True Self or identity.

If you have done this exercise with any degree of success, you should have tacitly acknowledged your own origins with the living spirit and affirmed your creation as an emanation of the consciousness behind Cosmos. This has been described as: "A thought in the mind of God," and that is indeed a beautiful simile. Now think about the symbology awhile. You began it by sitting in the dark in the center of a circle. Compare this with your biological beginnings. The circle represents the unfertilized egg in your mother's body. Its center or nucleus is about to be impregnated by a single sperm, hence the stirring of energy currents. The sperm arrives. Will it activate the egg or not? Are you to be or not-be? The decision comes with the moment of fusion, when the Divine Spark has been struck into light. You symbolize this with your "utterance" and lighting the candle.

That "utterance" has a wealth of symbolism. Note that it is triple. The O signifies zero or the *nil*-state. The I is your Self, your true Self. Note that the match is I shaped, and so is the candle; that is, it is phallic, or a "father" symbol. What shape is the flame? If it is steady, it has the suggestive outline of a female sex organ. You are looking at a father-mother emblem, and the light from that flame represents your Self. "And God said: 'Let there be *light.*' " After that comes the final M, not only meaning someone who IS, but also representing the humming of released energy completing the work of creation. In the beginning was the Word. It is given here as *O.I.AM.* for the sake of thinking in our own language. In Hebrew it is *Amen,* and the Druids knew it as *Awen.* The word of life is the same for all humans, but we might as well utter it our particular way.

Now comes the "Name-breathing" to the four quarters. You *are,* but who, or *what* are you? Esoteric tradition says that Divinity brought itself into being by the utterance of its own Name. That is to say It identified Itself, or specified Its Being. Naturally no human could be expected to know the exact nature (or Name) of Divinity, so early priest-magi invented symbolic substitutes for that "Name," and held those very sacred. Here we are symbolizing that "creative cry" in the simplest possible way, by inhalation and exhalation of breath so as to make a first and last sound of life. The newborn first inhale air, and the dying give a last outbreathing. What could be a more fitting salute to the Lord of Life and Death? Later we can make what sonics we may find more consistent with our progressed perception. However we resonate them, there will always have to be an indrawn or inspired breath, and a corresponding exhalation.

Why the division into quarters? Going back to the womb and elementary biology, we find that the fertilized egg first divides into two, and then into four parts, after which it continues subdivision and cell construction. We are here symbolizing the first four-fold formation which in effect makes a Circle Cross. Perhaps here also, we may find a connection between the Cosmic Cross showing the arrangement of our planets around their central Sun during the four seasons, and our own primal structure at the four-cell stage around our central life-spark. No wonder the esoteric concepts of Macrocosm (Great Cosmos) and Microcosm (Small Cosmos) were developed by earlier generations. In our way, we are miniature copies of creation as a whole, for the simple reason that our species was developed according to the same principles or laws of life.

So here we are sitting quietly before a lighted candle thinking about our origins and maybe wondering where we are going from here. Awesome, isn't it? When you feel you have had enough, rise, place both hands over the heart, right above left, make a slight inclination of the body toward the candle flame as symbol of the Divine Spark within yourself, then put everything back in place.

It is good practice at the end of a practical magical exercise to "switch off" and return to some quite mundane occupation. The idea of this is to return these currents of consciousness dealing with arcane ideas back to the inner levels they came from where they should mature and consolidate into an improved condition by the time we invoke them again. While they are in the early formative stages they need a lot of care and protection if they are to flourish and thrive. Consciousness has to be treated properly if we expect it to develop into anything we would value. Fresh ideas or formulations of them are not unlike new planted seeds, whether in wombs, soil, or any other nutrient medium. Those who know how to treat them get the best results every time. So concepts which are freshly conceived should not be immediately exposed to rough or detrimental conditions, but guarded carefully in the deeper layers of consciousness until they are able to emerge by themselves and survive through their own strength and ability.

This is why initiated members of Mystery Temples or Lodges were always cautioned not to talk about their spiritual experiences. It was not for the sake of secrecy itself, but to give those precious spiritual seeds a chance to grow undisturbed. To let well-meaning but premature influences interfere would be like a child pulling up a germinating seed to see how it was doing.

Therefore you would be very wise to begin a habit of discretion concerning your inner experiences, and *never* mention or discuss them outside the very small circle of those fully entitled to share them with you. Keep them *intimate* until they grow so solid that others will feel them for themselves without you telling. There is no harm in family or friends knowing that you are interested in meditation, and need time and opportunity for its practice. The chances are they will not bother you unduly because they will be far more interested in their own affairs. If you should be disturbed with a lot of questions or pryings, then just be good-natured and make as light as possible of the subject, even joke about it. Say something like: "Oh, well, it keeps me out of mischief," or "I got tired of watching TV. My mental programs are a lot more entertaining." Be a wise fool. Let people think you are making an excuse for a quiet little snooze, if you like. Anything rather than expose your inner spiritual state to inimical attention.

Since this is a very important exercise, carry it out at least three times the first week, and four times the second. Here is a point to note especially. In these exercises you are "recapping" a considerable amount of the preceding one, while adding a few further details each week. By now, you should be speeding up the recapping part and spending more time on the fresh material. This means that what took you several minutes at first, should shorten to a matter of moments as you make progress. Eventually you will aim to accomplish in seconds, processes of consciousness which once occupied a whole period. That may be some way in the future, but it is well to have the idea in mind.

Your additional exercise for this lesson is learning and practicing the sign of the Circle Cross on yourself. This is a rapid way of identifying youself with Cosmos by a symbolic gesture outlining the Western view of Divinity. Start with both hands to the breast, either in prayer position or right over left. Say the following (preferably) aloud, or mentally:

(Raise R hand and touch forehead and say:)	*In the name of the Wisdom,*
(Touch over heart and say:)	*the Love,*
(Touch R shoulder and say:)	*the Justice*
(Touch L shoulder and say:)	*and the Infinite Mercy*
(Trace a complete circle around these points, saying:)	*of the One Eternal Spirit.*
(Bring R hand to rest on breast again and say:)	*Amen.*

Practice this a few times by itself, then incorporate it into your ritual practice at beginning and end. From now on, you should automatically commence and finish your exercises with this sign. It is an affirmation of what you should believe a Supreme Being is capable of towards yourself, and also what that Being expects you to develop in your own soul—the four great qualities co-ordinated by the life-spirit in Cosmos—and in you. It is the signature of our secret tradition, and by using it you align yourself with everything this stands for. You are saying in effect: "This is what I mean to make of myself so that I may truly belong with others who dedicate their lives to the same Spirit." Wise, loving, just and compassionate, because of a belief in the Supreme Spirit of Life, and your hope of immortality therein. There are many more meanings which you may be able to figure out for yourself. For example, it is a Western form of the Arabian gesture of touching forehead and breast, then making an outgoing hand gesture, which briefly means "My head, heart, and hands are at your service." Our version signifies far more than that. In the next Chapter we are going to extend our quarternity a good deal further.

Questions

1. What is the basic pattern of the Western Inner Tradition? Why is it this way?
2. How does the *nil* concept come to be in your genetics?

3. How can you "think of *nothing*?"

4. Can you see the distinction between the real and the purely personal "you," and if so, how?

5. How do you "switch on" before an esoteric exercise?

6. How do you "switch off" afterwards?

7. How do you relate to the symbol of the Circle Cross on yourself? Discuss this particular practice.

8. In what way, if any, did the *"O. I. AM."* formula affect you?

9. Choose the ten most important sentences in this Chapter.

10. What did you find easiest to grasp in this chapter and what was the most difficult? Ask yourself after each chapter. It helps you assess your progress.

• 3 •

Cross Purposes

Y ou are now covering ground which has taken centuries of time, and Heaven alone knows how many incarnations of souls dedicated to the Western Inner Way, to discover and to be mapped out for your benefit. You, in your turn, will add your particular contribution to our tradition which will not only help others in the future, but might even help *you* when you incarnate here again. You might say you will be leaving a legacy for yourself. Strange thought, isn't it?

Experience of every kind of work in this world has shown that no worthwhile project can be done properly without adequate preparations. This is particularly true of all mystical and magical work. The ancients once called it "the Labour of Preparation," and it was mandatory for all students. No serious rite or practice was ever to be attempted without performing such obligatory preparation. Opinions varied on the nature of such primary work. Some prescribed prayer and fasting for a stated period. Others advised herbal baths and fumigations. Most practitioners had their own ideas of how to prepare for each mystico-magical operation. Possibly one of the most detailed preparations described in print is that of Abra-Melim the Mage.* It needed nine months of effort, the

---

*See *Western Inner Workings*, also by William Gray, for more information about Abra-Melim.

same as a pregnancy. Though commentators differ from each other, they do agree on one point: Without proper preparations, no work is likely to be worth anything in the end.

Very many years ago, "trainee-magi" were sometimes told to tramp or run round their smallish circles, literally, for quite long periods. This induced a semi-trance state due to exhaustion and vertigo. The result was increased psychic sensitivity with possible visionary experiences, which are very seldom reliable or desirable. Nowadays we should call this a stress technique. It used to be called "working the Mill." In those days, small mills were often powered by several humans scurrying around a squirrel cage type of wheel. Starvation and exhaustion nearly always produces illusory visions or voices. We would not recommend that such practices be carried to their extremities, nor that drugs be employed.

How did you learn to stand upright and move yourself around in this world so that it meant something to you? First, you had to distinguish between up and down, forwards and backwards, and side to side. Then you had to maintain your balance between all these and find out how to direct your course in relation to them in order to make movement purposeful. This is an early experience you have consciously forgotten, but which governs your active life today. Unless you could do this naturally and easily, your existence on this earth would be far from pleasant or profitable. Exactly the same is true in spiritual dimensions. The laws of life apply to *all* states of being. It is only a question of how they operate in differing conditions of consciousness.

So the first movements you make in spiritual dimensions should accord with alignments therein. Otherwise you will not be able to tell your ups from your downs, your right from your left, or your back from your front, and you are likely to become a very mixed up soul. Can you think of some humans this might apply to? They never seem to have any sense of inner direction, and often get so confused and even angry that they refuse to recognize any kind of spirituality at all, and fix the focus of their attention on physical effects alone. If you know people like this, please, for both your sakes, do not attempt to interfere with them in a spirit of mistaken missionary zeal. *Leave them alone* unless they ask you for help of their own will and accord. Pray for them privately if you wish, but let them find their own light in their own way. They will have other lives, other opportunities, and eventually they have to find their way along the path to perfection or perish. You have no right to start dictating what they ought or ought not to do. Ours is not that kind of inner tradition. Every one of us is individually responsible for his or her own spiritual progress toward "perfection." All we can do for each other is offer whatever is ours to companions in need if they are willing to accept it and use it for their spiritual advancement.

You are going to be different from those struggling with spiritual confusion and out-of-focus inner vision. Fortunately, you will be able to construct a "cosmic compass" which tells you how to stand upright and move around inner dimensions so as to make sense and meaning there.

As you might expect by now, it starts with the Circle Cross. Draw the Circle Cross and study it intently. Try extending the lines of the cross beyond the limits of the circle. In theory they go on beyond the edges of the paper and reach out to infinity. Or do they? If we are to believe the latest (and earliest) theories about our universe, those lines would eventually bend round the boundaries of the universe and meet again at some unknown point. We don't need something that big, but a symbol we can handle more easily. Circles of any diameter are always the same thing. Circles. A small circle is the same thing as the biggest one. So if we are designing a Cosmic symbol, we can make any size of circle we like. What happens if we make them all the same size?

The best way to find this out is by making a practical example. Can you obtain three identical rings of flat wire or similar material? At one time these were obtainable as children's bracelets from chain-stores, but a good handyman (or woman) should be able to make them up somehow. Once you have such available, proceed as follows. Pick up one ring and look at it. There is your zero-circle. Pick up another ring, and press it over the first at right angles. This is your first bi-section of the life-cell. Note it is a shaky affair which will fall to pieces very easily. Now get hold of the third, and press it carefully over the other two so that it holds them firmly together with equal angles everywhere. You have built a firm structure which is self-supporting. Place it on your desk top or some other surface. Flick it lightly with your fingers. It should roll around. You have made a model of the Cosmos in the simplest way (see Figure 1.2). How does it feel to be a creator?

What you have constructed with three rings amounts to a circle divided into four parts; the circle of the zodiac, the four seasons with three signs in each; a "cage of consciousness," something more fundamental to the entire symbol in relation to ourselves. So far as we are concerned, our consciousness of Cosmos around us is limited by three main factors—time, space and events. It takes time for us to live, space for us to move, and events for us to realize we are living and mobile beings. These are the three rings of Cosmos from our point of view. We are, so to speak, confined within these rings in order to experience existence. That is why this concept was once called the "ring-pass-not," a definition of our life-limits, but this did not mean they could not be extended indefinitely.

Our three rings have made a sort of compass with which we can stabilize ourselves in spiritual dimensions. They are not unlike a gyroscope which keeps an aircraft, submarine, or space-station in a steady position. Our earth itself is a gyroscope, and if we ever got

---

Figure 1.2. A simple model of the Cosmos

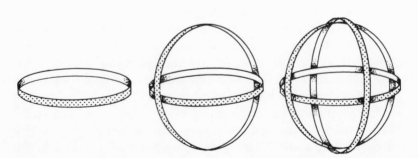

Figure 1.3. The Time Circle

---

away from its gravity, we would have to rely on artificial gravity supplied by a gyro-type of mechanism. In order to maintain spiritual gravity and stability for ourselves we shall have to work out an equivalent scheme inwardly. This is a priority in all mystical or magical work. Many fail to realize its importance, and fall blindly around in all directions. They are like sailors without a compass or airmen without gyro-controls. Stability is a primary necessity in the Western Tradition and this is where we learn how to gain it.

Go through the "creation ritual" from Chapter II, briefly yet carefully.

Now you are going to surround yourself with the three circles of Cosmos. Use the index finger of your right hand as a pointer to focus attention (see Figure 1.3). You could use a rod or wand if you like. A dramatic way of doing this is with the beam of a flashlight in a darkened room. After you have affirmed the *I AM,* trace the horizontal circle clockwise around you at about half your height, and intone slowly:

Throughout my time!

Think of this circle as the time factor of your life. If a flashlight is used, it may be switched from one hand to the other and back again in order to complete the symbolic movement behind your back.

Next swing your indicator round to trace a circle directly above your head and beneath your feet clockwise (all circles are clockwise or "deosil," like our solar track). This circle should be traced sideways at right angles to the time circle (see Figure 1.4). This time you intone:

Throughout my space!

As you realize, these circles would not hold together without the retaining rings, so this is traced last from front to rear above the head and below the feet (see Figure 1.5) while you intone:

Throughout my events!

Lastly bring your hands together at the central point upon your body, and intone *Amen* in this way, giving it a fourfold value: *Ah Mm Eh Nn*. Prolong each syllable somewhat, making almost a separate word of each. Now sit down and think about all this.

What you have done is provide yourself with a visualized spiritual stability which enables you symbolically to stand upright on your own inner feet and find your way around your inner world. This corresponds to an equivalent within Cosmos Itself. You have also provided yourself with a sense of inner time, space and events, which are not the same as those we experience with our physical beings. Naturally, you will find your first few footsteps around your inner world to be somewhat uncertain and teetering as they were when you were an ordinary toddler. You will soon gain confidence, though, and it should not be too long before you are walking quite well and steadily. Practice and patience are needed in all conditions of life.

Figure 1.4. The Space Circle   Figure 1.5. The Events Circle

Figure 1.6. The Individual within the Cosmic Cross

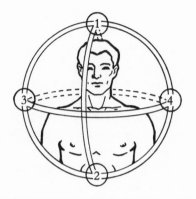

If you look at the solid, three-dimensional Circle Cross again, you will note that there are six crossings where the circles meet, six points of reference: above, below, before, behind, right and left. Strictly speaking, there is a seventh point in the center. Visualize these as points of spiritual stability in relation to yourself (see Figure 1.6). You have "Heaven" above you, "Earth" beneath you, and the four "Quarters" of your spiritual world around you. You yourself are the axis of this symbolic structure you are building up.

If you think back a bit, you should see that when you made the sign of the Cosmic Cross on yourself, you made a rapid summation of these three circles: one up and down, one across, and one round. So that is what it must signify to you in the future, and as you make it you should call up your three stabilizers around you by being conscious of them, then realize that whatever you intend to do will be within the sacred symbol of our Western Tradition.

This practice is believed to derive from a procedure in olden days of sticking an upright staff in the ground and trying to obtain guidance from "Heaven" by a shadow in daytime, and star positions at night. A staff in those times was often considered as a symbol representing its owner, and was usually cut to his own height. No one would dream of making any journey without one. It was weapon and walking-aid all in one.

The staff was taken up with the thought: "This is me." Then stuck upright in the earth while thinking: "This is where I am." The gaze was directed toward the zenith of the heavens above with maybe a prayer for guidance, then the horizon was studied carefully for signs of the best direction to take. Translate this into spiritual terms, and we have our Circle Cross. Try this one night under the stars. It is quite a rewarding experience, and a pleasing remembrance of so many that have preceded us along the Western Way. Quite often in those early days, ceremonial staffs ended with forked branches. Apart from utility reasons, such as tent supports and so forth, this signified the triple nature of primal life. It also pointed out the Golden Rule of living. "Between two extremities, try to find the Middle Way."

For the first week of this lesson concentrate on the practice described while continuing with your routine work. Set your own times and duration of practice. Remember to keep notes of any interesting thoughts which arise, or ideas which may suggest themselves. Do not overdo your efforts. Just keep going at a steady and comfortable pace which you can continue without a sense of strain. Remember the adage about always leaving the table while you are slightly hungry, and never stuffing yourself until the thought of more food makes you feel sick. It is the same with mental or spiritual equivalents of food. You need to regulate your intake so that it is no more than you can digest easily afterwards. "Digesting" mental or spiritual supplies means absorbing them into your mind and spiritual system so that they become part of yourself to use as you will.

As you perform this Cosmic Circle exercise, do not forget to sign in and out with the Circle Cross. Bring in "extra" bits this way. Start thinking about the locations where the circles cross each other. How shall we identify which is which? In our earthly equivalents we would simply say: North, South, East, West, Earth and Sky. Those are our space-limits. Suppose we start identifying the points of our inner compass by thinking something like: "Above is Divinity and all higher forms of life than ours. Let the top crossing represent that. Below us are all lesser forms of life than ours, animals, creatures of every sort, each as needful to the same universe as we are. Let the bottom crossing represent them. Level with us we have a circle of life supplying us with the essential elements enabling us to exist here. Let the four remaining crosses represent those elements."

Most literate people know that the olden four elements of life were supposed to be Air, Fire, Water, and Earth. What may not be so widely recognized, however, is that no initiate of the Mysteries believed this literally. The physical phenomena of Air, Fire, Water, and Earth were only meant to be *symbolic* of the unknown energies which keep us alive as conscious creatures of Cosmos. There was also a very arcane fifth element which kept the others together in a common connection. Some called this Aether, and others just Truth in the sense that unless all the things and people in Cosmos are true to each other, everything will fall apart and result in Chaos or total confusion and meaninglessness.

Perhaps you are wondering if these ancient concepts of elements can possibly be valid today, or if we choose more modern ideas. As actualities they never were valid, but as *symbols* they always will be. They are representations of life-energies, purely and simply, and also basic needs for our bodily survival. We need an atmosphere to breath with, body-heat to keep our functions going, fluids for cell nutrients, and solids for nourishment and replacement of tissue. As *principles* these old "elements" will apply while there is a living creature left on this planet—and beyond that point. So let us see how they sort themselves out at each quarter of our Cosmic Circle.

Assuming we are facing the coming of light represented by our Sun, this must be the East, or Air quarter associated with dawn. Turning deosil (clockwise) we find the South where the Sun is highest at noon as a manifestation of Fire. The next quarter must therefore be the West, where Sol was reputed to sink into the watery ocean at dusk, so the last quarter has to be the North, associated with night and the dark, silent Earth. The quarters will also align with the seasons of Spring, Summer, Autumn, and Winter. All these attributes are what might be called natural Cosmic phenomena. You have to connect them with your own Circle by any system of association you like best. There are many ways of doing this.

For instance, you could turn round in the center of your circle, pausing at each quarter and naming the attributes aloud. Rather pedestrian, though, isn't it? You might pace round the perimeter of the circle, stopping to face outward at the quarters and make mental pictures of the elements and their effects on yourself at the appropriate seasons. Make these pleasant pictures by all means. See yourself at dawn in springtime waiting for sunrise as a gentle breeze carries an interesting scent to your nostrils. Then visualize at noon with the Sun high while you are cooking something very savory over a campfire. Next, think of yourself sitting and watching a beautiful autumn sunset while you are drinking a very welcome refresher. Last, you may suppose yourself on a bitter winter night finding a lifesaving shelter in a dry cave with plenty of soft leaves to settle down in.

If you demand something more concrete than that, try placing a hand fan at the East, an unlit lamp at the South, a cup of water at the West, and a plate with a piece of bread on it at the North. As you go round the circle, stop at the East and fan yourself, light the lamp at the South, drink the water at the West, and eat the bread at the North. (Since bread is made with grain, which is "fruit of the Earth," it represents that element.) If you are poetically inclined, you may make up very short verses about each element and say them as you go round. There should not be more than four lines each. Rhyming is not so important as meaning.

However you choose to represent the life-elements, try to do so logically, and appropriately, yet at the same time artistically. We know that the elements are raw power and can be appallingly destructive when running wild. Do not invoke them in that form. Cosmos should always be *controlled*. We have reached our present state of civilization by learning how to control the elements to some degree. Whether we have learned how to control their spiritual equivalents with equal success is another matter. That should be what concerns us with these particular exercises.

This is not the place for long dissertations on the nature and peculiarities of the elements. You should go into that with your own reading material, and come to your own conclusions. Jot down any ideas you get, however disjointed they might seem. Keep a page or so for each element and add to your ideas. By this time, quite a few ideas should be coming to you from unidentified sources inside yourself. Greet them, and make them welcome as they arrive. Remember that you are a living human being trying to make friendly and valuable relationships with invisible, intangible, and incalculable energies behind your life. In mathematics if you do not know what some suspected factor may be, you make a symbol for it, usually X, then juggle around with other connected factors you know about, until their relationship eventually reveals what the unknown reality must necessarily be. Much the same applies to mystical procedures. If you do not know what some spiritual value might be, give it a symbol you hope is suitable, and work as old-time mariners once said: "By guess and by God." They are not a bad combination.

There is a side effect of this Circle Cross working which is rather interesting. The great psychotherapist C.G. Jung, towards the end of his life, when reviewing the thousands of cases he had handled, noticed a peculiar recurring factor. A high percentage of permanent cures began to have the same fundamental dream-image when the likelihood of a cure became possible. This image was the Circle Cross in one semblance or another. One person saw it as a rose garden, another as a design on a belt, another as a circle of friends she was trying to talk to from four directions. Everybody saw or felt the same "archetypal image," as Jung called these codings of consciousness. It was always associated with re-balance of mental and physical health, and a promise of cure to come.

One doctor whose wife was suffering from psychological, and consequently, physical trouble, read Jung's comments about the Circle Cross and tried a "wild experiment." He did no more than cut a large Circle Cross about four feet in diameter out of plywood, painted it with shining metallic paint, set it up in a shaded room with a spotlight on it, and told his wife to sit comfortably and contemplate the symbol for a time each day. She did this and was cured in the course of a few months!

Why should things like that happen? Mainly because the people concerned were Western people, and they were confronted with a symbol connecting them with their own roots. They did not know this with their ordinary objective consciousness, but their deep and normally dormant inner awareness recognized and responded to the symbolic signal for help. This was also a call to our cosmic companions for assistance along inner lines of communication.

Questions

1. What do you understand by a "Labor of Preparation?"
2. How do you conceive the "three rings of chaos?" Make a sketch.
3. Align the life-elements with the quarters. Why are they called "life-elements?"
4. Do you understand that your spiritual stability depends on an inner equivalent of our "time-space-event" components of Cosmos? How do you symbolize this around yourself?
5. Make up a short invocation for each element of life.
6. How do you understand your relationship with the Circle Cross of Cosmos? Discuss this.
7. Can you see why the Circle Cross concept should act as a spiritual safety device? Explain why this is so.
8. Choose the eight most important sentences in this chapter.
9. Think of six examples of the Circle Cross pattern in ordinary living and sketch them, if you can.
10. Discuss the "golden rule of life."

· 4 ·

Elemental Energies

What we are going to do here is assign control symbols at the principal points of our Circle Cross and add an appropriate code letter:

Quarter	Time	Element	Symbol	Letter	Sign
East	Dawn	Air	Dagger or Sword	E	△
South	Noon	Fire	Rod, Wand, Staff or Spear	I	△
West	Dusk	Water	Cup, Horn, Waterskin	O	▽
North	Night	Earth	Shield, Pentacle or Spade	A	▽
Encircling everywhere		Truth	Cord	U	○

We still need a top and a bottom axis to complete the scheme, and all must relate with the center:

Position	Symbol		Sonic
Zenith	A crown of a circlet and 4 bars	🜨	An audible breath
Nadir	A cube made from six pyramids	⬡	A very deep buzz
Center	A small brilliant star of light	☆	A medium hum

It is easy to spot that the elemental symbols are the four suits of the Tarot Cards or ordinary playing pack, but a lot of people get confused with them and cannot see why a Sword should not symbolize Fire, or the Cup be North, and similar ideas. This is where we have to come down very firmly and see basic truths as they are.

Originally the student of the mysteries was visualized as a Hunter, because he was seeking and questing for his Divine Quarry which was his own ultimate identity. He was seen as if armed with the ancient weapons of primitive hunting. First a bow and arrow or short throwing spear, which would whistle through the air towards his target. Next a staff or long spear, the end of which could be used as a lever for hurling the throw-spear harder and further. Combined with the bow-string or cord, it could be used as a fire-drill, or to carry fire safely from one place to another. Also the fire-charred end of a staff could easily be sharpened and hardened to make a lethal attack-weapon. The cup was originally a water-skin which carried the life sustaining fluid in arid areas, but if inflated with air, might be used as a float to get its owner over wide rivers or lagoons. The shield was not only that, but might be employed as an earth-shifter or for carrying building materials and so forth. Lastly the cord or rope had endless uses including making snares or fishing lines. The whole collection of "weapons" amounted to survival gear in ancient times. With these you might live, but without them you didn't stand a very good chance.

All you have to do is translate these old realities into idealized symbology for survival in spiritual life, and you should see why they evolved as they did. As it happens the five vowels line up with them with a certain amount of sonic semblance. An *E* sound whistles like Air, an *I* crackles like Fire, an *O* gurgles like Water, and an *A* thuds like Earth. Though nobody knows the sound of Truth, an *U* says several things. First it is a very old name of God: HU. It is also the sound of a question, UH? Or an assent, UH HU, which can turn to a negative UH UH. Those are virtually universally understood sounds in themselves. So the sonic could be translated as: who, what, or which will or will not. The meaning of all this is our concept of truth at any given moment.

Now we have the axial symbols left. The crown above is obviously a sign of "Heaven," and our ideas of highest attainment or "Kingship" while we are still human on earth. Note that a crown is really the top half of our three Cosmic circles. The sonic associated with it is a "pre-alphabet" noise of an inbreath or the "sound before sounds," to indicate some ultimate aim far above the heads of mere humans as we are now, but which we hope to reach eventually. The cube beneath our feet is the solidity on which we stand, or the cubic stone on which we sit as "Crowned Kings." It goes back to the old Sacred Stone idea, on which only an annointed King dared sit or stand. The Stone was supposed to speak secretly to the King while he uttered his edicts therefrom. Here we are seeing this cube as having lines crossed from corner to corner inside it, so that it is really six equal sized pyramids connecting at their points. The last symbol of the series is the star in the middle of all, which is simply a radiance concealing whatever may be concealed in its secret center. This is the divine spark of life. Its sonic symbol is the *M*, or humming of the Cosmos in motion. The old Hunter figure would have connected it with the humming of his bow-string as his arrow went into action. Masons might note the crown is drawn with compasses and the cube with a square, the sign of Heaven and Earth interacting.

Most people working in the Western tradition like to own actual representations of these symbols even though they may realize that the real symbols are those they create in their own consciousness. It was always believed that initiates should make as much of their gear with their own hands as they could because of the focusing of consciousness involved with construction of the articles. They are thus creations of the minds which are using them, and so much the more valuable than anything merely purchased. Fundamentally there is no real objection to buying mystical symbols, providing one is prepared to spend the same mental and conscious efforts on them *as if they had been made with one's own hands.* Remember that it is this concentration of consciousness over time which really "consecrates" any form of magical symbolism. Specific ceremonies only set a final seal on the procedure. They are worthless without it, just as a signature on a check would be useless without money behind it in the bank.

What does *consecration* actually mean? It is the specific dedication of anything to some form of mystical practice or purpose, such dedication being made through a human–divine partnership. "Consecrated" objects are to be used *only* for their specific spiritual purpose and nothing else. The whole idea, of course, is to keep streams of consciousness clear of contamination from other conflicting sources. You would not run a sewer into a stream you meant to draw drinking water from. You get much the same effect if you run currents of "clear" and "murky" thinking together.

The main function of your "magical symbols" is for keeping your channels of consciousness clear to the elemental energies of life. With the Sword you should only think "Air" ideas, with the Rod, "Fire" ideas, and so on. Of course, life itself is a constant combination of all these energies simultaneously, but you still have to see them as separate streams of energy before you can combine them properly. Each is theoretically a "pure" element, which means that it is unmixed with others. Strictly speaking, the word "pure" means unadulterated, unmixed with anything other than its own unique nature. That is the sense in which "purity" should be understood in mystical matters. Pure elements can be *combined* together without mixing them, just as oil and water can be combined yet will not mix. Fire and water can combine to boil a cauldron of liquid, but if mixed the fire might be extinguished and the water turned to steam, so both elements would be lost to the user. It is vital to see this difference, because it is the principle with which all magical "elements" are worked.

Before you start making or buying solid magical symbols you might want to gain a little skill in using them. The simplest way to do this is to take the four Tarot aces out of the pack, shuffle them face down, then pick one out and look at it. Whichever it is, keep thinking about the element it represents *only* for a few moments, then put it back, re-shuffle, and pick another. Never mind if it's the same card, just go on with the process. The important thing is to keep concentrating on one element at a time as they turn up in random sequence, switching quickly as the cards change. You can begin this exercise fairly fast, then gradually slow it down until you can hold the idea of a single element in your mind for at least half a minute. This could take you a lot longer than you suppose.

When you gain some success with this, you can make a complete set of "instrument cards," which are just plain cards on which you have drawn the symbols in whatever way you see them. There will be eight in all: Sword, Rod, Cup, Shield, Cord, Crown, Cube, and Star. The last four will be most difficult, especially the Cord. Who can imagine what Truth is? Nevertheless, you have to find *some* idea of this in your mind and hold on to it while controlling your consciousness with a Cord symbol. With the Crown, you may think of all or any of the wonders above your present reach which you are aiming for, and with the Cube, whatever you have already accomplished and passed by in your progress. The Star should give you ideas of your living and eternal present as a spirit illuminating the whole Cosmos of your being. Keep shuffling and laying out the cards, choosing one, and changing your consciousness to suit.

It is best to work on this exercise for a few minutes each day for about a week before proceeding to the next development. This is where things get a lot harder. What you have to do is pick *two* cards at once, keeping two streams of consciousness going together, each confined to its own element or other symbol. At first, you may have to keep jumping from one to another, but you should soon get the knack of dealing with two separate, but complementary concepts at the same time. Once your realize the "feel" of this practice, you can go from two to three, and then up by one at a time to the full eight concepts simultaneously.

Don't let the complexity of this task frighten you into thinking it might be beyond your abilities. You can already do it along other lines. Supposing you were lighting an ordinary campfire to boil a kettle of water. You would have to concentrate on all four elements at once, yet separately. There would be the fire under the water to think of, then stones around to keep it together, then the wind which might be blowing the wrong way, making you erect a screen. If you can do that much with ordinary physical things, you should surely be able to carry out a similar process with their inner equivalents. How many separate thought-streams do you have to handle when you are driving a car? Yet the separate streams do not *mix,* but combine towards a single end. You have only to manage the same on inner levels of life.

What we are concerned with here is binding ideas together so as to concentrate the force of consciousness. At the moment we are binding concepts of elemental life-energy to physical symbols which express their spiritual use. Suppose we start with the very simplest and easiest things. Remember it was traditional that equipment should be made from "virgin" materials, or those never previously employed for mundane purposes. This was so that no "counter-thinking" could possibly be attached to them. Therefore it is certainly permissable to buy a new knife with the intention it will never be used for profane purposes, like opening mail or cleaning your nails. It should have a decent cutting edge and preferably a black wooden (not plastic) handle. Choose and buy it, for cash, (not on a credit card). It was strictly forbidden to haggle over the price of any magical equipment. This was to prevent ill wishes and ungenerous emotions from attaching themselves, but such a contingency seems unlikely in modern fixed-price markets.

When you have your knife you can cut your Rod with it. The simplest form of Rod is a straight section of hazel or almond about as thick as your forefinger and the length of your forearm from elbow to fingertips (a cubit). When you have cut it, mark its middle, then peel the bark from one end only and scrape the wood smooth. Sharpen the scraped end to a blunt point. Cut a slight V groove across the other end like the notch of an arrow. You have thus given your Rod a "Male-Female" significance. Do be careful of the knife blade during this operation and *mind your fingers.* If you don't feel capable of this task, you can do just as well to buy a short length of plain wooden dowelling at a shop and stain half black with ink.

Next comes the Cup. If you cannot make this from clay, glazing and firing it yourself into a finished product, then you may buy one. Remember it is only a temporary symbol for practice purposes. It should be a reasonable size and easy to handle.

The Shield or Platter is another problem. Fundamentally it is a circular disc, often of wood, on which is traced a design representing *your own concept of the universe and your particular purpose within it.* You will have to work this out for yourself because that is an essential part of the process. Again, remember, this design will apply to the way you see things *now.* You may make several of such Shields during a single lifetime. If you can't think of anything else, get a circular wooden bread board or round place-mat, paste a picture of yourself in the middle and write some idea of your own, or a favorite quotation, around the edge.

So much for the four elemental symbols. The Cord may be made from any nylon rope suitable for a girdle. There should be an eyelet at one end and a tassel at the other. It is worn around the waist with the tassel looped through the eyelet so that this makes a noose which is secured by a suitable knot which pulls through the eyelet like a button through a buttonhole. The loose end of the Cord dangles from the center of the body down below the knees. There are other ways of wearing the Cord, but this is the most common method. For beginners the Cord is plain or white, but later it should change color to signify higher grades. Of course, a much shorter and thinner Cord could serve as a more convenient symbol.

The axial symbols are quite easy to simulate. If you do not want to make a Crown and hang it in the center of the ceiling, get a simple skullcap, paint or embroider the Crown design thereon, and put it on your own head when you need it. With gold edging you can show a handsome Crown with its cross bars going from back to front and side to side. A suitable jewel can be sewn on to locate the center of the forehead by touch. The Cube beneath the feet may be a small square mat to stand on. It should have one black and one white line connecting diagonals, and the center where these cross ought to be a gold or bright point.

The last symbol of the Star will naturally appear upon your breast. It either hangs from a chain round your neck or is pinned in place. As a rule it takes the form of the five-pointed pentagram or sign of Man the Microcosm, worn right way up with a single point at the top and two at the bottom. This may be plain or engraved of any material, but preferably of highly polished silver or gold. Brass is an excellent substitute, and so is copper.

When all these symbols have been obtained, the next thing to do is "place" them. That means locating them correctly in their places of Cosmo-control and associating them fully with the living elemental energies they represent. This is likely to take over half an hour of exercise time, so make sure you will not be interrupted, and have your symbols ready on a small table close to hand in any order you like. Run over the ritual for setting up your Cosmic Circles as rapidly as you can to the closing point of the last lesson, and when all is oriented in your consciousness around you, begin with the Star. After it is properly affixed upon your breast, try to feel it as a point of light *within* you. It shines quietly and steadily with a heatless holy light, proclaiming the presence of that spirit you hope to harbor in your secret heart. If you like to think of it as the Star of Bethlehem, then do so, for it indicates Divinity incarnate. Spend some time on this concept, approaching it from any angle you please. Hum its sonic *"mmmmmm"* so that you feel a tingling everywhere in your body, right down to your fingertips. Start turning round on your axis slowly, humming all the while and thinking of the Star with its associated meanings. On no account go fast enough to make you feel sick or giddy. Keep on a very calm and steady course, and don't prolong it too greatly.

Stop slowly, face East, raise your attention to the zenith of Heaven above, then place the Crown-cap on your head correctly aligned with its bars to the quarters. Concentrate on this symbol and see it as the "crowning" of your life with the acme of spiritual attainment you might expect in this incarnation which you earn with your own efforts. Breathe audibly through your open lips as if in ecstatic wonder at this, then "come down to earth" very firmly on the Cube symbolized by the square mat and contact of your feet with the floor. That is your "throne" which forms the fixed fulcrum for your magical Cosmos to move upon. It is also your "philosopher's stone" which will transmute your base nature to one of much higher value. Again, it is the mysterious "lapis exilis,"or stone of exile, which reputedly fell from Heaven and eventually became the Holy Grail, or Sangreal. As such, it is the foundation of your faith in life and should be so thought of. Now you must learn to control the elemental powers of life in action. Recognize these by a prolonged *"buzzzzzz"* like a mechanism in motion.

Pick up the Sword (knife) in your right hand with its blade pointing forward. Imagine a wind springing up in the East which soon turns to a gale, then a hurricane or tornado driving at you. Hark at the shrieking, howling, diabolical frenzy of it! None of it is touching you, however. The sharp blade of your magic Sword cuts the fury to either side so that it whistles harmlessly past you on left and right. What a cutting and bitter noise it makes! *"Eeeeeeee"* it screams. Throw this sound right back in its teeth as you form the upright triangle and bar sign of Air with your Sword symbol, then utter firmly and authoritatively the ancient formula: *"Peace. Be still."* As you say this, the wind drops, you are conscious of the Sun shining, and then a pleasant gentle breeze brings some refreshing scent to your nostrils. Lay down your Sword in the East, then turn right and pick up the Rod in your left hand.

Here you face South. Raise the Rod pointing forward and picture a fire starting as a small flame in front of you which rapidly rises to a roaring inferno, threatening your destruction. Feel the fierce heat of it and listen to the flames crackling as it comes closer. *"Iiiiiii."* Pick up the sound and echo it as you point the Rod right at the hottest part of the flames. Immediately picture the Rod projecting a flame-quelling energy. Make the upright triangle of the Fire sign while saying once more: *"Peace. Be still."* The flames die down very quickly, leaving in the end a small and friendly little fire which you poke casually with your Rod as you place it in the South of your Circle. Turn right again, then back to the center and collect your Cup in both hands.

Now you face West. Raise the Cup and extend it before you. The scene in your mind changes to a storm at sea. Huge waves are breaking over your ship. Rain is pouring down from a darkened sky, the "waters of wrath." Hear them as they threaten to overpower you. *"Ooooooooo,"* they wail, while soaking you to the skin, clawing at you as they drag you to doom in their depths. Call back their own cry as you make the sign of the down-pointing triangle and command them: *"Peace. Be still."* Troubled waters subside at once and become calm, the rain ceases and sun shines on gentle rippling seas. The Cup in your hands is filled to its brim with clear sparkling fluid, the water of life. You drink thankfully, then place your precious Cup in the West. Turn right again and pick up the Shield.

You are facing North. Raise the Shield with your left hand, its edge just below eye level. You are conscious of darkness and cold. You are in a huge cavern, but there is a very dim light which must be coming from some distant entrance. Ominous creaks and noises sound like rocks grinding together. One or two light stones fall near you, and you realize to your horror that the place is collapsing and threatening to bury you alive. Instinctively you raise your Shield above your head while stones and earth hit it. Listen to them. *"Ah ah ah ah,"* they sound. Everywhere echoes the awful noise. If you do not act now, you will be lost forever. Roar the note of the rocks back at them as you make the downward triangle and bar sign of Earth before you with the Shield. Again order: *"Peace. Be still."* There is silence once more, and holding your Shield in a protective position, you find you are facing the entrance to the cavern, through which more and more light is coming. You pass through it without quite knowing how, and find yourself in a most beautiful country place with fields and flowers all around you. Lowering the Shield, you hold it flat in both hands like a platter. Suddenly you realize the world is rather a wonderful place to be in after all. So you leave your Shield at the North, and pick up the Cord.

This time, make a small circle of the noose-end and let it lie on the floor while you hold the other end. Stand in the noose-circle. Pull the Cord sharply upwards as you try to walk round your Cosmos, and the noose should tighten and ride up your legs, restricting your movements. (Be very careful with this exercise or you are liable to fall.) Do you see that the more you try to pull the Cord free by sheer force the tighter it binds you? That is how you are hampered in a world full of lies when you struggle and tie yourself with untruths till you can't move any way at all without hurting yourself. How are you going to get out of this mess? Listen to yourself grunting as you go: *"Uh. Uh. Uh. Uh."* Realize you are just being plain stupid. Stay still and *relax*. Maybe it would be better if you changed the tune a bit. Try saying *"Truth"* with a long drawn-out *"U"* in the middle. Like this: *"Tr uuuuuuuuuu th."* Breathe out as long as you can. The noose should loosen and fall to the floor. Step carefully out of it and go the edge of your Circle, still holding the free end of the Cord in your right hand. Now you can freely walk round the Circle. What is more, if the Cord were firmly held by a peg in the center so that its tightened noose slid freely around it, you could walk the Circle blindfolded by keeping the Cord tight as you went. The same Cord which once nearly caused your downfall is now your infallible guide. That is the parable of Truth in life.

This brings us to the end of the present Chapter which should have given you a lot of hard, yet worthwhile work. Maybe you wonder if you have only been acting out childish fantasies with yourself. That might be what it would look like to an unsympathetic observer, (whom we hope you would not allow to watch your performances) but inside yourself, you should have been doing something of real importance. You have been organizing your own nature in relation to the fundamental energies of life, selecting and setting up by associative consciousness a series of control symbols for the forces which move you about and make you live. By thinking and concentrating upon any of these Symbols, you will eventually control the energies they represent in yourself.

For instance, by concentrating on the Knife or Sword Symbol, you should come to control the wildly airy side of your nature which blows about irresponsibly and ruffles other people's feelings, generally spinning you round like a weathercock without getting you anywhere in particular. The contrary wind is always blowing you off course in life, yet arises from within yourself the whole time. The same follows for the other elements of your inner character, which you should easily be able to work out for yourself now. You have been laying out a master-scheme for taming and eventually making good use of the natural forces of life within yourself. Surely that is something to feel justifiably proud of?

Of course, you won't do all of this at a single try. Nobody would expect you to. At first you will only be able to go through the motions, but that will mean a great deal by itself because it indicates your intentions are serious. This is only the beginning of finding a magical meaning to life. If you think this is hard, just you wait a little longer! You can make things a lot easier for yourself by following these lessons as best you can now.

Questions

1. Name the symbols at the doors of our Western Mysteries and state their functions.
2. How have you designed your symbols? Make sketches.
3. What did you understand about the symbology of the Cord and have you any new ideas about it?
4. How would you consecrate anything? Deconsecrate it?
5. Give the relationship of symbols, elements and vowels. Discuss.
6. How does the Hunter-figure come to be involved with our Western Mysteries?
7. Which quarter do you find most in harmony with your own nature? What part of yourself do you see in relation to them all?
8. Choose the nine most important sentences in this chapter.
9. What is the fundamental function of the "magical weapons" and why are they so called?

· 5 ·

Archangel Attributes

Many people have vague ideas about magicians of old chanting away in chalk-drawn circles while they summoned up spirits in all kinds of weird shapes whom they hoped would gratify whatever greed they felt at the moment. How much of this is true and how much false? It was certainly true about would-be magi standing in circles and chanting, but what, if anything, did they summon up? And did this do them any good or not? If it was a complete waste of time, then why should we bother to do anything of that sort today? On the other hand, if it wasn't an entire waste of energy, how do we set about the process in our times? Good questions.

Let us face the fact that a great deal of what magicians in old times "summoned up" were creations of their own consciousness due to drugs, lack of vitamins, starvation, stress, exhaustion, and other such causes of toxemia. *But, not all!* Sometimes their thought-creations constructed a sort of "body" which then became animated by an active intelligence with a behavior pattern of its own. Obviously, if they were making a nasty type of thought-body then a similar sort of intelligence would be attracted to it, and conversely if they made a pleasant kind of vehicle the opposite was likely to happen.

Have you ever thought of consciousness as what artists call a "medium"? This means whatever materials they use for a particular work of art to express their concepts. Thus a painter would use oil paints or water colors or acrylics, a sculptor stone or metal, a carver wood, a potter clay, and so forth. Well, consciousness is the direct medium of magical art. Magi are expected to "take a lump of consciousness" in its natural state, then mold and manipulate it around until it represents the will or intention of the magical worker. The difference between him and other artists is that they can exhibit their products to external viewers, while he is limited to inner beholders.

Try a little experiment, but don't let anyone watch because it would look almost insane to an outsider. Gaze into the cupped palm of your left hand and realize that your consciousness is being projected there. Think of a small amount of that consciousness as a sort of plastic substance colored red. It will not stick to the skin, nor discolor it. Now put the right palm down over it, and try to feel it between your hands. Start rolling your hands around as if making a ball of their contents. When you get the impression of a ball forming up there, stop, lift your right hand gently up and look at your visionary impression of a little red ball lying there in your left palm. Pick it up with the right thumb and forefinger and put it somewhere carefully. Go through the same process again, but this time make a yellow ball of the same size. Next, a blue one. Look at them, all three together. So you can actually construct anything with size, shape, and color out of consciousness alone, if you want to. Everything else is no more than an extension and elaboration of this principle.

Before you go any further, learn to be neat and tidy with your work and don't leave mental rubbish lying around in your mind. Banish your concept of the three balls by "sucking them back" into your mind and willing them to revert into original energy. See the place where you put them as being quite clear of their presence. Never leave unwanted or superfluous mental creations cluttering up the background of your consciousness. Reduce them down to stock as it were. That is what "banishing" meant in old magical terms. This doesn't apply to other than useless or unnecessary concepts. You need good ones to stay around and serve some purpose, which doesn't mean you mustn't ever alter them into better and improved versions.

We propose that you should now try to create a conscious semblance of an "Archangel" at each control-point of your inner Cosmos. Each will deal *only* with the specific energy associated therewith, but in combination with each other they can handle all energies within your life. They will present appearances of greatly superior spiritual beings and behave accordingly. Though they are factually "made out of your own mind," they should eventually act as contact-points and receivers for pure streams of inner energies linked with their symbology. Technically these creations are called "telesmic images," and because they are humanoid in character, they are convenient and natural to deal with.

This is where you will have to read up descriptions and details of these "Archangels" in other books and get the clearest concepts of them you can imagine. These Archangels are chosen as symbols because they represent the very best, noblest, and most beneficial nature of whichever elemental energy they stand for. They can only mediate forces for good purposes and are quite unsuitable to serve the slightest ends of real evil. That is a very important consideration.

A lot of workers just visualize the eternal appearance of an "Archangel" at each quarter, then hope for the best. This is not sufficient at all. A mere outer semblance is no more than a picture and will do nothing else than just look pretty. We need an active and capable creation of consciousness which will assist us in controlling and managing our magical Cosmos. Here is one practical method of "creating an Archangel."

First, get the right atmosphere in your working room with suitably dimmed lights of correct color and appropriate incense. There can be music to match, if this helps, but it is advisable to keep the volume low. Put a circular mat on the floor at center about two or three feet in diameter, maybe a little less. If you like being elaborate, you might contrive four of these mats with the colors and names of the quarterly Archangels on them. What you are going to do is use the mat for a "plinth," then go round it carefully, building up an "Archangel" figure exactly as a sculptor builds up a clay figure with his hands, except that instead of clay, you will use consciousness itself as a medium. In other words, you will be "making like Pygmalion." If you aren't familiar with his story, then please read it (you'll find it in Ovid's *Metamorphosis* and other sources on Greek mythology), or you'll miss the point entirely. Whatever you do, make sure it's the Pygmalion of *Cyprus* you imitate and not the one of Tyre.

Stand at whichever quarter you mean to start with, preferably the East. Face center, then go to the edge of the mat and close your eyes. Begin rubbing your hands together, trying to feel the element in question between them as if you were molding it. Think of the element as being alive and intelligent, mobile and conformable. Let it flow from you along your arms to pour continually from the palms of your hands as you work. Keep concentrating on that one element all the while, especially the spirit of the element, its meaning for you, its significance, qualities, virtues, and admirable properties, all its *good* attributes. This is extremely important.

Many magical workers make a mistake by concentrating on the exterior of a thought-creation alone. You should always begin on the *inside* and work outwards, leaving appearance till last. A thought-appearance is only an empty shell, a mere case with no mechanism in it, an envelope with no message inside. No more. So begin by assembling the inner active energy first, then mold it into whatever you will afterwards.

Start with both hands somewhat apart, just above your own head level. Imagine yourself pushing your supply of elemental energy in the rough shape of a human head, then a body, then arms and lastly legs. Don't attempt any artistic shaping yet, only assemble the barest outline of a humanoid body slightly larger than yours, like a sculptor slaps modelling clay on an armature. Keep going round the thing clockwise while you attempt to feel it building up under your fingers from whichever angle you approach it. Move your own body to suit your actions, stooping to do the legs and feet for instance, and raising your hands for the head. You can keep up a running commentary to yourself if you like, but at this stage it must only refer to the power, energy, or intelligence of the element you are using. When you feel you have actually formed something, it is time to begin the finer process of formation. If you want to break off and finish it another day, you can quite well do this if you make a clear visualization of what you have done up till now and pick it up from that point another time. Creative work of this kind can be far more exhausting than you would believe—until you try it for yourself.

The next stage of making up a telesmic "Archangel" is by shaping its appearance and sensing its movements exactly like a blind person interprets the looks and motions of another human by running fingers all over the surface of that being's body, then calculates impressions of them from such findings. Set up your invisible figure, and with closed eyes begin feeling very carefully all over it from top to toe, molding and setting as you go. Progress all around the figure, touching it from each quarter. Again you can invent your own descriptive commentary or listen to a tape, but this time it must only concern the appearance of the "Archangel" and your reactions to such.

Remember, you are not making a mental image of a statue, but the conscious semblance of a living and active creature. As you work, talk to the thing in your mind as if it were coming to life under your hands. Get the impression of warm flesh, yet consider that this is not a being with blood in its veins, but is energized by the *principle* of whichever life-element you are making it from.

Incidentally, Archangels are sexless beings, so don't try to be clever because you thought of sex organs for each. The legend behind angels is that they do not reproduce like us, but are specifically created for some particular purpose. Minor angels, for instance, could be created to fulfill some single end and when that was achieved they could be "de-created." The archangelic images we are dealing with here, being concerned with living energy, have a continuity factor co-equal with life itself. So far as we are concerned, that means an eternity. They are "beings" with representative qualities of both male and female creatures of biological existence.

Continue going round your "Archangel," stroking, smoothing, filling in details, correcting mistakes, or adding improvements to the structure. Feel the fineness of hair, the texture of garments, outlines of jewels or accoutrements, features and hands in particular. Say in your mind: "What well-shaped ears and straight nose. Magnificent hair, full and firm lips, good jaw-line and splendidly smooth cheeks." Add concepts of color to match until you feel the whole picture firming up nicely. Think or say something to the effect of: "What a glorious blue cloak. Clear, piercing gray eyes, windswept ash-blonde hair, delicate fair complexion," and so on. Use plenty of superlatives, because you should be building with words as well as will. Be very careful, of course, only to use appropriate wording or imagery for whatever telesmic image you are creating. If you should make an error, cancel it out and replace it with the correct version. This can always be done later if you get it wrong the first time.

It is actually best not to be too finicky or particular on the first occasion you try this exercise. Be content to get a rough semblance of an "Archangel," activate it, then go on "trimming up" a bit at a time later. You have to make it "come alive" by "pouring your will" into the thing through commands like: "So and So, be conscious of me through this body. Hear me with these ears. Speak to me through these lips. Move with these limbs. So and So." Go on uttering the name and giving "enlivening" instructions. Move away from the plinth holding the telesmic by its hand and feel it follow you. Sway from side to side and make it do likewise. Dance with it if you like, but on no account make it do anything which would contradict the characteristics of the "Archangel" concerned. Once satisfied, direct it to its proper Quarter of your inner Cosmos and leave it there. Place its mat as a position marker. *Do not "banish" the figure,* but let it live in your subconsciousness, from whence you should summon it by name when needed.

While you should be able to make quite good likenesses of the elemental Archangels, the others are more of a problem. Since nobody can visualize what truth looks like, the Archangel *Suvuviel* will have to be seen as a momentary flash which you know is there, can occasionally feel as it passes by you at unexpected moments, but which you cannot hold or compel in any way. You might sometimes catch an echo of what it says in passing, but you realize you could have been mistaken. You will just have to do the best you can in creating this concept. Everyone has to work this out for himself. There is no official way of visualizing this Archangel, because that would be totally contrary to the spirit this concept represents.

Although the zenith Archangel, *Metatron,* and the complimentary nadir Archangel, *Zandalaphon,* are usually thought of as separate beings, they are really opposite ends of the same concept. *Metatron* is usually imagined as having his head in the heavens and his feet on earth. He (or it) is assumed to be the only "Angel of the presence" who faces divinity directly, and legend says he was once a human being. He has seventy-five separate names, and while on earth was called Enoch—a man. He characterizes the supreme spiritual height it is possible for a human to reach and consequently cannot be seen very clearly. Can you remember as a very tiny child what it felt like trying to hang on to the hand of some very tall relative who was trying to guide your tottering steps? You hung onto that person's hand with all your strength, but the rest of them seemed lost in the clouds and very far away. The hand was more real to you than its owner, because it was in closer contact with you. That is the *Metatron* concept to foster, a guiding hand from Heaven.

Zandalaphon the "co-brother" is supposed to protect our spiritual feet from the pitfalls and perilous places of the "Path". He also has the specific work of weaving garlands out of human prayers and sending them heavenwards, where *Metatron* presumably catches them and hands the best looking ones directly to God. Again, the best analogy for this Archangel is a childhood memory. You are very small and confused by being in some crowd where all around you is a frightening jungle of human legs and enormous wheels. Suddenly your guardian catches you up and sits you on his broad shoulders, from where you can see over the heads of everyone and discover what is going on. Huge hands are holding your ankles securely so that you will be safe and not fall. Maybe you are hanging on to the grown-up's hair or ears, but he is good humored and only laughs while he holds your kicking legs tighter. Well, that is *Zandalaphon,* your co-brother. You can't see his face, but he is holding you up to find out what life is about. Deal with this concept the best way you can.

Now you may realize a little why "occult secrecy" is sometimes important. If an outsider were to witness you practicing this exercise, he could conclude you were totally insane and act accordingly. A lot of "magic" looks like madness on the outside. Yet what have you really been doing except "space-sculpture"? Why shouldn't space or time be as valid an artistic medium as any other in existence? A surprising or novel idea? Why not? A wheel was a novel idea once, yet look how it changed all our history.

Do bear in mind you can't create an "archangelic" image in a flash. It isn't something you can see a picture of once, think of a few seconds, and—bang!—Archangels are fawning all over you. You will really have to work on the thing for enough time, using space as a medium for your consciousness. They won't live very long either, unless you keep "feeding" them with occasional supplies of active consciousness. If you had a pet animal and never fed it or you gave it the wrong diet, the poor creature would either leave you or die. Here you have been creating a "creature of consciousness" which needs feeding from time to time, or it will fade out of existence from sheer malnutrition. All you need is to think *at* them now and again, especially before you need them for ritual work.

You might be wondering what you have accomplished by hopping about and waving your hands around. What you *should* have made is a mental mechanism which will link your consciousness with a source of inner intelligence corresponding to its symbolic significance. Isn't that worth something? You could say that you have been setting up a special receiver tuned to a particular life frequency. Communication may not be too brilliant to begin with, but everything improves with practice. You have to make a start somewhere.

Perhaps you are reminded of the "invisible friends" invented by some small children, and think there might be a connection between them and the "creations" you have been trying to make here. If so, you are right. The principle is the same, but the practice and purpose differs. A lonely child invents friends to play with whereas you are creating concepts to work with. The similarity is that both your "Archangels" and the child's "friends" can be inwardly animated by genuine intelligences of independent origins. Yours are specifically limited to certain classes of consciousness, whereas the child's "friends" may be picking it up from a wide variety of origins, some not always very helpful. Then again the child will usually lose interest in his "phantom friends" as he makes closer contact with "solid" people in the course of growing up, whereas your creations tend to get more "real" as you continue to cultivate them.

There is one disadvantage here you must avoid at all costs. In some cases, people foolishly allow their rational outlooks on life to become dominated and over-influenced by their inner concepts. Mostly this is because they are too lazy or indecisive to take responsibility for running their own lives. It is so much easier to let life slide along, blaming everyone or everything else for what happens to them. In the Middle Ages it was so convenient to blame the Devil for the evil in human nature. Moreover, we have to bear in mind some of the evil we commit in the name of God. Religious wars and persecutions through our history bear witness to humans attributing their own ambitions to a deity which reputedly made them in its own image. How many mean, unkind, and unjust actions against undeserving people have been inflicted because somebody thought a God meant them to do those things? It was their images of God in their own minds which instructed them, not the deity itself. They built the wrong ingredients into their God concepts.

So if you think you are getting messages from Heaven (or elsewhere) through your archangelic creations, you could be right, *but* the interpretations must always come through your conscious-ness, and that could be *wrong*, or at least mistaken. Listen to whatever comes by all means, but *never* accept what comes as authoritarian purely because of how you received it. *Always* weigh *any* inner information which reaches you with calm deliberation, think it out for yourself and when you have considered everything, decide *on your own responsibility* what you will or will not do.

You must realize that, especially at first, most "messages" which seem to come from the "Archangels" will be one part of yourself speaking to another part of you. Your telesmics will be like reflectors, bouncing back consciousness into your receiving mind which you might not otherwise have been particularly aware of. This is not a bad thing at all, because it is possibly alerting you to the fact that you *can* be conscious above normal and ordinary levels. However, you are still in the position of a ventriloquist with one side of himself talking to another aspect of himself through a dummy symbolizing his alter ego.

In olden days, would-be magicians were always told by those experienced in the art: "Do not allow any spirit to dominate you. You must always be their master, and never their slave." Excellent advice indeed. So take it. Even though the use of archangelic telesmic images makes it much less likely that you would be deliberately misled through them, they are not 100% foolproof, and only long and hard testing can possibly prove their integrity.

Once you realize and know exactly what each concept is supposed to do, and you recognize its correct behavior pattern, you should strongly suspect any kind of uncharacteristic action or suggestion. For instance, if you found Michael writhing to the latest hit music while putting obscenities into your mind, something would obviously be terribly wrong with its construction some-where, and it would most likely be your fault. Each concept should stay tuned to whatever stream of consciousness it was set for, and if it doesn't, there is a malfunction to deal with as soon as possible.

Archangel RAPHAEL

Pronounce	RAPH EEEEEE AEL	*Build,*	Slight
Element	Air	*Skin,*	Pale and elastic
Quarter	East	*Hair,*	Light blonde
Season	Spring	*Eyes,*	Light gray
Symbol	Sword	*Features,*	Aquiline
Time	Dawn	*Clothing,*	Blue-gray
Voice	Young and clear	*Ornaments,*	Crystal

Characteristics: Graceful, rapid motions. Quick changes of expression and mood. Enthusiastic and keen. Healer of hurt feelings and injuries. Encourages devotion to causes. Points out possible perils ahead. Feels stimulating and exciting.

Archangel MICHAEL

Pronounce	MIK IIIIIIIII AEL	*Build,*	Powerful, athletic
Element	Fire	*Skin,*	Sunburned, radiant
Quarter	South	*Hair,*	Gold
Season	Summer	*Eyes,*	Amber-hazel
Symbol	Rod, Lance	*Features,*	Classic
Time	Noon	*Clothing,*	Yellow, brass armor, red cloak
Voice	Incisive but friendly	*Ornaments,*	Golden, but has large Emerald in diadem

Characteristics: Decisive and firm motions. Leadership-like qualities. Insistent on spiritual and moral uprightness. Keen on health and fitness. Strengthens faltering resolutions. Gives out a feeling of warmth and expansiveness.

Archangel JIVRO'EL (GABRIEL)

Pronounce	GAH BREE IEL	*Build,*	Comfortable
Element	Water	*Skin,*	Creamy and moist
Quarter	West	*Hair,*	Chestnut
Season	Autumn	*Eyes,*	Greenish
Symbol	Cup	*Features,*	Full and round
Time	Dusk	*Clothing,*	Green and dark blue
Voice	Richly expressive	*Ornaments,*	Silver

Characteristics: Gentle and flowing movements. Kindly smile and sympathetic touch. Tolerant and forgiving attitude. Comforting and soothing approach. Calms troubled emotions. Feels cool and softly satisfying.

Archangel AURIEL

Pronounce	AUR AH IEL	*Build,*	Spare
Element	Earth	*Skin,*	Swarthy and dry
Quarter	North	*Hair,*	Black with some gray
Season	Winter	*Eyes,*	Very dark
Symbol	Shield	*Features,*	Craggy
Time	Night	*Clothing,*	Brown, dark green, white trim
Voice	Deep, slow, elderly	*Ornaments,*	Bronze

Characteristics: Slow and deliberate movements. Senior approach-style. Solemn manner, but sometimes quiet smile. Encourages learning and erudition. Always advises caution. Feels cold and solid, yet protective and reliable.

Questions

1. How would you define an "Archangel?"
2. Describe the Archangels of the quarters giving their names, meanings and positions.
3. Name and describe the Archangels of the axis.
4. What is a telesmic image, and how would you make one out of pure consciousness?
5. How do you understand the idea of using pure consciousness as a "medium" of creative art?
6. Do you see why you should always stay in control of your telesmic images and never let them attempt to control you? Explain.
7. Choose the eight most important questions in this chapter.
8. How do you conceive of the Archangel *Suvuviel?*
9. Do you truly feel a flow of force to your fingers while working the material in this chapter? If so, does anything seem to diminish or increase it?
10. What have your learned from the practice in this chapter and do you feel it has further possibilities?

· 6 ·

Thinking of Trees

This is where we start studying the now well-known design called the Holy Tree of Life. Before World War II, however, it was *not* well known. For a long time it was considered to be semitic arcana of an obscure and mystical nature, having little bearing on anything beyond that specialized field. Subsequent studies have completely changed that narrow outlook, and now we have many books on the subject which reach a wide readership. Quite ordinary people are beginning to realize that here indeed is something intended to represent factual relationships between human beings and the spiritual structure of the universe and the consciousness which created it.

To read all about the Tree in every available book is not necessarily to *understand* it or what lies behind its conception. How did it become connected with the Western Inner Tradition? How did it develop, and why should it be coming to public light in our times? What significance has it for our future? Why should the design be called a "Tree" anyway? Since the subject obviously demands a great deal of time and attention for study, will it really repay such an expenditure of effort? All these are vital questions to be considered before we settle down to tackle the enormous amount of work in hand.

Beginning at the beginning is very difficult here, but we might as well have a look at the Bible, where remote concepts of our human origins are recorded. This postulates humanity in a pristine state, dwelling in "Paradise" (an apple orchard) watered by a spring which divided into four rivers. At the center of this grows the mysterious Tree of Life and also the Tree of Knowledge. The fruits of the former cause immortality, and those of the latter give the ability to distinguish between Good and Evil. Since humans ate from the Tree of Knowledge, they were expelled from Paradise by God before they could taste the Tree of Life, and therefore they had to pass through the death-process instead of existing eternally in a condition of contentment and bliss.

So says the legend. It is interesting to note that the "Serpent" (the betrayer figure in the picture) told humans they would "become as Gods" if they ate the forbidden fruit, and the "Lord God" rather grumpily agreed: "Man is become as one of us to know good and evil." (Mark the plural "us" carefully.) Then the same Lord hastily drove disobedient humans away from Eden before they might: "Take also of the Tree of Life, eat, and live forever." Apparently God then posted Kerubims (a winged-bull type of angel) armed with flame-throwers at the East gate of Paradise, to prevent humans sneaking back under the fence when He wasn't looking.

Therefore the mythical Tree of Life is first presented as something humanity needs before the full process of "becoming Gods" is possible. Through the Tree of Knowledge we are represented as being *part* divine, but we cannot complete the cycle of change until we are in a position to partake of the Tree of Life. Thus the Tree is implicitly indicated as a quest-aim like the Holy Grail was a lot later on in our history. Gain either, and all our life problems would be solved at once, the panacea idea we have clung to down the centuries.

Another interesting point is that the concept of Paradise traces back to our Circle Cross pattern. Most visualizations of it are circular, surrounded by a protective perimeter, having the Fount of Life in the center with the twin Trees above it, while the four streams flow to the Quarters and beyond into the hostile world around. No actual description of either Tree is given.

The idea of a Tree per se is lost in antiquity. Trees have been objects of religious devotion since time immemorial. This could well go back to the days when we were reputed to be arboreal creatures ourselves. Certainly in very primitive cultures stone and wood were the basics of their technology. In all probability a broken branch from a shrub or tree was man's very first authentic implement. Holy Trees are common to all creeds and every mythology is full of them. They are central to thousands of folktales.

Tied up with the creation myth in which the Life Tree is a main item, comes the theme of the "Fall" in which humans lose contact with divinity and become somehow inferior to their original condition. This again is common to many mythologies, but however it is presented, the story amounts to a belief that before becoming purely earthly mortal beings, humanity had a higher and holier heritage with which we lost direct touch owing to some bad error in judgement or behavior. Since that sad moment we have been trying to regain our state of pristine purity, but undoubtedly we are a long way from that yet.

A modern way of interpreting this is by postulating the "earthfall" of some spacecraft bearing highly advanced beings from a distant galaxy. With no hope of return, most of the survivors decided the best way they could perpetuate their line was to breed with the primitive anthropoids they found on earth, relying on a prolonged genetic process to produce their true strain eventually. It was hoped that in the end, enough of the old knowledge would come back among later generations to make a return to the "heavenly homeland" possible. The stranded cosmonauts realized they were taking a very long risk, because if the spiritual development of their descendants did not grow in advance of their technical abilities, they would scarcely be fit creatures to be welcome in properly conducted Cosmic circles.

There are many other interpretations we could put on the "Fall" legend, but however we translate it, the concept remains of a difficult gap or "abyss" between ourselves as we are on earth, and the sort of beings we were meant to be when we were "invented." We just aren't what we should be. Who in his right mind would suppose otherwise? Still, the impression remains that *somewhere* in Cosmos there must be a plan of some kind which shows not only what we ought to be, but the specification of how we might be restructured to conform with that divine design. One way or another, humanity has hunted for this scheme over many millennia.

The Tree of Life we are about to study is one of those "perfection plans" which evolved during several centuries of study by mathematically minded metaphysicians. They were unwilling to accept an irrational, haphazard, and unstable universe governed by the whims and fancies of unpredictable gods and demons following illogical and unreasonable desires. These spiritual scientists were seeking a state of Cosmos designed and created by a Cause, Deity, or whatever else It might be. They were looking for order, intelligence, and competence on a cosmic scale. Since they could observe harmonies, rhythms, and patterns of behavior throughout nature, it seemed likely to them that there should be equivalents in purely spiritual dimensions. Early astronomers were trying to connect the predictable patterns of heavenly bodies with events on earth, and if only some arrangement of spiritual factors could be calculated, it was considered possible that mankind might be in a much better position to direct its own destiny through life in any dimension of existence.

Earlier man worked instinctively mainly on an action-reaction basis. As we evolved, rationality slowly but steadily replaced sheer impulsiveness as a control factor of our behavior. Humans were becoming calculating creatures. Causes were being consciously linked with effects. Schools of thought and systems of philosophy were springing up wherever intelligent humans were willing to devote time and energy for such purposes. As we might expect, a number of these concentrated in Greece which has been called the "cradle of Western civilization." True, the Greeks had drawn their traditions from Chaldea, Egypt, India, and other ancient sources, but they were "men of new minds," capable of putting old concepts through a mental melting pot to generate fresh nuggets of golden thoughts. Perhaps some very dormant genes were waking up in those days.

Mathematics was then laying the foundation of modern science and technology. Men had first become mathematicians because they were traders and needed to calculate exchange values on goods. Later on they discovered they could apply calculating principles to increasingly abstract topics. They were by now aware that the principles of *mathematics* lay behind every law in nature, and they suspected it might account for creation itself if explored far enough.

For a long time, traders had been dealing in a sort of decimal system for the simple reason that people who can't speak each others' language can still bargain and trade by finger-counting. Fractions could be indicated by finger-joints showing thirds, or thumb-joints for halves. Sooner or later it was inevitable that humans should start counting and calculating with their gods.

Even when monotheistic beliefs began to emerge it still remained a question of how many different aspects that deity had. One semi-secret school of belief based on Hebrew mythology decided to pattern their God concept on the decimal system utilizing the old Circle Cross scheme and the life elements making a total of ten concepts altogether. Remembering that the solid Circle Cross had three axis of two poles, these thinkers took the three letters of the Divine Name, Jehovah, י ה ו ה , Yod He Vau He. (Hebrew letters are always read from right to left). By leaving off the final He, and from IHV (Yod, He, and Vau) they made up six "God Names" which they attached to the direction points as follows:

Zenith	Nadir	East	West	North	South
IHV	IVH	HIV	HVI	VIH	VHI

Associated with this scheme were the life elements, seen somewhat differently from the way we have been viewing them:

First: The Spirit of the Living God.
Second: Air from that Spirit, plus a 22 letter alphabet.

Third: Water from Air, plus the idea of snowing on the letters until it became Earth.

Fourth: Fire from Water, out of which God made his own throne, angelic attendants, and dwelt in that divine court.

He created Himself King of the Universe.

Note carefully that no zero value was conceived at this stage, nor were the concepts arranged in what later became the Tree formation. They were however, termed *Sephiroth,* an interesting word of Grecian influence signifying spheres in the modern sense of *fields* or *areas.* The Hebrew part of the word meant *numbers,* and since there is a connection with the Latin *spiritus* or spirit, the complete meaning of the word Sephiroth should be: *numbered spiritual spheres.* The singular form of the word is Sephirah.

With this early scheme which is believed to date back to about the 4th century in a small treatise called the *Sepher Yetzirah,* or *Book of Formation,* attributions were made arranging the Hebrew alphabet into three classes: three "mothers," א , מ , ש ; seven "double" letters, ב , ג , ד , כ , ר , פ , ת ; and twelve "single" letters, ק , צ , ע , ס , נ , ל , י , ט , ח , ז , ו , ה .

מ			א		ש	
Merit			Normal		Guilt	
Cold			Temperate		Hot	
ב	ג	ד	כ	פ	ר	ת
Height	Depth	East	West	North	South	Center
Sun	Moon	Mars	Mercury	Jupiter	Venus	Saturn
ה	ו	ז	ח	ט	י
Aries	Taurus	Gemini	Cancer	Leo	Virgo
Sight	Hearing	Smell	Speech	Eating	Coition
ל	נ	ס	ע	צ	ק
Libra	Scorpio	Saggitarius	Capricorn	Aquarius	Pisces
Work	Movement	Wrath	Mirth	Meditation	Sleep

In this way it was postulated that God created His universe by means of numbers, letters, and words, ie: identification of intelligence with formalized will. You (and many) may not agree with these attributions, but you must admit that at least a system of classifying distinct streams of consciousness was started. Furthermore, each was "filed" under a reference number because, in those days, letters served as numbers also. Thus, if you agreed with the attribution you would be able to identify any classification of consciousness by a simple letter reference. Computerization was being conceived!

Once the idea was born of "grading God" into specific divine aspects, and associating metaphysical concepts, natural phenomena, and other factors with these, everything else became a matter of time and scholarship. Both were available then, but documentation does not go back much before the Middle Ages. This was chiefly because it was customary in most "secret traditions" to pass information along oral rather than written lines. That was why this type of study was called "Qabalah," because the word meant "from mouth to ear." There were many other good reasons for this, but it does mean we are forced to a certain amount of conjecture as to pre-recorded periods of teaching. The *Sepher Yetzirah,* one of the earliest books on the subject, was not printed until 1562 in Mantua.

Here is a fairly important consideration which seems strangely missed by modern commentators of Qabalah. Most monotheistic religions did not portray their concept of a supreme spirit under any formal symbolic guise. Semites in particular were expressly forbidden by their laws to attempt this. Druids also disapproved of trying to depict deity in any shape. All these people considered it was not only an impertinence for a human to define what God looked like, but it was also an insult and affront to the deity Himself which was likely to arouse His justifiable anger.

Christians were somewhat divided on this issue. The majority felt that if their God had consented to be born in human shape there was no harm in imagining Him as an anthropomorphic deity who, after all, had created man in His own likeness. They compromised by never depicting the Holy Spirit in human shape.

Apart from a dove, many artists indicated the Holy Spirit as "living flames" or radiances and beams of light. They dared not show a definite feminine element in any portrayal of a triple deity. Officially, for Semites and Christians alike, woman was an afterthought of God, who created her out of Adam as a "helpmate," for Adam's benefit. Besides, it was Eve who got poor old Adam flung out of Paradise.

Such rigid viewpoints were causing considerable discontent among scholars and others who were familiar with the older feministic faiths. They had come to the inevitable conclusion that if deity had any kind of human connections, it must necessarily be to both masculine and feminine aspects, probably with a neutral principle between both. The most intelligent of these dissidents decided the best thing to do was keep their theories private and "go underground" while they developed their life theme, and that is what they did for several centuries.

Some other minds reasoned this way: "God said we mustn't make images of him, so we won't. But he didn't say we mustn't make mathematical speculations about him, or calculations concerning his qualities, propensities, or powers. So why don't we do just this and come to closer knowledge of him that way? So long as we stick to pure mathematics in connection with abstract subjects we shan't be breaking the Holy Law, shall we?" That is exactly what metaphysicians of those early (but not primitive) periods did. They could draw geometric designs indicating divinity and its activities. They could write much of what they felt about God, provided they did not attempt to describe his actual appearance in living shape or form. Since letters were also numbers, they could combine and compute them in many different ways, coming up with different words which sometimes gave quite fresh and surprising notions about God's mysterious actions. It was a fascinating new game which they called "Gematria," again from the Greek "gramma" or rules of language. Another form of this involving capitals of words only was "Notaricon" from the Latin *notarius*—a shorthand writer. For a long while some supposed they might solve all the secrets of the universe that way. What it actually did was improve their mental training until their minds were capable of grasping more advanced matters than average humans could handle.

These early Qabalists probably didn't realize they were setting up a systematic mental discipline which improved their reasoning, widened their inner horizons, and raised their consciousness to a higher level of comprehension. They were just "looking for God" like everybody else, but *they were using a computational method of doing so.* It was this system and order in their method which was important. *What* they believed was of less significance than *how* they believed it. Once the method itself becomes established, the values should work out correctly like the answers to an ordinary mathematical problem.

No one can be absolutely certain when the idea of showing "God and all His works" as a geometrical design arose in men's minds. Our earliest ideas of Cosmos as we know it were shown as a simple Circle Cross. Since there were three axes to the solid version of this symbol, could this be shown diagramatically? It could, in a very interesting way, as the hexagram or double triangle now

Figure 1.7. The Hexagram as a reef knot

known as the "Star of David" or "Solomon's Seal." There is a great deal to this ancient design we shall have to consider later, but the present point is that it signified the sign of Cosmos or "Greatest God," in Greek, the Macro-Cosm. If this pattern was tied as a *knot,* (from which idea many old patterns were made) it formed the reef knot or "true tie" which always holds firm and will never slip apart as a "false" knot does (Figure 1.7 on page 71). This made the hexagram symbol doubly significant as a sign of "True-God."

Some early mathematician must have tried tracing circles of identical diameters with overlapping circumferences and centers. The beautifully harmonious nature of this arrangement cannot have escaped notice. A single circle intersected by three other equals showed the "knot of eternity" in the center, so called because it could be drawn indefinitely without removing pen from paper. The Celts, in particular, venerated this type of knot because of their sacred triplicity system, and now it is often known as the "Celtic Knot" (Figure 1.8).

Try making this design yourself. All you need is paper, drawing compass, ruler and a pen or pencil. Put a dot somewhere in the middle of the paper and let it represent the spirit of the whole enterprise. Set the compass arms half an inch apart, giving an inch diameter circle. Make a circle. Then put the compass point anywhere you like on the perimeter and make another circle. Spot where the perimeters of the two circles intersect, then use that as a center for making another circle and so on until you come back to

---

Figure 1.8. The "Celtic Knot"

Figure 1.9. Six circling   Figure 1.10. Six pointing

where you started making secondary circles. You should have made Figure 1.9. Note it takes six circles to do this round a seventh. Now with your ruler, connect the six centers together to form a hexagram or sign of the macrocosm, and you will have Figure 1.10, which represents the six points of our magical Cosmos together with its central seventh.

Next, mark out the points where the six circles intersect each other and set up another series of six more circles. This is where you have to be extremely exact, because even the slightest error becomes increasingly magnified as you continue to add surrounding circles to the group. After you have marked the second set repeat the process with a third. Then, using the sides of the original hexagram as a guide, fill each marked circle in with another six hexagrams. By this time you should figure out what is happening, but if you really feel you can stand it, carry on with the process a bit further. You should find you need another two surrounds of twelve circles each. It is a good plan to mark the center of each series of circles with different color dots so as not to get confused.

If you ever get to the eighteen-circle series, the pattern should be so clear to you, there will be no need to keep on repeating it. All you are doing is enlarging the original concept. Though all the circles are separate and all the hexagrams are separate too, they keep combining with each other to form an ever-expanding sign of the macrocosmos. Did this truly symbolize that though every living soul is a separate unit of its own, the divine spirit in each links up with those of the others, increasing its own identity all the while? Is this an adequate symbol of how God puts his universe together? Some of the advancing Qabalists certainly thought so, though they realized they would have to use a more concise version of the scheme.

Even though you have Figure 1.11 to look at (and it makes a good meditation subject) you should try and set up the scheme for yourself from scratch. You may know from a purely intellectual viewpoint what the thing signifies, but the actual effort and concentration on the work involved will be a valuable inner experience it would be unwise to reject. Do remember how exact and precise you must be in order to relate those centers and circumferences properly. The first few may not look too bad, but as you go on assembling the circles, the overall picture will get worse and worse.

That factor made the early experimenters wonder if God had made the slightest inconceivably minute error when he started

Figure 1.11. Circle multiplying

creating the universe, and, if so, how much would that imperfection have, magnified by now? They were eventually forced to the conclusion that God, the creative consciousness, had indeed made such an initial slip which accounted for the obviously imperfect state of human nature alone. Nevertheless, they assumed that divinity is in itself the perfection of life, and therefore deity was constantly concerned with correcting creation and would eventually succeed. They hoped their studies would help them understand this process of otherwise inexplicable divine behavior.

Who these early workers with "Qabalah" were, we shall never know. A number were certainly Semitic, though there seems a strong Greek influence. By the early Middle Ages, scholars from several schools of thought were developing the theme regardless of which official religion or nationality they were attached to. By the time some Qabalistic books were being written and printed, a very small scattering of European intellectuals were interested in formulating its theories into a more modern interpretation. Obscure and eclectic as it was, "Qabalah" was becoming a seminal influence within the Western Tradition. Its appeal was to "head" rather than "heart," rationality rather than romance. It thus attracted very few people, and those were limited to extremely small circles of scholars.

This is normally the way with most esotericism. A tiny nucleus, sometimes only a single soul, reaches ahead of contemporary thought into the unknown and *consciously* touches a fragment of truth. All that can be done is to record impressions of that truth and, perhaps, perhaps pass it on to others. This may stimulate them to reach for that truth themselves, and those that miss it either fall back and lose interest, or find other truths instead. It could be *centuries* of our time before any wide dissemination of that truth becomes possible, or it might be within a single generation. Qabalism is a seed which was planted a long time back in our tradition, and has only come to flower recently. The reason for this is because our modern "inner climate" has become suitable for this particular esoteric stream. Now the "Old Wisdom" can be recovered in ways to benefit modern mankind by *living* that tradition in terms of our times.

The Tree of Life and its associated symbology has preserved the inner meanings of our secret tradition through very difficult times. Now we must learn how to unlock its mysteries and turn them into contemporary forms of consciousness. The time has come when the musty mathematics which safeguarded our spiritual heritage must be translated into realities of Life, Love, Law, and Learning. Otherwise what would be the point of so preserving it?

In the next chapter we shall see how the shape of the "Tree" developed from what we have considered in this one. Everything step by step, even though strides may not always be the same length.

Questions

1. Why do you think a Tree was chosen as a symbol for life and knowledge?

2. Compare our "Fall" to early man descending from trees and living mainly on the ground. How do you interpret the "Fall?"

3. How do you think enumeration first began? Why should humans begin counting in the first place? What is the rationale behind figures?

4. Why would metaphysicians prefer to conceive deity as an abstract mathematical formula rather than an anthropomorphic being?

5. Trace a "Celtic Knot" on paper without removing the pencil from the paper. Speculate on this and comment.

6. Why is the hexagram the symbol for Great Cosmos, and what is the symbol for "Lesser Cosmos" and why?

7. Select the ten most important sentences in this chapter.

8. What does the word "Qabalah" mean to you?

9. Why would early thinkers associate defined ideas with numerals or letters?

10. Why should the practice of associating numbers with ideas improve mental abilities?

· 7 ·

Creative Concepts

In the previous chapter we were left with a complicated design which was an ad infinitum repetition of the Circle Cross and Holy Hexagram theme. If any of this was to represent the workings of deity in relation to our human condition, it was obvious that an abstract would have to be made. How many circles would be needed, and how should these be connected? We shall never know all the pros and cons of the argument, plus all the philosophical speculations involved, but in the end it seemed reasonable to settle for the number *ten*. That was the first unit of double figures which meant values could go on repeating themselves indefinitely. If nothing ever went further than nine, the universe would come to a stop at that point. Like the diagram, it was the extension to infinity of values by adding another numeral at every cycle which made the ten conceptually representative of God.

Ten was "nine-plus-one" and so a symbol of infinite repetition through every cycle of creation. It was also the sum of the first four numbers, or the total of the quarters: $1 + 2 + 3 + 4 = 10$. Add the primal numbers, 1 to 9, and you get 45, which adds to 9 again. By adding 1 to 9, you theoretically push the 9 back to first place again and start it on another round of increase and so on. This led early esotericists to conceive that God must have built up the universe by a similar process of starting with a fixed set of figures and constructing with them eternally. So 9 remained the original sacred triple-triplicity, but the "plus-1" factor enabled it to continue creating forever. Thus it seemed to them a sound idea to base concepts of divinity and all else in existence on a decimal basis.

So what would ten circles of the base-pattern look like? They looked like Figure 1.12, a nice representation of "God looking at God," so to speak, one hexagram reflecting the other. Here we have to remember the creation concept of God "brooding or hovering on the face of the water." Legend says that God *as a being* emerged from the ocean of infinity and first saw his own face reflected therein. As soon as his lips were clear of the surface he began uttering the Word and Words which caused the rest of creation to come to life around him. For that reason, it became a mystical practice to imitate this concept by wading slowly into a pool or lagoon until lips were level with the water and then uttering "Words of Power" or magical mantras. To be most effective this was supposed to be at dawn, because God called light into being first.

According to Genesis, man was God's tenth creation. These were, in order: light, space, earth, oceans, vegetation, stars, birds, fishes, animals, and man. In the diagram was a double Hexagram for God, but where did Man come into the picture? The sign of Man the Microcosm was a pentagram or five point star, for obvious reasons. It made a rough outline of a human body standing with arms spread

Figure 1.12. Tree marking	Figure 1.13. Wrong relationship

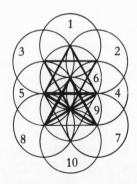

Figure 1.14. Unbalanced Fall   Figure 1.15. Balanced Fall

and legs apart. An attempt to relate these two important symbols was made as in Figure 1.13, but it was realized at once this could hardly be right since it was such an imperfect figure.

Eventually, it appeared that this imperfection was in itself the very factor needed to bring the whole system nearer truth. Man *was* imperfect, *had "fallen from grace," was* no longer "close to God," but had become separated from divinity somehow. This might be partly shown by the pentagram being upside down, but something still seemed wrong. The sphere of Man had to be shown as distinctly apart from that of God, yet related by "Paths of Power," since we were still connected to God by links of memory, hope, love, duty, and similar bonds between the two states of being. It looked right to put God at the top of the diagram and Man at the bottom, but how should the bottommost Sphere, representing "fallen" Man be related with the rest? Like Figure 1.14? Hardly. One glance at its awkwardness settles that. No, if Man's breakaway point is at closest contact with God, then the two Spheres connecting humanity most directly with divinity must therefore fall away at the same time to depict this division. This was tried and produced Figure 1.15.

As you can see, this produced a much more compact association, while yet indicating the direct disconnection by the irregularity of the centers. Surely these center-points alone should indicate the pattern without need for the circles around them. What would it look like if they were joined up by the most direct routes? This gives the result shown in Figure 1.16 and that remains the standard pattern of the Tree of Life today. If you count the contact-lines between the sphere-centers you will find there are 22 in all, the same as the number of letters in the Hebrew alphabet. It was only logical they would use a letter to each line (or path) for identification (Figure 1.17).

How should the Spheres themselves be identified apart from the numbers? If Hebrew letters *were* numbers used to identify connections between Spheres (which were called "Paths" since they joined the concepts together), how should Spheres be identified except by name? The old teaching was that God created everything by numbers, letters, and names, so if the first two had been used, names must be found next. Identification of Spheres by Arabic or Roman numerals while keeping the original Hebrew letter-numbers on the Paths came in much later.

In Hebrew and other forms of prayer, God was constantly being called "Our Faithful King" or "King of the Universe." The concept of Cosmic rulership had been attached to highest ideas of divinity for a very long time. The symbol for a king, then and also now, is a crown. This made an undoubted title for the primal

Figure 1.16. Related Paths

Figure 1.17. Paths and Letters

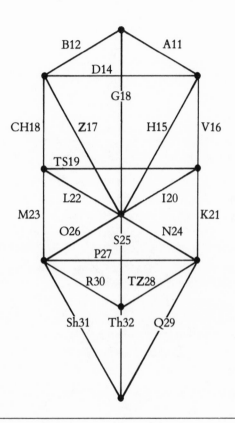

concept. *Kether* in Hebrew not only mean a crown in the monarchial sense, but also signified a summit at the top of anything high, such as a mountain or treetop.

The bottom concept where exiled Man lived was seen as the "kingdom" ruled over by the Divine Faithful King. In Hebrew, *Malkuth*—a kingdom, derived from *Malek*—a king or sovereign ruler. Between those opposite ends however, were eight other Spheres—three pairs of opposites and two mid-way ones—all interconnected, which had to be explained. There was also the important concept of the "Great Divide" between God and Man which came to be called the "Abyss" because Man could not

Figure 1.18. Tree with Abyss

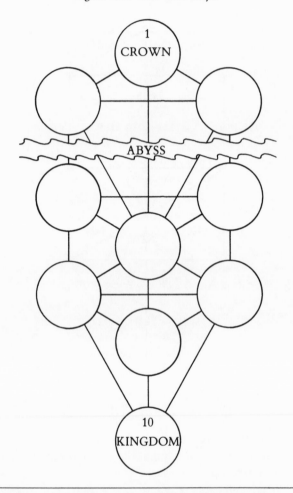

possibly cross it in his "fallen" condition. All this is shown in Figure 1.18.

What separates man from God? Consciousness, or rather the lack of it on the part of man. God has the perhaps unfair advantage of being all-aware, or omniscient, and so can be completely conscious of man, whereas man can only be aware of

God in very attenuated and limited ways. Our efforts at understanding or comprehending the real nature of divinity fall
pathetically short of the mark. On our side of the Abyss we can only
guess and speculate. All the understanding and comprehension is on
God's side, not ours. We only have what leaks across, as it were.

So the experimental theologians of that time divided the
intentional awareness of our supreme life spirit into two principal
categories: Wisdom and Understanding; in Hebrew *Chockmah*
(pronounced Hoch'ma) and *Binah* (pronounced Beenah or Veenah).
They considered Wisdom as the rational side of awareness, while
Understanding was intuitional. These made up the male (Chockmah) and female (Binah) sides of God's mind, and together made
him omniscient. They were complementary opposites, and were
therefore placed second and third in the scheme where they formed
a triad with the ruling spirit of life itself.

Now, how about man? What had he got at his end of the
construction to compare with this? Nothing nearly so noble.
Looking at human nature on the whole, straight in its unattractive
face, its dual drives are sadly seen as greed for gain and fear of
failure. There is a higher translation of these however, if we are
able to see above the lowest levels of life. If we can but conquer our
base and brutal instincts and stay victorious over them, without
hurting others in the process, we can gain spiritual states of honor
and glory in the sight of God. Our inner "victories" and resulting
condition of "glory" indicate the first steps we are taking on our
way to divinity. So the concepts of Victory and Glory, *Netzach* and
Hod in Hebrew, became attached to the human end of the life-scale
as shown in Figure 1.19 on page 84.

But what about the concepts remaining? Now we surely
have to think of some abstract yet recognizable quality which God
and man alike may *share*, albeit with differing degrees. Here, the
king concept comes in again as a starting point. What are the
greatest and most marked attributes of kingship which are
complementary opposites of each other? On the one hand,
undoubtedly a king's might or power over his people which is
supposed to curb and control them with law and order for their own

Figure 1.19. Creative concepts on the Tree

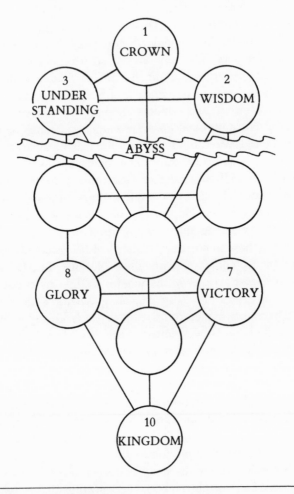

good, even if he has to use severe measures in extreme cases. Balancing this is his magnaminity and compassion for all dutiful subjects whose sufferings he should try to alleviate by generosity and kind treatment. In most old coronation oaths, a king usually swore to recompense the ill-treated and punish their persecutors. Never mind how few kings ever tried to keep that promise, it was still there to be broken. We would not expect a God to break faith in a spiritual world with his faithful people, even if it took him a long time to influence their affairs in this mundane sphere.

This principle of cosmic compensation had long been considered as "Karma," which is simply the natural law of cause and effect. If a human does *this*, then he must expect *that*; action and reaction. There is no question of punishment or retribution by a wrathful God. It is no more than an automatic rebalancing of disturbed cosmic conditions. Here however, this is seen as a conscious re-adjustment of unbalanced spiritual conditions caused by human carelessness, clumsiness, or worse still, deliberate and malicious mishandling. This is accomplished by twin curbs on creation, Mercy and Might. These concepts attach to Spheres 4 and 5 on the scheme. In Hebrew they are called *Chesed* (pronounced Hesed) and *Geburah* (sometimes Jivurah).

If curbs are needed to keep creation in balance then the immediate query is: balance in relation to *what*? Balance is a condition of poise or harmony among a number of factors relative to a common point. We usually refer to a "point of balance" when thinking of scales or measuring equipment, and it is normally the central distance between two extremities. Looking at our scheme as it stands, Sphere 6 plainly has this role but what exactly is it? We are more or less forced to one conclusion: the factor of harmony itself, which is idealized as beauty. Beauty is synonymous with harmony and poise, just as its opposite—ugliness— is linked with discord and unbalance. Therefore the concept of Beauty in an absolute sense has to be identified with Sphere 6 under the Hebrew name of *Tiphereth,* which means exactly that.

This leaves us with the last Sphere to identify. Left over from the previous concept is the idea that beautiful balance is a necessity of life throughout cosmos on all levels, but balance on what? In order to support any kind of balance, there has to be some solid point which will remain stable while balance is constantly re-adjusting. If there were no steady support for the center of a scale, balance would be impossible. There has to be this factor in life too, a supportive fulcrum which will maintain a proper sense of balance as the stresses and strains of living shift around in a continual effort to remain relatively constant to each other. We have to bear in mind that we are not constructing a dead and motionless concept of creation, but a pulsating, moving, *living* outline of energy and action. So far we have been designing a temple of the Living God, and here we have come to the foundations.

That is the word we need—Foundation. Something for our concepts to stand on and relate down to. So far as we are concerned on our side of the Abyss, this is where we would begin to build our ideas and notions of all which is above our heads as earthly humans. It would also be the basis of our humanity and the nature thereof: the life force focussed down to a point where its next emergence is our appearance on this planet Earth. So we settle for the concept of Foundation (or Basis) for Sphere 9, and its Hebrew name of *Yesod*, signifying the same. Then we can sit back and look at the complete collection of concepts in Figure 1.20.

Here is where we should see why this design is called the Holy Tree of Life. It is a tree in the sense of a family tree depicting the derivations and distributions of a line of human life from its inception right down to its present position. In ancient times, people of good birth were very proud of their family trees, tracing ancestry to long-past illustrious ancestors and showing links with "the Blood" leading back to a Sacred King. Here we have evolved a family tree for humanity to trace itself back to God, not through genetic lines of descent, but through linked qualities shared by divinity at one end and humanity at the other. It is then a Tree of Conscious Being. No wonder it was called the *Holy* Tree of Life and compared to its predecessor in Paradise. If we could but "eat the fruits"—that is, assimilate and absorb the living principles of this Tree—we should indeed become immortal.

The subtlety of the overall concept is so great, it is scarcely possible for a human mind to grasp without an enormous effort spent in study and contemplation. It was, in fact, the Einstein relativity formula, $E=mc^2$, of its time. Even now it is far beyond the comprehension of many mortals. They can look at it, read information about it, hear lectures or talks on it, and do everything except "take it in" so that it becomes an inner reality. Until it does that, the Tree will be no more than circles, lines and dots on paper,

Figure 1.20. Concepts complete on the Tree

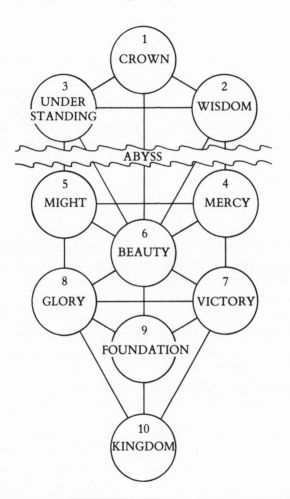

interesting perhaps, or informative concerning old-fashioned philosophical speculations, but that will be all unless the concept takes root in your soul and grows alive there.

It could be that you have read a lot of books on Qabalah and are inclined to say: "Oh this is all old stuff. I read that years ago.

When are we going to come to something more advanced?" If by any chance that is so, may we point out a valuable esoteric fact which is often missed by impatience or over-assumption. It is usually going over the same ground again and again by different methods and from various angles which produces the finest results in terms of inner truth. To cover any subject just one way reveals very little of its deeper value. We have often been told that truth lies at the bottom of a well, which means we shall have to keep digging deeper and deeper in search of it. To get inner truths from outside, layer after layer of covering concealments have to be stripped away until eventually the irreducible core of spiritual solidity begins to emerge.

Some old-time "teachers," when approached by eager pupils with demands for instant enlightenment, would set up some essentials in brief order, tell the pupil to study and meditate on this and return later with his findings. Presently, the pupil would come back with some cursory or perhaps long-winded and irrelevant result. The "teacher" would reject the work and instruct the pupil to do it again from a different outlook or approach. This process went on and on for perhaps a long time, but in the end bright students began to get the point: No matter how often good inner ground is raked over, there will always be something deeper to discover on each occasion.

That is so with the Tree. The best way to study it is by considering each stage carefully, then repeating and repeating the same material on different occasions just as one circle was drawn out of another according to the original plan. Every time, something *new* should appear to interest the serious investigator. It may not be anything very surprising or startling, and sometimes it will need careful scrutiny to identify it, but there is always something worth looking for when you go back to the beginning with re-opened eyes.

Something of this nature may happen if you have been studying with an occult organization for some time and then, for one reason or another, you want to drop it and start working with another. The second group is quite liable to insist you begin with them afresh at the basic level, and you might feel offended or annoyed at being "sent back to nursery school." One director of studies, on being told of an applicant's grade status with another school, replied with complete justification, "We know very well you have done all this before, but if you want to work with us you will have to do so *our way.*"

Although the Holy Tree of Life is a universal formula applying to all living beings as any mathematical calculation must, its major appeal is likely to be limited to souls who normally think in terms of mathematical relationships. Nevertheless, there is a strongly emotional element in the Tree which is capable of being experienced by those with no particular taste for arithmetic. Providing people can appreciate the nature and validity of the concepts of the Spheres, and form general ideas of how these relate with inner reality, there is no reason why they should not use the Tree as a background to whatever system they feel happiest with.

The Tree is not an object of religious worship, though its formula may well be used to regulate or even design devotional and mystical practices. Neither is it exclusively Jewish or Hebrew in essence. Semitic scholars have interpreted the Tree in their own way so as to give it meaning according to their esoteric beliefs, and Gentile scholars have done exactly the same. So the Tree of Life *as studied by Westerners today* carries the interpretation and practical applications arrived at by centuries of study by Western minds and souls. It could be that exclusively Semitic students might pour scorn on the way in which Gentiles have presented the Tree for a modern readership. All are entitled to work out the same formula in whatever way seems best for their type of consciousness to follow. Furthermore, *the Tree formula is not yet a finished or finalized one.* It is *as we know it now*, and that is all. Who knows what it will reveal to future investigators who approach its concepts with open, enquiring, and genuinely interested minds. You may have such a mind yourself. If so, may we salute and honor you for services to our tradition.

As you read on, you will see why the Tree scheme became absorbed into the Western Inner Way and came to be a modern means of co-ordinating our channels of consciousness. Apart from other considerations, its sheer utility alone would be sufficient to recommend it. You can think of it as being like a slide rule or calculator. Forget about who, or how many minds in which centuries combined to invent and improve the thing. How many professional carpenters could tell you who invented the jack-plane? How many mechanics know who discovered wrenches or when they were first used? What matters is learning how to use such aids properly, and that is the principal function of the Tree as an instrument of intelligence for inner living.

At this point, go back to the beginning again and soak yourself in the ten concepts, one at a time and then in combination with each other. There is no point trying to think of them in Hebrew, unless that language is either native to you, or you have great fluency with it. Use your consciousness in its most natural and effective way. Link your feelings with it and try to experience what you are aware *of* by what you are aware *with*. Think this out carefully if it is a strange idea to you.

Note that the concepts *above* the Abyss are not approachable by feelings, while those *below* the Abyss *are*. One cannot very well *feel* wise or understanding, but one can feel merciful, mighty, harmonious, victorious, and glorious. In the Kingdom, of course, one exercises all types of feeling in the experience of life. Though many workers with the Tree tend to neglect the Abyss concept, it is an essential part of the great plan and has a vital function to fulfill. The point here is that everything above the Abyss is pure consciousness while everything to do with our human nature lies below that level of life.

Think of things this way. Unless our fallible and imperfect type of life existed, there would be *no need* for mercy, might, balance, victory, glory, or stability. Pure consciousness alone could make a closed circuit of itself, and live in a perfect state of self-perception. Life without end, *Amen*. The Abyss is a demarcation line past which, in a "downward" direction, spirit materializes and, in an "upward" direction, matter spiritualizes. "Up" and "down," of course, are purely relative terms here.

Let us take a quick climb upwards through the concepts in the direction of divinity. We start by standing on Earth and reaching up towards Heaven. We can do this nowadays with a reasonable belief that one day man *will* reach those realms in physical reality. Whether or not this might be a good thing depends on whether we reach them spiritually first. Here we are in the *Kingdom* of nature, contemplating our cosmic chances as the countdown comes to the *ten* mark.

Stability or Foundation. Before launching ourselves anywhere, we have to be certain of the ground beneath our feet and also of our ability to keep a steady course aimed on target, once we are clear of the earth. Watch any cat or athlete preparing to leap. Study the way they position their bodies with the utmost precision before they make a spring. If they don't feel exactly right for the move, they won't make it. Think of this before attempting to step out into spiritual space. Are you absolutely positive where you are and at what you are aiming before you hurl yourself around the inner universe? If not, then why not? Do you feel absolutely stable and confident in your spiritual stance and intentions? If you don't, hadn't you better do a lot of re-thinking? That is one function of this Sphere from a human viewpoint. It supplies factors which help stabilize ourselves when setting our course through an inner cosmos. Assuming we have found these and aimed accurately, then launched ourselves "lightwards," where do we go next?

Glory or Honor. Here we are aiming ourselves as much by human feelings and ambitions as by sheer spiritual purpose. After all, we *are* humans, and we do have human instincts which prompt life drives. Most of us are not noble, self-sacrificing souls at all, but just ordinary folk who enjoy feeling good and having some purpose in living which gives a glorious sensation of being really alive in the best meaning of the word. If we weren't, we might not be encouraged to leave the ground and start looking for the stars. Perhaps we might think of this Sphere as the encouragement we receive from higher levels of life to come out of Earth conditions and seek above ourselves for something better. Most people know that if a small child isn't encouraged almost constantly by its elders, it will seldom achieve very much, purely on its own account. Maybe you think life can be very *dis*couraging and so it can be on the outside, but here we are not talking about the outside, we are speaking of inner living. You won't find encouragement there handed to you on a plate. You have to "go inside" and ask for it. Then it is there, perhaps only enough to get you going, but it is sufficient for the purpose. So once you get it, where next?

Victory or Achievement. There isn't much point in feeling encouraged unless you can actually achieve something thereby. Humans live to achieve. Most humans are only too happy if they gain plenty of physical possessions and social success, money, position, and power over other people. That is the ultimate limit of their ambitions. They want nothing else, so they get nothing else. They utterly ignore the indisputable fact that such "success" can only last for the lifetime of their physical bodies. They don't care about a "what then?" but we assume *you* do or you wouldn't be reading this. At this life Sphere you will still be aiming at success or victory, but on spiritual levels rather than material ones. It doesn't follow that you can't have both but your prime aim here is victory on an inner field of struggle: things like conquering the worst side of your own nature, achieving some spiritual status because of the efforts you have devoted to such a cause, developing whatever qualities you have in yourself, and building up those you may need but are deficient in your nature, such as patience, fortitude, generosity or tolerance, gaining control of yourself. Maybe you aren't making any big or spectacular victories in this field yet, but as long as you are actually seeking them, that is what matters most. You will get there eventually.

Harmony or Beauty. Have you ever in the whole of your life felt that everything in and around you was absolutely just *right*, harmonious, and couldn't be improved on? It might have been only a fleeting moment, yet it was unforgettable. Maybe you have never had such an experience in this life up to now. Unfortunately, it is difficult to define this life Sphere to those who can't realize what it might mean. Things very seldom do go completely right in this world, but that doesn't stop all of us from wishing they would.

"Rightness" means different things to different people, but all would agree that rightness means being balanced. We know this is very much of a theoretical state so far as this world goes, but that is no reason we should not strive to attain it inwardly. This is the life Sphere where we seek at least a semblance of such an ideal cosmic condition. If we can't find this in ourselves sometimes, how can we ever hope to establish anything like it on Earth or reach its ultimate reality at the end of our existence? So let us keep looking. If we can maintain it for even a moment, we shall next come up against an extremely formidable factor of life.

Might or Severity. This is where we shall need every bit of the poise and balance we gained in the previous Sphere to compensate for the shocks we are likely to receive in this one. Surely nobody in their right mind would expect life to be all sweetness and bliss right up to the top of its Tree? This is where we get cut down to the size of souls we really are rather than those we imagine we might be. Here is no place of punishment or retribution, however; nothing of that kind exists in this concept. There is no such thing as hate, malice, or vindictiveness on any part of the Tree. Nothing more than plain justice and righting of wrongs. It has been said: "The Lord chastiseth whom he loveth," and the meaning of this much misunderstood message lies in the old sense of the wording, to chasten, make chaste and clean, to purify or restore to order. We talk about having "a chastening experience," meaning one which might take us down several pegs but which nevertheless has made a better being out of us. This is what has to happen in the Sphere of Severity here. It may be likened to spiritual surgery where any malignancy gets cut and burned out of us in order to make us fit for life on higher levels. One way to think of this is like a decontamination process to destroy any infectious impurities still inherent in our systems before we may be permitted to approach divinity any closer. When this is properly done, we may enter the following Sphere.

Mercy or Compassion. The quality of Mercy is indeed not strained. It rises completely out of fellow-feeling (or com-passion) between living beings. Here is the Sphere where this state of Mercy exists between a loving God and living mankind. Mercy is not pity or sentiment, or any form of weakness whatever; Mercy can only be extended from a strong being towards a weaker one. Nor is Mercy to be confused with forbearance or tolerance. One may forbear or be tolerant because of a sense of justice or duty. Mercy can only exist where there is Love in the true sense. It was once said: "God loves the sinner yet hates the sin," an old-fashioned truism maybe, but illustrative of the idea here. Mercy does not mean just abstaining from punishing or inflicting something on someone, which they may entirely deserve, because they grovel in hopes of avoiding such. No, Mercy means a condition of consciousness wherein you could not do anything to another soul without feeling the effect magnified in yourself. If you were to hurt them only a little, you would automatically hurt yourself a lot more. This is no question of a sententious schoolmaster mouthing the old rubbish about "This is hurting me more than you." It is a purely spiritual state of sympathy between divinity and humanity in which the sufferings of the latter are felt by the former because of a common life system. Theologians once thought the "sins" of man offended divine dignity, so God punished man in return. Though they are getting away from this idea now, it must still be considered that we might harm other orders of life by our behavior to them, and this ill-treatment must have inner repercussions back to very deep levels. What about our mistreatment of animals and helpless fellow-creatures for instance? Yet we may take life mercifully to spare undue suffering. That is it. Mercy is a condition of mutual love wherein all partakers spare each other any suffering because of the love-bond between them.

The Abyss. We will be going more deeply into the philosophical implications of this concept later, so for the present be content to see it as a division between divinity and humanity which is more than difficult for any human soul to cross completely. Yet this crossing may be possible, but only after long preparation and training plus superhuman courage inspired by sheer self-affinity for the Absolute. Legend tells of a "Sword Bridge" over the Abyss which souls had to cross with as much care as if they were walking along a sword blade. Many myths have comparable bridges between ideal and ordinary worlds. In Norse mythology it is a high, arching bridge of brittle ice. With our Grail legend it is a bridge to the Grail Castle which is a bowshot long and only a foot wide which is supposed to broaden out when a brave man begins to cross it. Let us imagine for the moment that we have braved the dangers and crossed the dreaded Abyss. What shall we first find on the other side?

Understanding or Intuition. This is sometimes thought of as the feminine faculty of cosmic consciousness. Now we may realize why Mercy was projected to the other side of the Abyss, and even how we managed to cross it to this point—because of complete understanding behind the whole of life. When we say we "understand" something, we usually mean we know a lot about it, but much more than that is meant here. Intuitive understanding means consciousness, that is, being aware of something through and through. Not objective consciousness but subjective awareness; a consciousness which does not need to be informed about anything because it *informs itself.* Should a mother need to be told about the nature of a child born from her own body? Let us set aside the sad human exceptions to this dictum and look at the natural examples of animals. Does a mother cat need her kittens *explained* to her? Certainly not. She understands kittens since it is in her nature to do so. If you care to think of it as instinct on a divine scale, you might be approaching the mark. Do not make the dreadful mistake of despising or belittling instinct in any living creature. Understanding is something without any words or formalized communication. It is consciousness which simply *communes* and empathizes from inside. If you have understood any of this, you might be ready to approach the penultimate Sphere.

Wisdom or Comprehension. Wisdom is not knowledge, but a faculty and ability to co-ordinate consciousness in ways which keep it in closest contact with truth or "ultimate reality." Someone whose mind is stuffed with information may be a knowledgeable person, but by no means really *wise* at all. Wisdom always implies an element of judgement, taking everything into consideration before authorizing action. When we say: "Is it wise?" we really mean is something in the best interests of all concerned. That is what Wisdom means here, the authority behind creation, an active consciousness which will not act at all unless such action is right. Old Qabalists said of God: "He is all Right, and in Him there is no Left." Much later it was said: "A thing is not right because God wills it, but God wills it because it is right." That too applies to the Wisdom concept. It means the priniciple in life which intended right in the first place and will set everything to rights in the end. So a truly *wise* human is one who lives rightly.

The Crown or Summit. There is nothing greatly to be gained from speculation about the origin and end of life. That is something we have to take for granted and leave on its own. Some see it as a "Divine Spark" or truly immortal part of ourselves which has to be earned because of our own efforts in life. Man has been called a "mortal" being, not because his body dies, but because his "soul," that part of him which survives bodily death, can also perish through the spiritual equivalents of disease, neglect, or contravention of laws on other levels of life. Old-time theologians used to call such conditions "mortal sin" because they led to the destruction of a soul. They then made the extraordinary contradiction of postulating an immortal life for sinning humans in a Hell of diabolical tortures designed for no other purpose than making them suffer. Surely if a soul were dead it was extinguished forever together with the human it belonged to. The immortal part of that being is God's and returns thereto. Would any God condemn pieces of himself to a condition of Hell for no useful purpose? Qabalistic teaching is that a human soul either evolves until it "unites" with its immortal principle in the end and so lives eternally, or else it degenerates to a point where it becomes useless anywhere as it is, so it goes through a process of downgrading and breaking up into original energies which are then fed back into the cosmic stream of life via the Abyss, and used again to create something else. Nothing is wasted. A human soul is extinct as such, and that is all. This process is compared to leaves dropping from a tree and dying, but turning into valuable humus which the tree absorbs through its roots and uses to make new leaves later on.

Further teaching is very clear that this "spiritual death" cannot take place without the full will and consent of an individual soul. In other words, you must intend your own spiritual extinction before it will happen to you, and this is the Sphere where such a final decision is propounded. To be or not-to-be. That is the eternal question you will face here.

Questions

1. How is the order of creation given in Genesis?
2. How is the "fall" shown on the Tree of Life?
3. Why are the "archetypes of awareness"—Wisdom and Understanding—shown where they are on the Tree?
4. How does the Tree compare with the $E=mc^2$ formula?
5. What differentiates the concepts on the Tree above and below the Abyss?
6. Describe and name the ten concepts of the Tree of Life briefly.
7. What is the fundamental use of the entire Tree concept?
8. How does the "Kingdom" at the foot of the Tree relate with the "Crown" at the top?
9. Pick out the ten most important sentences in this chapter.
10. Define the Qabalistic concept of "soul death."

· 8 ·

Continuing Creation

So far, we have covered the basic outline of
the Holy Tree of Life and considered its ten major concepts, called
Spheres. Nothing could be added to it in theory, because the
original definition distinctly said: "Ten, not nine. Ten and not
eleven. Understand very carefully and calculate with care." That
was thought to be a stopper until some mathematical genius solved
the problem. If nothing might be added to the Tree, then they *would*
add *nothing* to the Tree, literally, the all-important concept of zero.

The zero or cipher (0) was not used in early figuring, and is
believed to have reached the mathematical scene from either Arabia
or India relatively late in the history of mathematics. It revolution-
ized the science, because instead of starting to count from one,
calculations could then begin at zero and reach one by a step
through non-existence into existence. The importance of recognizing this factor of life can scarcely be over-estimated.

By commencing or ending a count with zero, we tacitly
acknowledge that all emerges from *nil*. This implies a creative
energy which must produce something out of nothing. Strictly
speaking, every time we speak of nothing, we are acknowledging
the fact of God. God is No-Thing, being beyond *every* thing, yet
remaining the spirit behind *all things*. The Cipher symbol (0), a circle

Figure 1.21. Commencing concepts

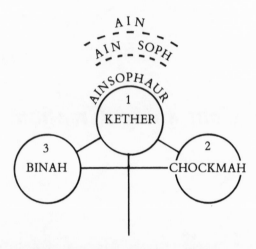

containing nothing, is an emblem of God as a circle "whose center is everywhere and circumference is nowhere."

What is matter? Most modern scientists tell us that matter is far from being solid or substantial as we formerly thought. To the contrary, it is an arrangement of electrically charged particles called electrons, which form patterns around other differently charged particles in the nucleus which combine to produce an atom which is the smallest part of any substance. No atoms ever make direct contact. All are floating free in an unimaginable field of— *nothing.* If all the atoms making up this world (including our bodies) *were* in direct contact with each other, they would make a mass about as big as a large orange. There is more of nothing than the whole of existence combined. That is how important it really is. The only reason we seem "solid" to each other is because we exist in similar states of energy.

"Nothing" is really the potential energy source from which divine consciousness constructed our Cosmos of life. It was said to have done so by impressing its intention or will upon this "nothing" by means of "Words." "And *God* said: Let there be Light, and there was Light."

Figure 1.22. Condensation of concepts

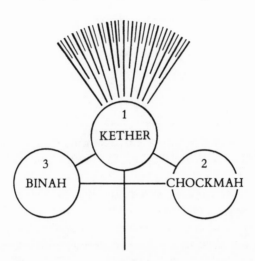

The question was how to indicate this pre-creative state of *nil* on the Tree of Life. It obviously could not be shown as an extra Sphere since these were limited to ten. Eventually it was shown as a "condensation-condition" immediately before the first concept, *Kether* the Crown. Since God's initial creation was light, the formless void was conceived as a state of darkness and limitlessness combining with the principle of light. From this, God condensed light into brilliant manifestation. Some modern esotericists term this *nil* state the "Great Unmanifested Universe," or just the "Great Unmanifest." Old Qabalists called this pre-Ketheric condition of non-being the *Ain Soph Aur*, which they postulated this way:

0	AIN	Nothing
0 0	AIN SOPH	Limitlessness
0 0 0	AIN SOPH AUR	Limitless Light

The pictorial method of showing *Ain Soph Aur* above *Kether* is illustrated in Figures 1.21 and 1.22. There are other ways of indicating the zero-factor of life, but they all amount to the same concept—an intensification of light out of darkness until its maximum focus at Kether produces a laser-like effect enabling God

Figure 1.23. The Chi-Rho Sign

to create Cosmos. Here note in passing that the name of a Celtic creative deity was Gwyn ap Nudd (pronounced Gwin ap Nuth) meaning Light, Son of Night.

Here we come to perhaps the most interesting development of all, the exact significance of the Hebrew word *Ain*, normally translated as "nothing." It does *not* mean nothing as we understand the word, but indicates it from a totally different angle which reveals amazing depths of hidden meaning. The small word derives from two even lesser ones—*eh na?*—What then? *Ain is a query*, the Eternal Question to which there is *no* answer.

Eh na? was a Hebrew way of saying: "What now?" "Where do we go from here?" "So?" It was an interjection implying that the speaker has come to the end of his understanding and is asking further enlightenment if any is available. Hebrew people are famous for concluding their comments with a final question which invites continuation of an argument. That is exactly the case with the Ain concept here. It says in effect: "All right, God, so we've come to the end of the road, have we? Then what next? We can't go any further unless you make more tracks for us to follow, so what are you going to do?"

There is a nuance of interpretation to that little word *na* which needs to be taken into account. It bears the sense of an old English word "prithee" or "pray thee." It is a hope that something will conform with the speaker's intentions because of a prayer uttered in the heart. Therefore, Ain is meant as a cry from the heart direct to deity itself. It does not mean "Extinguish me!" It means: "I've come to the end of myself at last, so please take me into You to live eternally."

That is really what we are looking for at the top of the Tree and beyond. Our own True Selves and Immortal Identities. Mystics of all schools have usually called this "Divine Union," or identification of a soul with its immortal spirit, ultimate liberation into light "from whence there is no returning." Buddhists seek this state because it liberates them eternally from the "Wheel of Birth and Death" putting them past all need for reincarnation, and transforming their once human natures into an "essence of the eternal." We in the West call that same state *Perfect Peace Profound*. To this day the motto of the Benedictine Order is *Pax* in Latin, and that is what they mean.

A brief but meaningful digression here may be of interest to Christian students. Pax by itself means "peace." As it stands, it is an A in the midst of P and X. Now if we turn those two letters into Greek, we shall get *rho* and *chi*. The Chi-Rho Sign is known as the Labarum of Constantine, or the Banner of Christ under which he fought (see Figure 1.23). Put together, they formed the first two letters of CHRistos. So a Christian could interpret the sense of PAX to mean: "The peace of Our Lord Jesus Christ," and feel this is the ultimate at which the whole Tree scheme is aimed.

Why not consider an improvement to the Tree by making the Ain Soph Aur into the form of a question mark as in Figure 1.24? With this method we can see the spiral of creation starting with the dot over the I as a sign of true identity, and continuing to

Figure 1.24. The Ain Soph Aur as a question mark

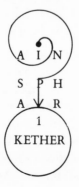

Figure 1.25. The Sphere of Daath

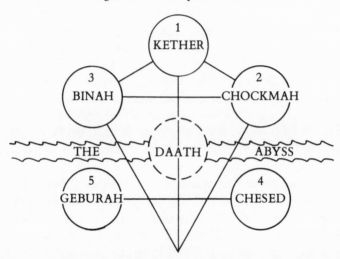

indicate the eternal enigma of existence. If Ain means "What now?" maybe we could interpret the term "limitlessness" to mean freedom, and "light" to mean illumination in the spiritual sense. So this will signify that when we have attained the maximum of emancipation from matter and full intensity of illumination in our souls, we shall reach our ultimate reality beyond all being.

If we read the words on this arrangement downwards, we shall find some fascinating interpretations from Hebrew roots:

ASA	To be strong, and heal.
IPV	Very beautiful.
NHR	To flow. Figurative for gathering of people.

Surely the story of the Tree cannot be put much plainer than that? A flow of beautiful power that heals (makes whole) all people gathering together in its name. In Arabic, the word Ain means a spring, especially a holy one, so here we see the wellspring of Life, the *Fons et Origio* of being behind ad infinitum.

There is another vacancy calling for an equal degree of comprehension. That is the clear central space bounded by the first six Sephiroth and crossed by the Abyss. You may have seen sometimes a dotted circle drawn there and read of references to a mysterious "eleventh Sphere of Daath" (pronounced "Dawth") which means "Knowledge gained by Experience" (see Figure 1.25).

Now since there cannot be such a thing as an eleventh Sephirah, you should realize this has to be a misleading or mistaken nomenclature at the start. Also, since Malkuth is commonly called the "Fallen Sephirah," it must surely make sense that it has fallen from somewhere, and the most probable place is that upper central vacancy on the Tree. If you remember the original "perfect pattern" outline, it shouldn't take much working out to see that you only have to push the three lower central Sephiroth up one place each, and the "perfect plan" appears again (see Figure 1.26).

Figure 1.26. The "Pre-Fall" position of Daath

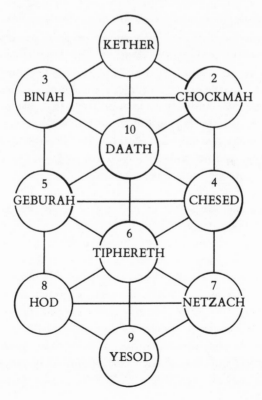

All that has happened is that the Spheres have gone back to their "pre-fall" places. Malkuth, the Kingdom of matter and physical life has disappeared and is absorbed into Yesod, the Foundation. Yesod has been drawn up into Tiphereth which has projected to its original position and now appears as the old-new concept of Daath. The dangerous Abyss has been sealed forever, because there is no need for it in a "closed circuit" Cosmos which is totally self-regenerative everywhere.

Daath signifies knowledge which comes through experience, and that is just what we are in this world to gain. It is knowledge won the hard way by bitter experience of life and all its problems which will eventually set us free from bondage to bodily matters, and let us live on far higher levels as creatures of energy and consciousness. That may be a very long way away for the mass of humanity, but if some of us don't start thinking and wondering about it in advance, few of us are likely to achieve it.

Knowledge in the sense meant here is something gained from life to life and passed along to future generations through genetic links. If life ran as it should, each generation of humans ought to be a little more intelligent and knowledgeable than the previous one. We know from history alone that this is only so to a small degree. In the last few generations we have increased our technical knowledge very considerably, but our spiritual knowledge has not developed proportionately. That is obvious to anyone with the least amount of inner perception.

A soul is born with a mortal body and inherits a genetic strain from ancestors somewhere in line with that soul's status. Through its body, the soul has a lifetime of experience on Earth as a human being. Because of that experience the soul gains knowledge according to the meaning of the word Daath. After the body dies, the soul "digests" all that knowledge, boils it down to essential energies, and reduces a whole lifetime of human experience to a sum total truth. If this is properly done, it conditions that soul for rebirth into a family with compatible genetic requirements. In that incarnation the soul concerned not only has those genetic faculties to draw from, but also its own past potentials which are brought over from one incarnation to another. Thus, theoretically, it should increase in status from one earthlife to another until it is fit for living in better conditions of being other than human.

This is the meaning behind folktales that tell of someone being set to stir a magic cauldron for a whole year and a day until the murky contents have simmered down to one single golden drop which, when swallowed, will impart immortality or universal knowledge. Alas, in the tales as in reality, something has to go wrong somewhere, and so the story takes a twist according to the teller's fancy, and meanders along to a contrived conclusion. Life in this world rarely goes as it should.

So Daath on the Tree should never be seen as a separate Sephirah, but as something we should be trying to build back into place bit by bit with inside knowledge gained by experience of life at this level. Nobody quite knows when Daath was attached to the Tree, but it does seem to have misled a great many commentators.

Daath in old Qabalistic terms was called the "Beautiful Path" whereby Wisdom was conjoined with Understanding, and Tiphereth of course means Beauty. What this seems to indicate is that if male and female types of consciousness were combined to form a single stream, life would be approaching perfection. Now it should be apparent why Qabalism was considered heretical by strict orthodox Jewry. It admitted a feminine element in its concept of deity. To impute a feminine side to the officially adopted masculine deity Yaweh was a dreadful things to do in the eyes of His chosen priesthood. Religious Jews were solemnly thanking God every day that He had created them in His own image and not as "a camel or a woman"—the two most unpredictable and awkward creatures desert-dwellers could imagine. Yet here was a mystical sect reconstituting the ancient matriarchal faith by including a Mother aspect of God in its concept of Cosmos, and making it co-equal with their Father-God.

Daath, then, is to be taken as a higher level of life-knowledge we may gain when the most advanced awareness of men and women alike unify and become a common consciousness above all sex polarization. This will theoretically complete the creative quarternity with the concepts of God-the-Spirit, God-the-Father, God-the-Mother, and God-the-Issue. Without getting involved too deeply in very complicated mysticism, esoteric teaching was to the effect that the ideal life form should be an androgyne figure or man-woman combined, capable of self-reproduction if it so willed. Whether this is looking very far back into our past as a species, or towards our remote future as an evolving type of creation is uncertain. Perhaps both. At any rate, Daath indicates a much more advanced state of consciousness than either mortal men or women can command at present.

Christian students may be interested to know that Daath is called "The Son" in a Qabalistic classic entitled *The Lesser Holy Assembly*. Verses 295-296 say: "Since the Son assumeth the symbols of his Father and his Mother (Chockmah and Binah) and is called Daath Knowledge, since he is the testimony of them both. And that Son is called the first-born, as it is written Exodus iv:22 'Israel is my first-born son.'" Further on the text quotes I Samuel ii:3: "Since Daoth is Tetragrammaton, Daoth or knowledge properly speaking, for he acquireth Daoth by Inheritance."

The use of the plural here seems to suggest that Daath is both the source and sum of Knowledge throughout life shared by every single individual conscious creature. Imagine the knowledge of every human and animal alive on this planet collected together as a unity, and you may gain a few more ideas about what Daath means. "Tetragrammaton" only means "a four letter word" and signified the Secret Name of God which might never be uttered. Masonic legend tells of a mysterious "Lost Word" which Adam forgot when he was expelled from Paradise. If mankind were ever to regain that Word, it would bring us the Knowledge (Daath) needed for restoring us to Paradise again. This may indicate that such Knowledge is buried somewhere deeply in our genetics, and eventually the long process of human breeding will produce the right combination which will bring this "Lost Word" to our Knowledge again.

Legend in general is full of tales about lost knowledge from previous generations of mankind. The famous Atlantis is only one such account of a highly developed civilization on this Earth which was totally destroyed because of its wickedness. After sending the Flood to chastise humanity, and burning out Sodom and Gomorrah, the Lord is said to have disapproved of the Edomite Kings who reigned before there was a Kingdom of Israel. Though there is mention of them in Genesis 36, the Qabalah likens them to mythical rulers of primordeal times who were destroyed because of their unbalance and chaos. Those times were called the "Prior Worlds" which God erased because he was unsatisfied with his apparently experimental handiwork. The Qabalistic text compared these pre-creation periods to sparks which fly out when iron is being forged and extinguish themselves almost immediately. It continues with the following interesting passage:

> And therefore have we related in our discourse that the ray sendeth forth sparks upon sparks in three hundred and twenty directions. And those sparks are called the Prior Worlds, and they perished. Then proceeded the workman unto his work, and was conformed namely as Male and Female. And those sparks became extinct and died, but now all things subsist. From a Light-Bearer of insupportable brightness proceeded a radiating Flame, dashing off like a vast and mighty hammer, those sparks which were the prior worlds.

Could this be a dim and distant race memory of an atomic explosion? Or might it describe the burning up of a nose-cone on an early spacecraft entering the atmosphere of this Earth, carrying some surviving colonists from elsewhere in the universe? The odd mention of 320 degrees of a circle inclines a belief in favor of the latter possibility since it leaves a distinctly cone-shaped gap to account for (see Figure 1.27). Speculation here is unlikely to be fruitful, but it is another item to include in a long chain of related incidents throughout legendary history. There is a fair comparison here to be made with the Hammer of Thor with which that Norse deity is said to have knocked creation into shape with a typically heavy Nordic hand. The hammer was called Mollnir, and was

Figure 1.27. "...the ray sendeth forth sparks upon sparks in three hundred and twenty directions. And those sparks are called the Prior Worlds, and they perished."

RADIANCE

320°

represented by a swastika symbolizing force in motion. The same symbol is also employed at Kether on our Tree.

This completes the general outline of the Tree, but there is an endless amount to learn about it yet. We have only just begun and cannot possible come to the end of its story because it is still being written every day of our lives. However, there is a great deal we can cover in the way of supportive concepts which help to develop and bring the theme closer to reality in our consciousness.

Questions

1. Why is the Zero concept so important?
2. What does the word *Ain* mean and how was it derived?
3. Why can there not be an eleventh Sphere on the Tree of Life?
4. What does *Daath* signify?
5. Pick out the ten most important sentences in this chapter.
6. Why do you suppose the Creator would wipe out previous creations?
7. Explain the position of the "pre-Fall" Spheres.
8. Why should we become "living questions marks?"
9. How is the Zero concept symbolized by Christians? Buddhists? Qabalists?
10. Why is *Daath* sometimes called the "Beautiful Path?"

· 9 ·

Pillars and Powers

Here we consider the supporting ideology
of the Tree, most noteworthy of which is the Three Pillars. Again,
it is uncertain when these ancient symbols were attached, but it was
most probably during the post-Christian era. To understand the
Pillars properly, however, we shall have to go back to prehistoric
days. They are as old as that and common to nearly all cultures.

The notion of sticking an upright into the earth and leaving
it there to mark a spot for a special reason must be almost as old as
humanity itself. As time went on, all sorts of ideas began to
accumulate around this "staff-to-see." It pointed the way to
heaven, it marked out a path on earth, it proclaimed whoever had
passed by, it staked a claim to territory. Its shadow indicated the
passage of the Sun-God over the world. It marked the stars by night.
All these things were magic to primitive people, but note carefully
they were first of all *practical*. They served a definite purpose
connected with the problems of living in this world. Early man was
practical first and mystical afterwards. He had to be.

Sticks, however, are not very durable, and upright stones
soon took their place. Since small uprights were not easily seen at a
distance and were easily moved by malicious hands, marker stones
became a lot higher and larger, needing a small team of men to set

Figure 1.28. The Druidic three-ray A.W.N., still used as a "broad arrow"

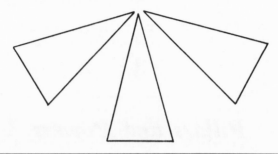

them in place. It could not have been long before selecting, shaping, and putting such stones in position became a craft of its own. The first masons on earth were learning their trade. Many of these early menhirs, as single standing stones are called, remain in their original places to this day. The pillar was man's first attempt at raising durable records of his progress on this planet.

Later in history, mystical and magical ideas grew up around stone pillars. The earliest were probably phallic and connected with the fertility factor of life. A standing stone would suggest a Father-God entering a Mother-Earth in the act of generation which might hopefully raise good crops and herds. The stone itself could act as a body for the local deity, and the first idols were only crudely shaped stones. There is a whole fascinating cultus of stone well worth studying in order to understand our human approach to deity through such means.

Eventually the stone-circle civilization began to evolve and became sophisticated enough to construct masterpieces like Stonehenge, which is still the finest example to be seen. By its day, designers were combining pillars to form patterns connected with cosmic phenomena. It had been discovered that by aligning two or more pillars, calculations could be made from stars, sun shadows, and seasonal changes of these. Man was beginning to learn his tempro-spatial relationship with the rest of the observable universe. It proved easier to take sights on far away points if two pillars were used, and accuracy was improved if a third was interposed between them.

By this time, triplicities of divinity were coming into wide circulation. There were three visible phases of the Moon. Celtic Druids were adopting the "three-ray" symbol for the Life-God. They called it *Awn,* pronounced Ahoon (see Figure 1.28). It was probably condensed from the many-rayed solar symbol of the Egyptian monotheist Pharoah, Ankh-en-Aton (see Figure 1.29). These three rays were seen as the beginning, middle, and end of the solar spectrum shown by a rainbow: red, yellow, and blue. Additionally, they represented the three possibilities of life: yes, no, and maybe. We can see them also as positive, negative, and neutral. Druids in particular promulgated their teachings in the form of poetic triads.

Another combination of threes which had become very meaningful in temple practice was the portal, two doorposts and the lintel above them. The design of a portal was being carved on Egyptian tombs as a "spirit entrance" for the soul to come and go on its visits to the mummified body, and some early long barrows had a false doorway made from three blocks of stone for the same reason. Some think the great Trilithons at Stonehenge represent "Gateways to the Gods." Many initiation ceremonies involved episodes of being formally admitted to the sacred precincts through a guarded entrance which was only opened after the correct passwords had been exchanged, and to this day in some lodges a

Figure 1.29. The multi-ray Solar Disc (Aton) of Ankh-en-Aton

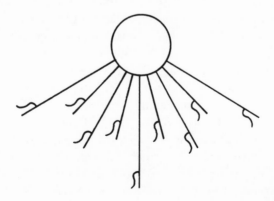

Figure 1.30. The basic design of the female date flower

relic of such a procedure is called "passing the Pillars" or sometimes "passing the Pylons." In the Christian church, a Bishop in full pontificals still knocks three times (ostensibly to honor the Trinity) with the butt of his crozier on a closed church door which then opens to admit him.

Another, perhaps more primitive, association with twin pillars was the birth custom of some tribal peoples. Two suitable stakes were hammered into the ground and the birthing woman knelt between them gripping one with each hand to gain leverage for the bearing down process of expelling the child from her body. Other women were there to assist, of course, but the mother herself formed the Middle or third pillar. American Indian women were doing this up till the last century and possibly later.

So deeply had the theme of sacred pillars entered the human consciousness that they had become integral to most forms of worship one way or another. Though the Jews had been strictly forbidden to raise any sort of stone idol, they compromised in the Temple of Solomon by including two ornamental pillars as part of the architecture. These were in front of the Holy House, their capitals were decorated with chain and pomegranate designs, and they were given names. The right hand one was called Jachin (He shall establish) and the left one was Boaz (in it is Strength) which clearly suggests they were male fertility emblems. Representation of these Pillars can be seen in modern Masonic and other "occult temples," while the chain and pomegranate decorations are integral to Masonic aprons.

Now although an upright tree trunk is an obviously phallic symbol in itself, it had been discovered that certain trees are unisexual and will not bear fruit unless properly paired. That is to say, among a grove of fruit-bearers which would be female trees, there had to be a small proportion of male trees in the vicinity to pollinate them. An important example of this is the date palm, which is dioecious or has male and female flowers on different trees. The male flower is small, yellow and five petalled, while the female is round like a berry, but has a backing which is almost a perfect hexagram against a trifoliate cup. There is a virtually perfect symbol for the whole Tree design: one in the center of six with a three-fold basis, ten altogether (see Figure 1.30).

On the strength of this, the background for the Tree of Life seemed best represented by a male and female pillar of two stylized palm trunks, one white for male and the other black for female. Here there could be a hint of Solomon and Sheba since she was reputedly dark-skinned. The Middle Pillar, however, would be a pure column of light represented by the stars, Sun and Moon, illuminating the Earth. It also symbolized the "Pillar of Fire by Night" said to have guided the Israelites in their desert wanderings. We are now in a position to put these important Pillars in their proper places behind the Tree. (See Figure 1.31 on page 116.)

At last we see the Tree as it is usually represented in most Mystery Temples. The remainder of its attributions are normally just imagined by those who should know them by heart. Its immediate message says on sight: "This is the Golden Rule of Life. Between two extremities, always choose the Middle Way." We can scarcely go very wrong if we keep that rule throughout our lives on Earth. It was said the black Pillar consisted of Severity, the white one of Mercy, and the Middle Pillar of Mildness. One could call them the Pillars of Pain, Pleasure and Peace.

Our whole lives are mostly formed by bouncing between these "pillars" and trying to keep a central course between them, so they are an excellent symbol of an average human's progress. From

Figure 1.31. The Holy Tree of Life with Triple Pillars

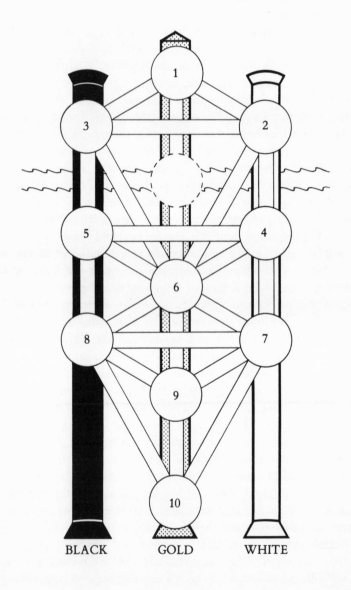

BLACK   GOLD   WHITE

an occult viewpoint however, these Pillars indicate the three broad paths of spiritual dedication by which initiated souls seek ultimate light. Most of us are mainly on one particular Path, but it is possible to find elements of all three in some who have varied their approaches from one incarnation to another. The Paths in question are these:

I. *Hermetic Path* (Black Pillar).This is named from Hermes Trismegistus (the Thrice-Great) who is the old "Initiator" from whom the Mystery Teachings of the West are reputedly derived. This is the Path mostly followed by ritualists who prefer formalized and intellectual ways of working. It is the way of caution, scientific application, and painstaking research. Here is where you would find Qabalists, Rosicrucians, and "Temple" types of occultists, satisfied to make step-by-step progress as they climb the Tree. It is a serious and plodding Path on the whole, though there are highly rewarding episodes to be encountered. Among ordinary human beings you might find here: accountants, mathematicians, physicists, surgeons, doctors, lawyers, technicians of all kinds, writers on learned subjects. orchestra musicians and so forth, all drawn by specific themes calling for considerable study and application.

II. *Orphic Path* (White Pillar), so called from Orpheus, patron of joyous living and popular music. This is the Path for nature-loving pagans who cannot be bond by chains of convention and artificially imposed rules for living, people who do not take kindly to discipline and restrained behavior because someone else dictates how they ought to behave. Here we find spontaneity and exuberance contrasted with deep tragedy and heartbreak. This is the Path of emotion and pure unguarded feeling. This is where you might encounter artists and poets, "show-biz" folks, sensationalists, romantic and fantasy writers, revivalists, enthusiasts of all types, animists who find God in natural phenomena. Very often souls are drawn to this Path in youth and gradually change over to the Hermetic Path in later life.

III. *Mystic Path* (Middle Gold Pillar), is the hardest Path of all for a human to attempt and relatively few may expect more than initial progress here. It is the Path of sheer single-minded self-sacrificing (in the real sense) devotion to deity however idealized,

Figure 1.32. The Tree of Life aligned on the human body

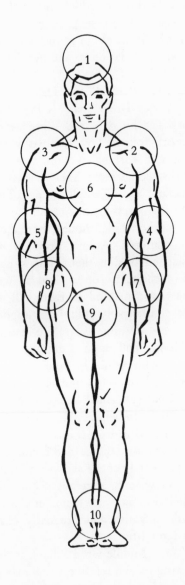

which gives all to attain nothing. No one unprepared to "suffer for the cause" should devote themselves to this Path unthinkingly. It is a Path usually undertaken by souls who have had long experience of the other two in former incarnations and have reached a stage of development where they know the risks and problems involved, and are willing to launch themselves lightward in a final fling for liberation into Perfect Peace Profound. It is a Path for Avatars and Sacred Kings.

If you have any uncertainty which of these Paths you belong with, you are strongly advised to settle for the Hermetic as the safest and most reliable. It is also supposed to have some elements of the other two in it. The Hermetic may be the slowest and often the least spectacular Path, but followers are less liable to encounter serious spiritual injuries thereon.

Do bear in mind that since you are facing the Tree design, the black Pillar is on the left and the white on the right. If you "pass the Pillars" and turn around, the Pillars are reversed in relation to yourself and right then becomes left. The Middle Pillar, of course, remains unchanged relative to your central axis. From a magical viewpoint, it all depends on whether you are taking in or giving out the qualities of the Tree. In the first instance you face it, and in the second, you project it.

There is a rough alignment of the Tree with a human body which is mostly used for visualizing the Tree around your own person in order to be conscious *as* the Tree instead of just being aware *of* it. The disposition of the Spheres is then consider to be as per Figure 1.32: *Kether* at the head and slightly above, *Chokmah* at the left shoulder and *Binah* at the right, *Chesed* at the left arm and *Geburah* at the right, *Tiphereth* at the heart and solar plexus, *Netzach* at the left leg and *Hod* at the right leg, *Yesod* at the genitals, and *Malkuth* at the feet.

Many interesting and instructive occult exercises can be done with this distribution of the Spheres. For instance, close your eyes and raise both hands to the top of the head, there visualizing Kether. Let the left hand fall away and conceive Chokmah on the left shoulder. Do the same with the right hand and Binah. Extend the left arm as Chesed and then the right as Geburah. Bring both hands, left over right, to mid-belly between heart and solar plexus. (This signifies that Might is kept in control by Mercy.) Take a step forward with the left leg, thinking of Netzach, and follow it with the right leg, thinking of Hod. Clasp both hands at the genital position, concentrating on Yesod, then finish by bringing the hands to the sides with forefingers pointing to the ground while you think of Malkuth.

You can do likewise with your face alone. Make the center top of your forehead Kether, your left eye Chokmah and your right Binah, then your left ear Chesed and your right Geburah. Tiphereth is just under your nostrils. Netzach is your left lower cheek and Hod your right. Yesod then becomes your lips and Malkuth your chin. Try making patterns over your face like that with your right of left forefinger and closed eyes.

Then you can experiment with the Pillar idea by standing just outside a closed door and imagining the "outside" Sephiroth in place on each doorpost and the Middle pillar at the center of the door. Identify them all in your mind, and touch the doorposts with each hand so that you have Mercy in your right hand and Might in your left. Make up a little invocation calling the Tree into your consciousness as strongly as you can. If you can't think of anything clever on the spot, just call the names of the concepts clearly to mind one after the other, *not forgetting to start with zero*. When you are ready, open the door and enter quite slowly while you try to feel the Middle Pillar pass into yourself as you go. Finish up with Might in your right hand and Mercy in your left. You may imagine yourself grasping a Sword in your right hand and a Rod or Scepter in your left, if you like.

Always try to use quite commonplace or available facilities of household provenance for routine magical exercises if you can, because this helps bring inner meaning into your ordinary living. Affairs of your soul should not be apart from your normal consciousness but a vital part of it. Otherwise you are likely to become like nominal Christians who lock God up in church during the week and make a condescending call on him every Sunday. Old time practitioners had nothing like the facilities of a modern home to employ, yet they managed to get quite good results with their limited equipment. This could have been because they were more or less forced into using their constructive imagination all the time, whereas we tend to accept only ready-made images pushed into our minds mostly for commercial or political reasons. Sooner or later, if you mean to accept real magical discipline in your life, you will have to learn how to control this invasion of your mind, and take the responsibility for setting up your own individual "teachers of truth." That is all part of the Western Tradition practice.

Now we come to two more ideas which are attached to the Tree from one outside Pillar to the other. The first is a bow (Qesheth) and its arrow (Chutz) which is visualized as being just behind Yesod, the arrow pointing straight up the Middle Pillar (see Figure 1.33). This bow shot idea is a very old one. It was something a man could do to hit an object at a much greater distance than his normal throwing ability. The bow here is visualized as a *rainbow*, made from all colors of the spectrum. The arrow is a golden one, and signified *desire*. They are probably the symbols which inspired William Blake to write his famous line:

> Bring me my bow of burning gold,
> Bring me my arrows of Desire.

The Qabalah does not see the bow as gold, however, only the arrow. The bow has an ideological connection with the rainbow set in the clouds by God after the flood (Genesis ix: 14-15). "And it shall come to pass when I bring a cloud over the earth that the bow shall be seen in the cloud. And I will remember the covenant which is between me and you, and every living creature of all flesh." In other words, when mankind's view of heaven was clouded and obscured, there would still be a sign of promise that brighter times were coming shortly. An ideological arrow fired with a bow of promise would be winged on its way by faith, hope and optimism. Thus the arrows were likened to hopeful thoughts aimed in the general direction of God by optimistic humans, our intentions shooting ahead of ourselves.

Figure 1.33. The bow and arrow on the Tree of Life

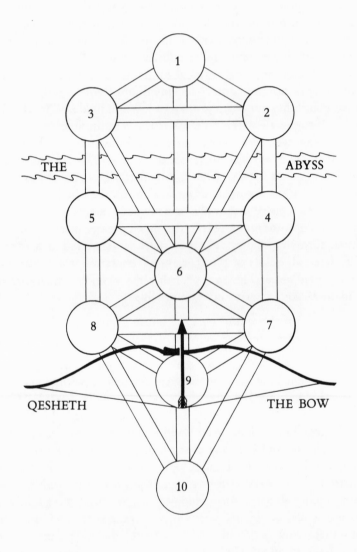

Today we might liken this notion to a spaceship aimed into deep Cosmos, bearing living beings in search of greater knowledge concerning the origins of life and its meaning. Why not? We should always try to see fundamental ideas in Qabalah or any other traditional system in terms of our our times. In olden days, though, arrows had other significance than simply aiming at marks. They were often used in divination. One method was just to fire an arrow straight up in the air and see which direction it pointed when it fell to earth. The shooter would then follow that direction as an indication that his fate led that way. The gods had decided for him.

We have to remember the arrowhead itself was a symbol of the "three-ray" sign of divinity used by the Druids as a symbol of the "sacred breath," A-OO-N which breathed forth life into the creation. Another connection of the arrow (as a flying Sword) was with the element of Air. If attached to the Staff, it became the Lance of Light with which the Dragon of Darkness was defeated. Sometimes archers would scratch symbols on the shafts of their arrows indicating their intentions. In the same spirit, soldiers of both world wars would scrawl rude messages to their enemies on missiles they were about to fire or drop. So there is a lot of meaning to be had from the bow and arrow notion on the Tree.

Further up we come to the second of these transverse conceptions. This is a "sanctuary veil" in front of the Abyss called Paroketh. This word literally means a divider, especially a curtain. These were used in Tabernacles such as the Israelites carted around in the desert to mark out the holy places from those admitting the ordinary congregation. Only consecrated priests were supposed to pass behind the temple veil. It was a common custom in most religions to veil especially holy objects from unentitled eyes. In the old mystery processions, such items were always covered from public view. In modern Christian churches, tabernacles or aumbries containing the consecrated Host and sacred vessels are veiled with seasonal colored curtains. In the Russian and Greek orthodox churches, the whole sanctuary is concealed by a huge screen called the iconsstase (image screen) with its three "Holy Doors." Synagogues still veil their "Ark" and scrolls of the Law.

So this sanctuary veil added to the Tree is a very ancient sign of reverence for holiness. It is a reminder of the admonition: "No man shall look upon the face of God and live." This is what the veil was supposed to hide. The first Sephira, Kether, is viewed from one angle as "The Vast Countenance" or face of Macroprosopus the Great Cosmos, which is so tremendous and terrible from a human standpoint, it would destroy us to encounter it directly. Many are the legends of humans reduced to ashes because of rashness in God-gazing. So here the mercy of God is shown as hiding his fatal Face behind the veil of Paroketh. The lower Sephiroth on the Tree are considered to compose the features of Microprosopus "The Lesser Countenance" which man *might* look upon and live. The "Great Face of God" was called *Arik Anpin* in Hebrew, and the "Small Face" was *Zeir Anpin*.

In other words, this "Lesser Countenance" of Micro-prosopus was thought of as the image and likeness of Himself in which God created man, the "face of nature" which we can see for ourselves all around us. Beyond that, a merciful veil was drawn across the concepts of pure consciousness which we dare not lift our mortal eyes toward any more than we may gaze steadily at the Sun without risking physical blindness. We can only stare safely at the reflection of the Sun mirrored in the Moon. Nevertheless some religious fanatics were known to stare at the Sun until they lost their sight or impaired it irreparably.

A practical purpose served by veiling across a sanctuary was to give approaching worshippers a chance to pause and adjust their consciousness before passing beyond that point. That is to say, they had an opportunity to put themselves in a proper frame of mind prior to encountering the Presence in the Adytum. Try this out experimentally: Stand before a curtain drape and collect your thoughts. Say to yourself: "Before I pull this curtain aside, I must be quite sure I am prepared to see what it will show. How do I know for certain what it will reveal? I may *think* I know, or *suppose* I know, but can I be *positive* until I actually remove this veil from before my eyes? What if everything were totally changed? Suppose I found myself looking into a strange parallel universe? How can I prove there will *always* be the same scene behind this curtain? Am I prepared for some terrible shock if a strange thing like that should happen?"

Go on asking yourself such questions a while, then finally make the effort and draw the curtain aside gently. Your familiar scene may indeed come to you as a slight shock when you do, because you have been conditioning your consciousness in another direction. Now do you get the idea? This is the sort of thing you should do before you approach higher concepts of deity in any system. That is the reason why in the Christian church it is customary to pause and make a slight sign of reverence before pronouncing the name of Jesus Christ. It is the reason why in a synagogue a reader pauses, bows, and substitutes the word Adonai (Lord) for the forbidden term IHVH (Yahweh). They get the most out of their Gods that way.

Finally, we have to think about another twin-idea concerning the Tree which was added during its construction. This is the time or rate-factor as applied to progression along its Paths. Everybody knows it is quicker to fall from a tree than to climb one. Most of us have done the first, but how many are prepared to pick ourselves up and start climbing again to where we fell from and higher? How fast dare we climb, and what is the most sensible rate of progress? Is there some kind of guide we can rely on?

The fastest thing the ancients knew was lightning. They described Lucifer, the archangel who defied divinity, as falling from Heaven like lightning. We were reputed to have "fallen" from Paradise ourselves because the same archangel tempted Eve in the form of a serpent. So what happened to the serpent? It was cursed by God to lose its limbs and crawl on its belly. Nevertheless it could still climb trees if it were long enough, by winding its body round the trunk and twisting in an upwards direction. Early man was quite accustomed to seeing large snakes ascending trees this way, frequently in a clockwise manner.

Now it seemed reasonable to earlier thinkers that if Lucifer had been hurled out of Heaven like a lightning flash and also cost us our place in Paradise almost as fast, it was only justice if he showed

Figure 1.34. The Sword Flash or Lightning Flash

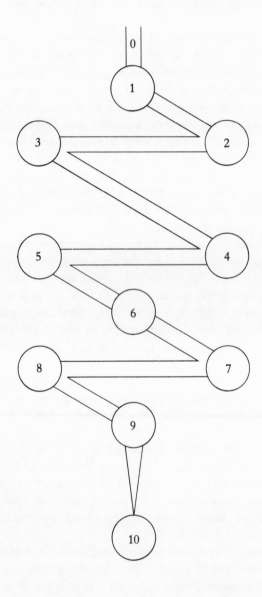

us the way back eventually. In his serpent form he seemed to be doing just that. With a strong, steady crawl, the reptile progressed from branch to branch in search of prey or shelter, transferring the weight of its body carefully from one branch to another before unwinding its tail from the lowest branch. A serpent did not leap like a monkey. It investigated every inch of its way with care, making absolutely sure of its grip as it went along. Even if it encountered a prize in the shape of young birds or small mammals, it still kept a firm grasp on the tree with its tail before it struck with its head.

All these actions were moral lessons for would-be climbers of trees, whether Holy or not. In the case of the Holy Tree, they visualized the Fall of both man and archangel as a lightning flash (sometimes seen as a sword), flashing from one Sphere to another until it reached Earth (see Figure 1.34). The image of a sword was chosen because of the "Flaming Sword" wielded by the Kerubim to prevent us getting back into Paradise after extradition. The return way of the serpent is seen in Figure 1.35 (on page 128) where the creature is shown crossing every Path in sequence on its upward journey. The moral here is that evil can indicate good by contrast, if we know how to study its behavior for such a purpose. Truth may be reached by means of lies.

So now we should know and emulate the serpent way of the Tree, steadily, carefully, taking things in turn, checking everything, pausing if in doubt, governed by caution throughout and keeping a firm hold on whatever we find to support us. All these supplementary ideas of the Tree are meant to help us approach and deal with it if we understand why they are included.

It may be that Semitic scholarship built up mystical and mathematical concepts of the Holy Tree of Life in earlier times, but since then, Gentile esotericists have made, *and are still making*, very important contributions and improvements to its original construction. This has been most valuable in the field of commentary, presentation and development of the theme in ways which capture the imagination and inspire further spiritual action among serious students of the Western Inner Way. Had the texts remained in the

Figure 1.35. The Serpent Path

first state of literal translation from the Hebrew originals, it is very doubtful if more than a handful of people would be interested in them now. What we are really following at present is Qabalah as interpreted and reconstructed by Western Initiates in order to make it more suitable for our particular mental and spiritual outlooks.

Questions

1. What are the three Pillars of the Tree and what do they signify?
2. What colors are the Pillars and why?
3. Describe the Three Paths of life.
4. How does the Tree pattern align with the human body?
5. What is the symbology of the bow and arrow?
6. Describe the symbology and function of the dividing curtain.
7. Choose the eight most important sentences in this chapter.
8. Describe the symbology of the serpent.
9. Describe the symbology of the Lightning Flash.
10. In what way do you feel the Tree pattern represents our cosmos?

·10·

Worlds Within and Without

Here is where we come to the "Four Worlds" of the Tree. Though this often confuses many people because of elaborate Hebrew titles, the idea is basically simple enough. If we go back to the three pre-stages of the first Sphere, Kether the Crown, as *Ain, Ain Soph,* and *Ain Soph Aur* and see:

0	Nothing
0 0	Nothing but Limitlessness
0 0 0	Nothing but Limitless Light
1	Kether the Crown

so that three nothings make a something, you might get the idea of four somethings making a Sephirah. Remember we started all our studies with the concept of a quartered circle, and here we are back to it again from another angle.

The general notion is that God doesn't think something into existence and—bang!—there it is like that. Creation is a *process*, and everything has to go through the same cyclic laws of life in order to reach the world of physical matter we live in here. Qabalism postulates this process in four distinct stages which are:

1. *Origination*. Atziluth, in Hebrew. This is where God actually originates anything by conceiving the archetype in his own

awareness. Hence this principle in each Sphere is identified by a God-name. If God means it to go further than his own mind, he hands it down to a somewhat lower life stage.

2. *Creation.* Briah, in Hebrew. This is where the concept is carried further along its line of life by leading orders of creative spirits termed "archangels" because they condense and make the archetype ready for processing by a lesser order of spiritual technicians.

3. *Formation.* Yetzirah, in Hebrew. Here, as the name implies, shape, form, arrangement, and all other detailed specifications are given to the concept by spiritual workers with very specialized yet limited skills called "angels." Each "order" of angels is designed to fulfil one function only, but all are experts at their particular job.

4. *Expression.* Assiah, in Hebrew. This is where the concept emerges into existence as we recognize the term. That is to say, it reaches us through natural laws and channels of consciousness. The "powers that be" at this stage are symbolized by cosmic phenomena we can appreciate with our normal perceptions such as stars, planets, zodiacal signs, and elemental energies.

In other words, it is all just like an ordinary production line in any factory. First of all you have the "top man" with some original idea. So he hands it over to expert designers, estimators, draftsmen, and other specialists who work everything out on paper and make a feasibility report. Those specialists correspond to "archangels." If they give the go-ahead, everything is left to the technical workers (angels) who actually produce the product in terms of material, shape, size, and all other such specifications. As yet, however, the produced goods are still "warehouse stock." Before they can actually reach users where their whole purpose will be realized, a whole army of handlers have to shift them into shops or somewhere making them available to consumers. This is where wholesale dealers, advertisers, and marketers of every description come in. So there we have the earthly equivalents of elementary and planetary influences.

That is what the "Four Worlds" amount to—cosmic consciousness focusing itself into material existence through creative cycles of energy seen from four angles of approach. Each Sphere on the Tree of Life is considered to project its principles into life by those four stages, and naturally each stage will correspond with one letter in the Great Name of God—IHVH. With those letters God is imagined as saying:

1. I Conceive. *YOD*
2. I Create. *HE*
3. I Form. *VAU*
4. I Express. *HE* (final)

Did you realize that you and the rest of us went through the same process? You may have been thinking you originated because of a sex act between your parents, but strictly speaking, you *didn't*. Your origins, like ours, lay in the thinking and feeling which took place *before* the sex act. Without such awareness and intentions in the first place, none of us would be here. We originate with *consciousness*, not copulation. That comes afterwards, and is the second creative stage. Then follows gestation as the formulative stage, and lastly parturition or birth as the expression of us into existence in this world. Now do you understand the "Four World" idea of the Tree a bit better? Let us take the Sephiroth one by one down the Tree and see how each "gives birth" to its own concept by this quarternal process.

KETHER, The Crown or Summit

1. The orginative stage is caused by God under his aspect of *EHIH*. This is not a word to pronounce, but to be *breathed*. It is the *I AM* of Existence, the first and last breath of life, the Holy Breath that consecrated Creation.

2. The creative stage is operated by Archangel *Metatron*.The name means "near thy throne," and is derived from Greek. Tradition says he is the youngest of archangels and is responsible for communicating Qabalah to mankind. He was said to have been human himself once, under the guise of Enoch, who "walked with God." He seems to typify a hope that the rest of us may one day

stand face to face with deity if we ever reach the level of *Metatron* on the Tree.

3. The formative stage is worked by an angel order known as the *Chioth ha Kadosh*, Holy Living Ones. These are the life elements raised to their highest degree of perfection. There were said to be four types of Chioth, and their main function is "keeping God alive" in relation to our Cosmos. They are to God what their counterparts are to us at our end of the Tree.

4. This is the expressive stage. The ideal symbol here is a nebula, cosmic matter just beginning to appear in evident existence. Another attribution here is Uranus, the oldest God, who, as Coelus (Heaven, the Sky), mated with Terra (Earth) and was later castrated by his offspring, Saturn. The blood shed with this act fell in the sea and produced the foam from which Venus was born. In other words, the virility of the Sky God stimulated the sex instincts of mankind.

CHOKMAH, *Wisdom*

1. The originative cause here is God as *IHVH*, Yahweh, possibly man's oldest name for God. *IO HO* is another form representing the "mighty shout of laughter" said to accompany creation (the Big Bang). Jove is a romanized form of the name. The Celts knew it as *IEU HU*, "He. Him up there." This is essentially a masculine form of consciousness.

2. The creative influence here is Archangel *Ratziel*, Herald of God. He is said to proclaim the secrets of the universe aloud every day for those willing to listen. The Wisdom of the Ages is available for anyone learning the "language" of the Spheres. No one can be sure if any humans have learned or listened yet.

3. The formation process is carred out by an angelic order known as the *Auphanim*, or the "encirclers" in the sense of rolling around. This could refer to the "mills of God" which grind slowly but very thoroughly, or maybe just the "wheels that make the universe go round." They seem to typify whatever mechanism keeps the cycles of life in action.

4. Expressively this Sphere is best represented by the zodiac, called in Hebrew *Mazloth*, the stations. Here we see the

complete circle of cosmic life in the heavens, theoretically determining which types of mankind will be born under which sign. Sometimes Neptune is placed here as the Earth-shaker God, presumably because Neptune is a Father figure and true wisdom is metaphorically an "earthshaking" force which can destroy a lot of false concepts and erroneous ideas.

BINAH, Understanding
1. Originatively, God operates this Sphere until the title of *IHVH ELOHIM*, an odd description amounting to "God the Goddesses." Here is the feminine aspect of divinity whose intuitive awareness makes up the other half of an omniscient deity. Here are also the aspects of *Ahmah*, the Dark Mother, and *Aimah*, the Bright Mother because she is pregnant with the seed of light.
2. Creatively, an archangel called *Tzaphkiel*, the Watcher of God, takes care of things at this point. He (or It) observes in an understanding fashion the ongoing work of Cosmos, and presumably communicates with the creator thereon. We could think of this archangel as God's "eye in the sky," or facilitator of cosmic comprehension.
3. Formatively, this Sphere is served by an angelic order termed the *Aralim*, thrones, in the sense of being supporters or upholders. True understanding needs both insofar as not even God can understand anything properly without supportive means for structuring consciousness. This is where such a process takes place.
4. Expressively, the symbol here is Saturn, a steady, sobering, cautious, and time-consuming influence. Just what one would expect is needed for gaining understanding. Care, prudence, and age are associated with this planet, factors needed to produce understanding through experience of life on all levels.

THE ABYSS
Yes, the Abyss has a guiding genius too, *Abbadon*, who presides over lost souls and causes. The Abyss itself was entitled *Masak Mavdil*, or place for rejected failures. A being called *Mesukiel*, or "Veiler of God," tactfully hid divine and human failures in this dumping ground. Through the Abyss everything and anyone who

was useless to life had to be "recycled" back to basic materials fit for reuse. Even deity had to appoint its "waste reclamation officers" and their "sanitary squads." Some spiritual orders have to do the dirty jobs and mess-clearing routines of cosmic life.

CHESED, Mercy, Compassion

1. The originative aspect here is simply *EL*, usually translated as "God," but meaning just "The." Many early religions rather feared naming their deities too specifically in case this might give offence or seem presumptuous. So they often referred to divinity as "The One," "That," "Her," "It what IS," or other oblique nomenclature. In this case of the Mercy concept, it seemed best to adopt such a procedure.

2. Creatively, the archangel *Tzadkiel* operated the construction of this Sphere. His name means "The Righteous of God," or one who does the right thing in life every time because that is his nature. It is always right to be merciful *after* the wrongs have been cleared up by other departments of deity.

3. Formatively, the angel order of the *Chashmalim* (Bright Shining Ones) shape up Divine Mercy. They are said to have the gift of cheerful encouraging speech. We can think of them as warm, friendly, and kindly beings telling us to trust in a compassionate creator.

4. The expression here is naturally Jupiter, the so-called "generous" planet whose gifts are not always the blessings they might seem. Nevertheless, this was the ancient concept of a benevolent Father-God in his most indulgent mood towards his mortal "pets." It was "God-the-Giver" personified.

GEBURAH, Might and Severity

1. The God origination here is *ELOHIM GIBOR*, the Gods of Might and Power, the "no-nonsense" aspect of deity which deals with delinquency as it deserves. There is no suggestion of punishment or retribution here whatever. It is simply a restoring to rights by which ever means happens to be most expedient.

2. The creation of restorative conditions with this Sphere is the responsibility of Archangel *Khamael,* the Burner of God. He seems to be another "divine decontaminator" who burns out

corruption and infection with his surgical laser on a spiritual level of life.

    3. Formation is carried out by an angelic order called the *Seraphim,* "Fiery Serpents." These evidently intensify the work of their superior, *Khamael* and set up circumstances or arrange conditions needed for cosmic correction to operate properly.

    4. Expression is considered to be the work of Mars, the God of War. Yet war on what? War on evil, wickedness and wrongs wherever they are encountered in life, God declaring war, not on human sinners, but upon the sin or imperfections in them.

TIPHERETH, *Beauty and Balance*

    1. The originative aspect of deity in this wonderful Sphere is *ELOAH va DAATH,* God-Goddess of Knowledge, the experience of existence. This shows the Sphere which eventuates Daath in the end. Here is the "know-how" of life which keeps all other powers in poise.

    2. Creation is carried out under the auspices of the solar archangel *Mikal* or *Michael,* whose name means "like God." Many are the splendid legends about this beautiful being whose championship of humanity has well earned him the title of "Leader" in our perpetual battle against darkness, disease, and ignorance.

    3. Formation is shaped up by the angel order of the *Malakim,* which name signified kings or controllers. They are masters at restoring lost balance, are the regulators or life and could perhaps be compared with pacemakers in human hearts, without which we would soon die from accelerated or slowed down heartbeats.

    4. Expression of this Sphere is naturally the Sun, our central source of life energy in this universe, our sure sign of God-in-Heaven and nucleus of our planetary system without which we would perish forever. What else but our Sun could represent beauty and balance for us on Earth?

NETZACH, *Victory and Achievement*

    1. The God-origin of this Sphere is *IHVH SABAOTH,* usually translated as God of Hosts, but which could mean God in everyone, the divine principle in life inspiring all that lives to achieve its highest functions for its species.

2. Creatively, the necessary work is accomplished under the direction of Archangel *Auriel,* the Light of God, or alternatively *Hamiel,* the Grace of God, and *Phanael,* the Appearance of God. These titles are apparently interchangeable. As *Auriel,* this is one of the Great Four responsible for steady and careful achievement while consolidating whatever victories we may attain on lesser levels of living.

3. The formative order of angels are simply called the *Elohim,* that odd word for feminine Gods with a masculine plural. Seemingly, they help us come to victorious terms with the dual sides of our own nature, the male-female in each of us regardless of bodily sex.

4. Expressively, this Sphere is typified by Venus, usually thought of as the planet of sexual love, but she also signifies feeling, emotion, sense of soul, and achievement in the sense of being loved in return for loving. A human reflection of divine love satisfying souls who search for such a reward.

HOD, Glory and Honor

1. Originatively, the God-title here is *ELOHIM SA-BAOTH,* another difficult one to translate accurately, but possibly the nearest is "the God-Goddesses of everyone." We all have our individual ideas of God, and this is where we get them from.

2. The Creative work of this Sphere is left to Archangel *Raphael.* We have met him before in his capacity for healing human injuries, and here we meet him again as instructor of the intelligent. Just as the last Sphere was emotional, so this one is intellectual.

3. Formative working here is entrusted to the angelic order of the *Beni-Elohim,* Sons of the Gods. They are responsible for forming our codes of honorable conduct so that we may reflect credit on our creator. We should all live by some kind of civilizing rules of decent behavior, and this is where they ought to come from.

4. Expressively, this Sphere is represented by Mercury or Hermes, the so-called "Psychopompus" or soul-conductor of Heaven. Apart from being Messenger of the Gods, he is supposed to act as an instructor and guide in the Hermetic Mysteries. He is to be

thought of as an initiator into occult schools, especially ritualistic ones involving full formal ceremonials.

YESOD, The Foundation

1. Divine origins of this Sphere are with the aspect of *SHADDAI el CHAIIM*, the Overlord of Lives. This is God in the sense of being Lord of human lives on Earth and the reproductive process thereof. It is the spiritual source of our sex ability.

2. Creatively, the supervision is alloted to Archangel *Gabriel* or *Jivrael*, the Virile One of God. *Jiv* in Sanskrit means "life force" in terms of the livening principle of bodies. He is capable of vitalizing minds with fertile ideas, too.

3. Formatively, the work of this Sphere is done by the angel order of the *Aishim*, another difficult word to translate. "Souls of Fire" is a close literal translation but it should carry the implications of being fit and proper in a sense of worthiness. Their job seems to be ensuring that whatever is born should justify itself. Cynics might suggest shortcomings in this department!

4. Expression is symbolized by the Moon, well known for its association with birth cycles. The four phases of the Moon bring us back to the Circle Cross theme of cosmic life and our places in it as reflected rays of spiritual solar light.

MALKUTH, The Kingdom

1. Origins in divinity here are with *ADONAI MALAKH*, or Lord King, God appearing as "Master of Matter" or ruler of the world. Pious people of old often termed God "Faithful King," and believed this world would never be properly governed unless deity itself did so directly. There are still sects who believe this in our times.

2. Creation in our earthly Sphere is carried out by *Sandalaphon*, from the Greek word meaning "co-brother." We have met him before, and recognize him as the "other end" of *Metatron* whose job he would be doing if this were Kether.

3. Formation is controlled by an angelic order called *Kerubim*. They are a composite of Ox, Lion, Eagle, and Man, or

Taurus, Leo, Scorpio, and Aquarius. These are the "Holy Living Creatures" at our end of existence. They represent the qualities of strong patience, noble courage, lofty aspiration, and imaginative intelligence. We need all these and more for survival here.

4. Expression in, on, and as the Sphere of this natural Kingdom of God is made possible by a low but powerful order of angels sometimes called *elementals*. We have met their energies before as Earth, Water, Fire, and Air. These are the last of spiritual structures behind what we know as "matter."

That is the making of the universe from spirit to matter as seen through Qabalistic eyes. Maybe modern scientists would see it as energy converted into electrons, and specify their theory differently, but those are only two ways of looking at one and the same thing—created cosmos. Each is as valid as the other insofar as both are human viewpoints.

In order to call up the concepts as clearly as possible, pictorial images were made for each one as a visual symbol of its characteristics. Magi of olden and modern times found that sensory associations were of great assistance in concentrating consciousness to effective degrees along specific frequencies for working "magic," in other words, to raise and apply suitable inner energies along correct lines of consciousness. The "Sephirotic Images" used in conventional Qabalism are these:

1. An old King seen in right profile, just head and long beard which often displays *IHIH* (I AM) in Hebrew letters among the hairs. His crown is made from nothing but Light.

2. A bearded male "Wisdom" figure with a book of law. Sky background.

3. A Mother figure with ark or closed chest. Earth-sea background.

4. A throned and crowned "Benevolent King" figure.

5. A "Conquering Warrior" figure, sometimes with a chariot.

6. A triple image of a Child, Sacrificed God, and Risen King. This symbolizes incarnation, crucifixion, and resurrection.

7. A lovely naked woman bearing palm branch or victor's laurels.

8. An Hermaphrodite in Hermetic form.

9. A strong virile male.

10. A young woman, throned and crowned as Nature, the Bride of Man.

In addition to these rather lovely pictures, continue working on your lists of attributions which you feel apply to specific Spheres. These will vary somewhat according to individual taste and reaction, but in the main they will follow a consistent sort of pattern. We suggest you try to make up your own list out of your reactions with Sphere concepts. That could be quite a fascinating experience. Say to yourself: "When I think of...(whatever the Sphere is), what do I imagine in terms of sight, hearing, taste, smell, and touch?" Run through whole gamuts of sensory stimuli methodically, either from memory or practical experiment. Make as long a list as you can, then pick good examples from each category and line them up with your list. Make sure you know *why* each item applies. It is no use just picking something more or less at random and then wondering why later, without ever finding an answer. Such a specimen list (called "Attributions of the Spheres") will be found on page 142.

You may not agree with the list supplied, but if you don't, it is important to find out why, and specify what you would have put in its place. You should learn a lot from this. It should enable you (if you have done the job properly) to be like God at the center and circumference of your own Cosmic Circle, in almost instant contact with all your consciousness in every direction on every possible topic. *It is much more than an elaborate memory system. It is a method of making yourself the creator of your own conscious Cosmos.*

Suppose you had access to an "all answering" computer. Once you knew the right codes to punch, you would only have to frame your intention for information, codify that and instruct your computer accordingly. After the short while needed for processing, the response you needed would flash up on the visual display unit.

Attributions of the Spheres

Sphere	Light Type	Aural	Smell	Touch	Visual
1. Kether	Bright spot	Highest audible sustained note	Amber-gris	Fine point just felt	Focal point
2. Chock-mah	Alternat-ing flashes	Repeated rhythm	Musk	Oscilla-tory vibration	Circle
3. Binah	Very dim	Saturn suite from Holst	Myrrh	Heavy weight	Triangle
4. Chesed	Blue	Jupiter, Holst	Cedar	Firm comfort	Square
5. Gebur-ah	Red	Mars, Holst	Ammo-nia	Sharp, painful	Pentagram
6. Tipher-eth	Yellow	Hymn to Sun, Rimsky-Korsakov	Frank-incense	Warm, friendly	Hexagram
7. Netz-ach	Green	Venus, Holst	Rose	Soft, pleasant	Heart
8. Hod	Orange	Mercury, Holst	Storax	Light, springy	Caduceus
9. Yesod	Pale, silvery Yellow	Moon-light Sonata, Beethoven	Jasmine	Cool and smooth	Crescent
10. Mal-kuth	Normal	Bolero, Ravel	Dittany	Rough, knobbly	Cube

Why? Because all the basic formulae were already in the machine waiting to be called up as the code ordered.

That is what you should have been doing the the Qabalistic Tree of Life code, classifying and storing consciousness in such a way that it will always be available *for you to live with* as an immortal entity. It is the *arrangement and availability* of consciousness which is of such importance, the system, method, structure, and development of it. Furthermore, it will not be just your consciousness alone. It will be *your consciousness in contact with that of others* who are using the same system as a common means of communication with higher levels.

Questions

1. What are the "Four Worlds" of the Tree and how do they function?

2. What "Letters of the Name" indicate these Four Worlds and can you verbalize why?

3. Recite the "God Names" for each Sephirah and explain them.

4. Give the archangelic names for each Sephirah and explain them.

5. Give the angelic names for each Sephirah and explain them.

6. Give the Assiatic attributes of each of the Sephirah and explain them.

7. What are the "Magical Images" of the Sephiroth? Describe them, or better yet, draw a rough sketch of them.

8. Select the nine most important sentences in this chapter.

9. Are you beginning to get an idea of how the Tree fits together?

10. What do you think the function of the Abyss is?

·11·

Paths and Placements

Now we have to tackle the idea of the Paths, or connections between one Sphere and another. Sometimes we hear these called "channels," but the original meaning was distinctly a footpath to be trodden on rather than be ridden over in a vehicle. In other words, a step-by-step Path to show the method of progression expected of travellers thereon.

Now what actually *is* a Path on the Tree of Life? It is a changing of consciousness from one Sphere to another involving a flow of force or exchange of energies between the concepts. One might say it is an "energy-encounter" relating the concepts with each other. For example, what happens when the concept of Glory makes contact with the concept of Victory? When such an event occurs it creates a stress-condition giving rise to specific states of consciousness associated with that particular junction. Thus, all the Paths have their special "frequency" or "harmonic" from top to bottom of the scale of life they cover. In a way, you could think of each one being like a single note on a keyboard designed to cover the whole of creation.

As you might now know, there are twenty-two actual Paths which join the ten concepts. Why, then, should the Paths be numbered in such an odd way starting with eleven, as if there were

Figure 1.36. Path numbers with the Hebrew alphabet

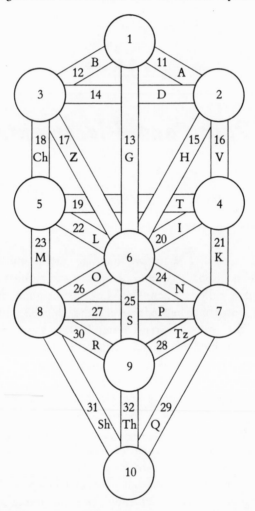

ten previous Paths (see Figure 1.36)? Also, why should letters of the Hebrew alphabet be attached to the Paths in the order they are? Why shouldn't the Paths have started with 1, 2, 3, etc.? All this could be quite confusing so we will set the matter straight at once.

First of all, the Hebrews used the same symbols for letters and numbers, A for 1, B for 2, and so on until it came to 10 at I

(Yod), then by stages of 10 up to Q for 100, and last till the final Tau for 400. There is obviously something very peculiar in using the sequential Hebrew alphabet to number the Paths of the Tree. For instance, if a reference was being made to the 12th Path, the correct way of doing so would be by using the Hebrew letters IB (10 + 2 = 12). But on the "orthodox" presentation of the Tree this is *not* the way Path 12 is indicated. It is shown as B, the second letter with a value of 2. Then again the 29th Path, which should read as Path KT (K=20 + T=9 = 29), is indicated by the letter Q = 100. Something seems a bit out of gear, doesn't it?

Natural Sequence

Path Number	Hebrew Letter	Sphere Conjunctions	Variant Paths	Path Number	Logical Sphere Conjunctions
11	A leph	1- 2		11	1- 2
12	B eth	1- 3		12	1- 3
13	G imel	1- 6		13	1- 6
14	D aleth	2- 3		14	2- 3
15	H eh	2- 6	X	15	2- 4
16	V au	2- 4	X	16	2- 6
17	Z ain	3- 6	X	17	3- 5
18	C heth	3- 5	X	18	3- 6
19	T eth	4- 5		19	4- 5
20	Y od	4- 6		20	4- 6
21	K aph	4- 7		21	4- 7
22	L amed	5- 6		22	5- 6
23	M em	5- 8		23	5- 8
24	N un	6- 7		24	6- 7
25	S amech	6- 9	X	25	6- 8
26	O in	6- 8	X	26	6- 9
27	P eh	7- 8		27	7- 8
28	T zaddai	7- 9		28	7- 9
29	Q oph	7-10		29	7-10
30	R esh	8- 9		30	8- 9
31	S hin	8-10		31	8-10
32	T au	9-10		32	9-10

There is only one possible explanation. The Hebrew letters were not there to identify the *number* of a Path, but the *significance* of it. The Roman or Arabic numbers were most probably added later in the scheme by non-Semitic scholars, and what we are looking at today is a combination which has slipped out of alignment. This seems evident when we find that the Paths have not all been numbered in their logical order, but some are out of sequence to follow the order of the letters. Let us have a look at the Path picture which is shown by former works.

As you see, there are only six Paths at variance—15, 16, 17, 18, and 25, 26. If there is a definite reason for this it is most unclear. Possibly earlier workers felt that the nature and character of the Hebrew letters concerned fitted those particular Paths best in that order. For instance, on Paths 15—16, H and V are transposed. They are the 2nd and 4th letters of the "Ineffable Name," IHVH. They mean respectively a window and a nail or holdfast. A window is possibly a better concept to join Wisdom and Harmony than a nail, while the latter could be taken as better than a window to connect Wisdom with Mercy. That is, one should fix oneself firmly to Mercy if one is wise. Then 25, S, meant a prop for a tent, usually a forked one, yet the next letter *Oin,* an eye, would have made a better symbol for this Path between the "Eyes of Heaven" or the Sun and Moon. Nevertheless, the staff-prop was indeed used to cast a shadow which indicated times and directions and the eye-symbol could be taken to represent the Glory of a Divine Vision. Most symbols can be meant to apply from very many angles, so we dare not be too critical.

What about the 11th Path? Where are the other ten? The Spheres do not count as Paths, yet there are indeed ten previous Paths before the 11th begins. They are the *Paths of the Lightning-Flash.* (Figure 1.37). Note that the first Path has to begin 0 - 1, yet having no cypher-symbol, the *nil*-value has to be taken for granted as 1. Having gotten down to the bottom of the Tree in a literal flash, the next thing to do seemed to be a reversal of the process by climbing back up it step by step, or Path by Path, *in reverse order.* That way we start with a maximum amount and finish with a minimum. After all, each Path ascended meant one less before

Figure 1.37. The first ten Paths as Lightning Flash

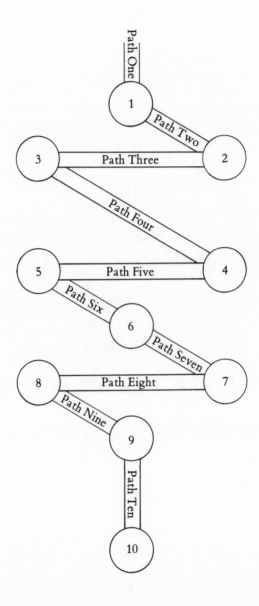

150 • CONCEPTS OF QABALAH

Figure 1.38. The Serpent on the Tree

reaching the top. That is why the Paths begin with 11 at the top
instead of the bottom. It was like a Zero count-down. You were
meant to start counting at 32. This produced some odd bends and kinks
in the Serpent-symbol trying to follow the lettered Paths upwards
(Figure 1.38).

To understand the process more simply, take a narrow strip of card and mark it in inches up to ten on one edge, and centimeters on the other beginning from the same end. Hold it so that the 1 is top-side. Run your forefinger down the inch side. That represents the "Fall" from 0 to 10 down the Tree. Now you have to go back up the other way 1 centimeter at a time. You will have to start from 25 centimeters. It is just the same distance but in *two different scales of measurement*. So the Spheres are the units of measurement *down* the Tree, and the Paths are the units *up*. That is all there is to it. You could jump down thirty feet in ten jumps of three feet each, but you would need to climb back by a ladder with rungs about a foot apart making thirty in all.

Now then, why should the Paths be identified by letters of an alphabet, Hebrew or otherwise? Letters are units of words, and therefore of consciousness among literate people. If each Path connects with a specific fraction of consciousness, this should mean that if we could combine these like words, we might be able to comprehend some workings of Cosmos more clearly.

Each Path is actually a particular type of spiritual energy existing because of contact between two distinct Spheres supplying one component each. Thus the energy is not unlike electricity which is a differential between two power potentials, positive and negative. Because these are connected by a conductor, energy must flow or move through that conductor. That is what the Paths *do*, they connect two Spheres so that a specific life-energy is generated between them. That is to say, each Path could be considered as a "Middle Pillar" with respect to its terminal Spheres, and its nature is uniquely that of both (see Figure 1.39). Thus we end up with 22 types of energy in our concept of creation as the Tree of Life, or the 22 divisions of the one energy which is life itself.

Figure 1.39. Path 19 as a blend of both end Spheres

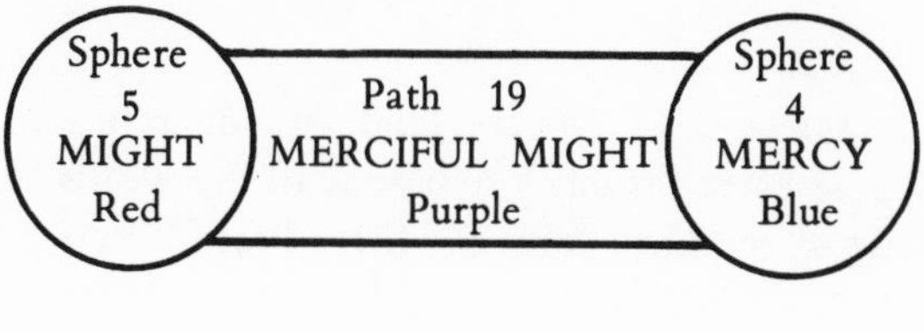

To symbolize or identify each level or Path of Life and label it, a letter of the Hebrew alphabet was used. The old teaching was that God created existence by means of numbers, letters, and words, our three categories of formalized communicative consciousness. We think of values in terms of numbers, and ideas as words which have to be formed from the units of speech and writing, or letters. Therefore if the Spheres showed spiritual values (which they do), and each Path showed a single letter (as it does), then by consciously combining Spheres and Paths we should be speaking the language of life, or "talking to God."

As a matter of interest, let us see how the arrangement worked out with the Hebrew allocation of letters to the Paths (see table called "Hebrew Allocation of Letters to Paths" at the end of this Chapter). Each letter was the full name of some item connected with the human body, animal life, or agricultural and piscatorial use. It was the sort of alphabet we might expect from a people who lived by a mixture of farming, fishing, and occasionally fighting.

11th Path

Spheres 1—2, Crown and Wisdom, letter Aleph. This meant an ox that drew a plough, worked a waterwheel, or trod grain, the "power plant" of an ancient farm. In one sense it could be argued that since this Path connects with the power source of life and consciousness on the masculine side, the ox-letter is an adequate symbol. On the other hand, the ox is not noted for being a bright beast. Nevertheless, he is a plodder and a strong one at that. Again we have the step-by-step significance, this time shown at the top of the Tree. Patience, plodding, and steady progress associated with achievement of the penultimate Path on the Tree. The ultimate, of course, is 32—0, or attainment of the *Ain Soph Aur*. This is the meaning of the 33rd degree in Masonry being purely honorary.

12th Path

Spheres 1—3, Crown and Understanding, letter Beth, a tent or dwelling. We are instantly reminded of the words "I will dwell in the House of the Lord forever" (23rd Psalm). In old times, tents were not so much for living in as for shelter and sleeping. They were places for begetting children and tending them in early babyhood. All such happenings align with the feminine faculty of intuitive comprehension implied here. The human womb is a "house" in a sense, with a live, yet not *objectively* conscious inhabitant, life in a state of "prebirth," not yet projected across the Abyss into independent existence from which the only return is over the same Abyss in the reverse direction of death. So in its old meaning, a tent is a reasonable symbol here.

13th Path

Spheres 1—6, Crown and Beauty, letter Gimel, a camel. Some would say there is nothing very beautiful about a camel. It is ill-tempered and very difficult to handle. Legend says that God confided his Secret Name to the camel as a sort of compensation for having made it so awkward. From a practical viewpoint its value lies in its unique ability to carry saleable materials or passengers across desert trade routes with a minimum consumption of food and water. Camels represented actual wealth to their owners, and constituted a means of survival in territory hostile to human life. This particular Path is the longest and loneliest on the whole Tree, involving a crossing of the Abyss by a bridge so narrow it was compared to a sword-edge. Now, though a camel cannot cross a literal sword-edge, it can cope with remarkably narrow pathways since its feet are moved one behind the other while its toes in their large soft pads have a very firm and definite grip. Where a horse might slip, a camel would stay. So the symbol of this surefooted creature bearing the Secret Name of God somewhere at the back of its brain might indeed symbolize the treading of this hazardous Path on the Tree.

14th Path

Spheres 2—3, Wisdom and Understanding, letter Daleth, a door or tent-flap. Otherwise a means of ingress and egress. This seems a reasonable symbol for consciousness going in and out of itself like the outgoing faculty of Wisdom, and the intuitive capablity of Understanding, or "taking something in." By various inner "doors" we are "let into the secret" of many mysteries in life, and from those doors we obtain viewpoints which broaden and enhance our understanding of everything we experience on our way to Wisdom. Doors are guardians to treasures, protectors of privacy, ways of welcome, means of escape. Quite an adequate letter-symbol for this Path.

15th Path

Spheres 2—6, Wisdom and Beauty, letter Heh, a vent-hole or window. This letter stems from "to breathe" and signifies something permitting air (inspiration) and light (illumination) to pass freely. It is also the 2nd letter of the Divine Name. Seeing and breathing are two vital aspects of life. Insofar as these abilities imply a rhythmical harmony and wise insight on living experience, they do seem to be connected with the window idea of this letter. A window is, in itself, a viewpoint, and in the old days would signify clear vision undimmed by the dark and smokey interior of a tent or dwelling. Since we need both the faculty of Wisdom and a sense of balanced Beauty to appreciate the multiplicity of human views on life, we can fit the letter Heh here.

16th Path

Spheres 2—4, Wisdom and Mercy, letter Vau, a hook, nail, or holdfast. Here we have the idea of holding something firmly by "pinning it down." It is certainly a wise person who hangs on to the quality of Mercy (or Compassion) for without it what are we? This is the 3rd letter of the Divine Name, and would signify the holding fast to life by every means.

17th Path

Spheres 3—6, Understanding and Harmony, letter Zayin, a weapon, sword or spear. Here there seems to be very inadequate ideological associations between the principles involved and the meaning of the letter attached. It would have fitted better on the "natural" sequence of this Path, Spheres 3—5, Understanding and Might.

18th Path

Spheres 3—5, Understanding and Might, letter Cheth, a fence or enclosure. This is another transposed Path where the' ideology of Zayin would have been more appropriate. Might should never be employed nor the sword used without complete understanding. Also Cheth would be more applicable to the last Path in that Understanding and Harmony need to be protected from would-be predators by secure surroundings. The only possible interpretation is that on Path 17 the principles of 3—6 should be defended if need be by force in order to maintain Balance and Harmony, while on Path 18 a mighty and protective perimeter should be set up with Understanding. Either way, the read-out is to the effect that the principles of the Tree-concepts here are worth defending both actively and passively.

19th Path

Spheres 4—5, Mercy and Might, letter Teth, the coiling of a serpent. A snake usually coils in order to gain power before striking. If, however, it is coiled with its tail in its mouth it cannot very well strike or it would poison itself. So everything depends on *how* it is coiled as to whether it signifies Might or Mercy. A coiled snake signifies potential power, that is, energy in hand which can be released into action in a moment, but is not actually being employed. We should keep the destructive energies of life ready for use if need be, while maintaining a merciful control of them. In modern terms, keep your gun loaded in enemy territory but don't shoot unless you have to. In biblical terms, "A strong man armed, keepeth his house."

20th Path

Spheres 4—6, Mercy and Beauty, letter Yod, a hand with outstretched fingers. Somehow this seems to tie in with Ankh-en-Aton's God-concept of a solar disc with rays ending in outstretched hands bringing the benefits of life to everyone they touched. It is also the first letter of the Mighty Name of God, the bringer of blessings in life to every soul. Hands are for touching with, and here we should certainly touch and be touched by the hand of God offering Beauty and Compassion to us all. This is the Path whereon we may experience such beneficence.

21st Path

Spheres 4—7, Mercy and Victory, letter Kaph, a hollowed hand as if to hold liquids. Note how the hand idea comes together, first outstretched and next cupped. Neither gesture can hold a weapon, the first being extended in offering, and the second being cupped in reception. Here the implication seems to be an acceptance of achievement (Victory) through Divine Mercy which permits such holdings. Note again it is not the closed grasping fist shown here, but the open trusting hand which holds things supportively so that they may be given or taken away again as divinity decrees.

22nd Path

Spheres 5—6, Might and Beauty, letter Lamed, a beater or ox-goad to control the course of animals, a prod. This is certainly symbolic of something we need to keep prodding ourselves with along the Paths of the Tree to correct our courses when we stray from them. To maintain our balance and harmony in life we have to constantly apply impulses of the right kind in the correct way. That is what this Path means, and where we are supposed to learn this art.

23rd Path

Spheres 5—6, Might and Glory, letter Mem, or water, particularly sea water as indicated by waves. Might is well represented by the strength of the sea and its tides, while Glory is often as transient as the waves, ebbing and flowing in turn, or just calmly reflecting the glories of heaven in the splendid mirror of the oceans. The "Power and the Glory" of God are both qualities of a *fluid* nature. Remember also that the purely human pursuit of power and glory in this world can lead to fatal issues, and we may be overcome by the tide turning against us, or drowned in the depths of the "waters of wrath." There are many implications of danger on this Path.

24th Path

Spheres 6—7, Beauty and Victory, letter Nun, a fish. Note the connection with the last letter and the uncertain association with this Path. To catch a fish is certainly a victory of some kind, but not necessarily a particularly beautiful one, though of course it could be so in the eyes of professional fishermen, which seems the way it was regarded here. Many Semitic fishermen worked by wading waist deep into the water, throwing a white stone or baited weight ahead of them into the sea to attract the attention of fish. When they thought fish were investigating this, they cast circular nets loaded with stones round the edge which settled flat in the water, then sank to the bottom, hopefully enclosing a fish or two for collection. It was a beautiful, skilled maneuver. This was probably what is implied here, since it calls for extremely harmonious action if fish are to be taken. This is the Path for learning, achievements, and accomplishments.

25th Path

Spheres 6—9, Beauty and Foundation, letter Samekh, a prop or support. This is one of the transposed Paths where the significance might have been better the other way around. An eye could have been better here than a prop, because the Sun and Moon associated with Spheres 6 and 9 were regarded as the "Eyes of Heaven," one open by day and the other by night. The only significance of a prop here is that the basis of our beliefs supports our ideas of celestial harmony. Not entirely satisfactory.

26th Path

Spheres 6—8, Beauty and Glory, letter Ayin, an Eye. It could be said that we have been given eyes to observe the Beauty and Glory of creation, but it could also be true to say that faltering beliefs can be supported or propped up by the same spiritual factors. Humans are in constant need of support and encouragement, and the "houses" or "tents" we build round ourselves have to be held up purely by beliefs in heavenly harmony and happiness which is the principal "prop" of old age. On the other hand, unless we can see some signs of this for ourselves with our inner eyes, even the strongest faith is liable to falter considerably.

27th Path

Spheres 7—8, Victory and Glory, letter Pe, a mouth. Here we have a connection with a mouth which is full of the glories and gains of life, but is it an open mouth or a shut one? Here we are reminded that there are times to speak and times to keep silent. This is the Path where we have to "watch our mouths," especially when tempted to boast or brag vaingloriously. The mouth is a weapon which has caused many a slaying or suicide, and to gain victory over it is a glorious achievement from a spiritual viewpoint.

28th Path

Spheres 7—9, Victory and Foundation, letter Tzaddai, a fishhook. There seems a connection here with Path 24, a Fish. If you can't net it there, then hook it here. Victory is the common factor to both Paths. There appears to be an implication between the two that victories or gains in life depend more on skill and cunning, like a fisherman, than anything else. Here on this Path it is indicated that the basis for Victory of any sort in life is like fishing with a hook. Use the right bait, choose the right place and time, set everything up and wait patiently. When the exact moment comes, strike! Then haul in your prize, if you can.

29th Path

Spheres 7—10, Victory and Kingdom, letter Qoph, the back of the head. Here it seems plain enough that Victory in life is what humans have at the back of their minds all the while they are in this world. We all want to "win" somehow. The thought of Victory in one sense or another is what keeps us going. Often it is *all* that keeps us going. Even if we feel we can't win in one incarnation we might do so in another, that is still an incentive to go on until we *do* succeed at something. This looks like the Path whereon we have to believe that there is Victory in the background eventually, and one day the Kingdom of this world may be worth living in.

30th Path

Spheres 8—9, Glory and Foundation, letter Resh, the whole head. This is the last Path amplified. Here we seem to be told we shall have to use all our faculties and everything our brains have in them if we are to live with any sense of honor and stability. A stable and reliable brain is a truly glorious human possession, and this appears to be the Path for developing such a thing. How often in life are we told to "use our heads," meaning to employ our commonsense and initiative? On this Path we shall be told that all the time, so we might as well keep our ears open for inner messages.

31st Path

Spheres 8—10, Glory and Kingdom, letter Shin, a tooth. There is not much of a connection here unless it means we shall have to fight tooth and claw to get any Glory by living in this world. There could be some link with eating the apple in the Garden of Paradise, by which act we lost the Glory of Heaven and fell into earthly estate. We have to remember God's curse on Adam: "Cursed is the ground for thy sake; in sorrow shalt thou eat of it all the days of thy life. Thorns and thistles shall it bring forth and thou shalt eat the herb of the field. In the sweat of thy face shalt thou eat bread until thou return into the ground, for out of it wast thou taken. Dust thou art, and dust shalt thou return" (Genesis 3:17-19). This could be a warning to those seeking glory in this world, and a timely reminder that "The Paths of Glory lead but to the grave." It might also be a hint that we often dig our graves with our own teeth.

32nd Path

Spheres 9—10, Foundation and Kingdom, letter Tau, a mark or sign, especially a cross or an X. It is interesting to realize that the custom of an illiterate person making a cross-shaped mark as a signature is so very old in practice. There seems no doubt that the message here is that we are in this world to make a mark of some kind and leave our signatures here for a memory after we have gone. Odd to think this world bears some kind of mark made by every human who ever lived in it. Even if someone lived here who did no more than displace a single grain of sand in a whole lifetime, that would count as having marked our planet. Hence the instinct to carve initials or dates on durable stones. At any rate the message of this Path is possibly to tell us that each life in this world should amount to a signed statement or account of ourselves for presentation to the Lord of Life so as to show what we have done to earn emancipation from re-embodiment.

So there is a quick glance at the Paths of the Tree as aligned with the Hebrew alphabet. It would of course be possible to distribute the letters a totally different way and get another set of meanings altogether. What we have to look at is not so much the literal lay-out as the principles involved. Strictly speaking, it does not really matter what letter is attached to which Path so long as an overall system is adopted for making sense by means of the spiritual values related with the letters. Once we have worked out such a scheme it has to be adhered to for the sake of making sense in any language. It is only because we have settled methods of spelling and speaking words that we are able to understand each other by speech and writing.

This is like setting up a computer. What we have done so far is set up a basic keyboard specifically arranged to print out in Hebrew. That is to say, when we manipulate the keys (or "tread the Paths") it will answer us in terms of *spiritual values* as associated with words and letters in the Hebrew language. If we are accustomed to thinking and consciousness formulated in that language, this will help greatly, but if our intelligent dealings with life are normally in English or a modern European tongue, we shall need the Tree set to an alphabet of that type. The Tree does not *have* to be set in Hebrew, for it will speak in any language. It is only a matter of correct alignment. Think of it as being like a translation machine which only needs the selector switch set to whatever language is required.

Suppose, for instance, you had a totally new kind of typewriter. You type a letter in ordinary English and it comes out as symbols of spiritual energy understandable only by higher orders of being who normally think in those terms. They would be able to make sense of your thoughts on their level of awareness. Then we reverse this, and *you* receive a communication which means nothing to you because it is in purely spiritual symbology. So you type that out on another machine and it appears in normal English. If such a thing were possible (which it may be one day), you would have what poor old Dr. Dee was trying to work out with his "Enochian tongue," a communication-code between humans and "angels." That is precisely what the letter-Path association on the Tree of Life was set up to do—in Hebrew.

Let us look at the basic principles of the thing. Take any Hebrew word to start, say a familiar one like *Adni*, Adonai, meaning "Lord or Noble One." Write it with its Path meanings letter by letter, and you get this:

$$\begin{array}{cccc} 1 & 2 & 6 & 4 \\ A & D & N & I \\ 2 & 3 & 7 & 6 \end{array}$$

Now take the letters away, but keep the Path meanings in mind. 1, 2, 6, 4 and 2, 3, 7, 6. Next try to read this formula purely in the sense of its spiritual significance:

Crown	Wisdom	Beauty	Mercy
Wisdom	Understanding	Victory	Beauty

Try to grasp the *wholeness* of this, as you would with any word. Don't see a set of concepts you have to string together, but see them *all* as having one meaning together. If you can't, it is only a matter of practice, the same as when you were very young learning your alphabet, letter by letter, before you could assemble words.

Now we will go a little further. As you know, the Spheres have associated colors as attributes. By combinations of these we could "speak" exactly the same word, *Adni,* which would be comprehensible to anyone thinking in terms of color. We would only have to combine:

White	Light Grey	Yellow	Blue
Light Grey	Dark Grey	Green	Yellow

Hebrew Allocation of Letters to the Paths

Hebrew Letter	English	Pronounce	Meaning	Linked With	Path
א	A	Aleph	Ox	Poise	11
ב	B	Beth	House	Wisdom	12
ג	G	Gimel	Camel	Wealth	13
ד	D	Daleth	Door	Fruitfulness	14
ה	H	Heh	Window	Sight	15
ו	V	Vav	Nail	Hearing	16
ז	Z	Zain	Sword	Smell	17
ח	Ch	Cheth	Fence	Speech	18
ט	T	Teth	Serpent	Taste	19
י	Y	Yod	Hand	Coition	20
כ	K	Kaph	Hollow Hand	Life	21
ל	L	Lamed	Ox-goad	Work	22
מ	M	Mem	Water	Merit	23
נ	N	Nun	Fish	Motion	24
ס	S	Samech	Prop	Wrath	25
ע	O	Ayin	Eye	Mirth	26
פ	P	Pe	Mouth	Dominion	27
צ	Tz	Tzaddi	Fish hook	Meditation	28
ק	Q	Qoph	Back of Head	Sleep	29
ר	R	Resh	Head	Peace	30
ש	Sh	Shin	Tooth	Guilt	31
ת	Th	Tau	Cross-mark	Beauty	32

We could do the same with scents, sounds, or anything specifically connected with the concepts; providing the sequence is right we can "spell" whatever we like in inter-dimensionally recognized symbology.

Try codifying a few easy Hebrew words for yourself just to get the hang of it. You can either write the Sphere concepts out in full, or use their number combinations. If you want to use plain Path numbers for each letter, that will do so long as you can visualize the concepts concerned. That is the important thing. Realize that each unit of any word is a conjunction of two distinct spiritual concepts on the Tree of Life, like the right and left sides of your own body, or the two hemispheres of your brain, while *you* are the meaning in the middle. Here are a few simple Hebrew words connected with the Tree:

RVCh	Ruach, *Spirit*	ShDI	Shaddai, *Almighty*
QDVSh	Qodesh, *Holy*	OTz	Otz, *Tree*
ChKMH	Chockmah, *Wisdom*	ShLVM	Shalom, *Peace*
AMTh	Amath, *Truth*	AHIH	Ehehih, *I Am*
ShRPIM	Seraphim, *Fiery Serpents*	MIKVTh	Malkuth, *Kingdom*

Don't worry, you will not be asked to learn Hebrew. There is an English version of the Tree which we are coming to next, but first you need to see the principles and ideas which are "back of everything." It is nothing you have not already done when learning English. First you had to struggle with the "A is for apple, B is for bed" stage until you could spell words letter by letter, then sentences, word by word, and stories, sentence by sentence.

Questions

1. What is the "Path of Life?"
2. Why are Paths in descending order from Kether rather than in ascending order?
3. What is the relationship of the Paths with the letters of the Hebrew alphabet?

4. Draw the Tree of Life and name the Paths (Hebrew letters).

5. Why does the Tree apparently start at Path 11?

6. Express your understanding of the spiritual significances of the Path.

7. How is the Serpent related with the Paths?

8. How is the Sword or Lightning Flash related with the Paths?

9. Choose the eight most important questions in this chapter.

10. Do you have a "favorite" Path? If so, what is it and why?

·12·

Learning by Letter

Now do you see the function of lettered Paths on the Tree of Life? They make a consciousness-code for communication with higher than human orders of intelligence. Here some bright student may say: "Aha! But in order to send back communications in the same terms they would have to know the original language of transmission. So why don't they just reply directly in the same language without all these tedious translations?" Clever? Yes, but there is a very good reason.

Alphabetical letters or words per se, do not transmit across the barriers between our type of consciousness and that of higher levels, but waves of sheer inner awareness *do* transcend this difference. It is similar to radio in a way. A word is spoken into a microphone. It does not get past the mike *as a word,* but is converted into impulses of pure electrical energy. These in turn modulate or vary what is called the "carrier wave" which reaches receivers many miles away. They convert this vibrating energy back into airborne sounds which reproduce the original word. Thus the word spoken in the studio and the one heard at a distance are not *strictly speaking* the same, identical word, because the one received is a *duplicate copy* of the first.

A clear description of the process is given by the King in *Hamlet* when he says:

> My words fly up, my thoughts remain below.
> Words without thoughts never to Heaven go.

It is the thoughts which reach Heaven, not the words. They are only the "carrier waves" of prayer which get there across inter-dimensional divisions between "Heaven" and Earth. The use of words is for modulating thoughts which in themselves are wordless. Words are purely an invention of intellectual consciousness by which we communicate with other humans.

The question is *how* and with what do we modulate our consciousness? A human can think really nasty, vicious, and destructive thoughts if activated by motives of fear, greed, hate, and other evil-intentioned drives. What classes or categories of inner consciousness would such types of thinking be likely to contact? Obviously those of similar frequencies. In olden times they would have been classed as "devils" or some other species of anti-human entities. Whatever they may be factually, they are most unlikely to help humans make this a better world.

If we really want our inner consciousness to make contact with types of intelligence which will be helpful to us, which will lift our minds and souls a little higher up the Ladder of Life, and bring us benefits of spiritual development, then we shall have to communicate with them in some way which will strike responsive chords in their scale of awareness. That is precisely what the Tree-scheme does. It "speaks" in terms of spiritual values appreciable and understandable by those who live in such conditions of conscious-ness as their normal state of life. Therefore the Tree-code can *only* communicate with what used to be called "Angels" or "Good Spirits" since it has no reference terms for any kind of evil.

This is because the concepts of the Tree are quite meaningless to active agencies of positive evil. What could such a type of consciousness possibly know of a Mercy-Compassion concept? That would convey nothing except, perhaps, weakness. Might could only be seen as domination by brutality and cruelty. Beauty and Harmony would certainly be entirely beyond compre-hension unless as some kind of condition disturbing their normal state of unbalance and discord. Something that ordinary humans find almost impossible to understand is that genuinely evil entities see the spiritual concepts of the Tree as threats to their chosen conditions of being, which bother, annoy, or otherwise interfere with their "life-styles." The last thing they would want to do is learn the language of the Tree. It is entirely outside their general pale of perception.

The "spiritual speech" behind the Tree of Life is structured for communicating with classes of consciousness once called "angelic" because they were considered to bear messages from God. In Hebrew they were called *Malakim,* or agents sent by God for some intelligent purpose. Every human soul had such a being allocated to it for the specific task of keeping that soul in communication with divinity. Legend said that these "Guardian Angels" seemed to be the opposite sex of their human charges, even though angels were supposed to be asexual. It was entirely up to us whether or not we paid any attention to our "angel guides." The Abramelim system of religious magic in the Middle Ages was completely dedicated to making conscious contact with Guardian Angels which would then continue to instruct human pupils in whatever was needed for their advancement to life on higher levels.

We may interpret all this on somewhat different lines today, but the fundamental of attuning our awareness to better than human conditions of consciousness by all available means still remains with us. The Tree shows a practical, though demanding way of doing this by deliberate and painstaking re-arrangement of our mental methodology. This amounts to superimposing spiritual significance on everything we normally deal with consciously. Every single word in our minds and mouths has to be given its spiritual counterpart from combinations of Tree concepts, and thus our ordinary everyday thinking must necessarily continue to lift our consciousness to successively higher levels. The interesting thing here is that not only special or "holy" words accomplish this, but quite common or crude ones also if directed intentionally. It was once supposed that magic was largely a matter of knowing secret "Words of Power" which accomplished miracles by themselves. With this Tree-system it is a matter of *every* word having its own "magic" if "uttered" in the right way.

In very primitive times, attaching definite meanings to sounds made by human voices was a truly magic art. It later extended to making the same meanings out of signs scratched by human hands on surfaces where they could be interpreted by other humans. Both eye and ear conveyed the same meaning to mind so that one human might meet another by such audio-visual channels. Speech and writing were greater magic in their day than radio and television in ours. The wonder of words which convey consciousness is with us yet, despite our devaluation and misuse of them. It is time we learned how to put some of the magic back in our words so that modern living may regain something of its lost qualities.

Long ago it was said that special magic words like names of archangels or potent spirits should always be uttered very slowly and sometimes letter by letter. Nobody explained the real reason for this, but it was actually because this method gave the utterer time to attach the inner meaning consciously. It was that inner intention which constituted the "magic." The audible sonics were only a symbol representing such meaning for human listeners. Non-incarnate listeners could only catch this meaning from the inner utterance. The slow enunciation was purely for the benefit of the human who needed that much time to formulate and focus a spiritual significance into the otherwise meaningless "word." Quite often the "secret words" employed *had* no sensible meaning to them for that very reason. If they meant nothing in the ordinary way, then they might bear *nothing but* spiritual sense which could be interpreted by those familiar with such levels of life.

So human words may be made "magical" or "non-magical" entirely by the attachment or non-attachment of spiritual significance according to the intention of the user. Let us try a word or two in this way just to get the feel of things. Since we are still looking at Hebrew originals, it will have to be a simple Hebrew word linked with Tree-Path meanings. Why not begin with the conventional greeting, *Shalom*, which means "peace." It is spelled with just three letters, ShLM, because the Hebrew alphabet did not have proper vowels like ours, but inserted vowels afterwards to make different meanings of the same words. In this case the three Paths concerned would be:

Sh, 31st Path, Glory—Kingdom, Tooth, Guilt
L, 22nd Path, Might—Beauty, Goad, Work   *PEACE*
M, 23rd Path, Might—Glory, Water, Merit

That of course only supplies the *written* word. In order to speak it, the A and the O have to be added, though the O sound in this case is indicated by the letter Vav as a short "uh." So we get:

(spelled and pronounced like this:)

Sh	31st Path	Glory-Kingdom, 8Sh10, Shhhhh
A	11th Path	Crown-Wisdom, 1A2, Aaaaaa
L	22nd Path	Might-Beauty, 5L6, Llllll
V	16th Path	Wisdom-Mercy, 2V4, Uhhhhh
M	23rd Path	Might-Glory, 5M8, Mmmmmm

Which means there are five combinations of double concepts to be conscious of while the sonic symbol for *peace* is being uttered.

What you have to do now is utter the word quietly, syllable by syllable, taking enough time over each to concentrate consciously on each Path or pair of concepts. It may help if you have a small diagram of the Tree in one hand and a pointer in the other with which you visually indicate the Paths in turn so that your eye helps your mind. This will be difficult at first, but it is only to get you accustomed to the idea of dealing with two principles simultaneously and striking a balance between them. The thing to do is not look at one concept and then another while trying to contrast them, but consider both at once while harmonizing them into a single structure, as if you were striking two notes together and listening to the results.

For instance, what do you think a combination of Wisdom and Understanding might result in? A junction of Might and Mercy? Or Glory and Victory? We shall not even suggest answers here, because the relevant answer is whatever this means to *you*, not anybody else. So here and now get your pen and paper, make a list of the Path-concepts and consider them until you form *some* definite ideas of what each combination means *in your mind*. Then write this down. It need not be your ultimate answer, but simply as you see things *now*. Your views can change as they broaden out and raise themselves. In fact they should. So realize that however you see the

Paths, it is just your present viewpoint which gives you something to be going on with. Try, if possible, to sum up each Path in as few words as possible, preferably one word for each.

All human beings are naturally connected to their spiritual levels of living, but not, as a rule through their ordinary thinking and verbalized types of thought. This is not exactly a disadvantage, but is a kind of limitation since so much of "civilized" consciousness depends on our objective styles of thought. Our so-called spiritual thinking is mostly in terms of reference to written scriptures or literature that we have either read for ourselves or heard other people talk about. This means that there is relatively little spiritual experience among humanity at first hand, in contrast to what has been written or recorded by previous commentators. However interesting or informative the literary field of spiritual enquiries may be, there is no real substitute for self-experience. That is precisely what the Tree-code is designed to do for its users.

Now if you think this might mean you would obtain conscious contact with "archangels" and supernatural beings who would supply you with all kinds of secret and astonishing information from which you could make untold profits, you would be wrong. You are going to get only what you are entitled to anyway because you are whom and what you happen to be. *But* you will find this coming to your consciousness along clearly intelligent lines instead of drifting around in your distant depths from whence you might never bother to dredge it up for your surface perception. Once these lines start opening up, they can lead almost anywhere, depending again on your inner identity.

What this means is that you do not have to depend on learning the spiritual facts of life from what someone else has said about them or you have been told to believe by authorities. If you learn how to use your consciousness-code corrrectly, you can "go inside" and learn for yourself at first hand. Do realize, however, that whatever you learn will be as things apply to *you* and have reached you through your own intellect. This may not seem very impressive to you, but it is much more important than you may think. It shows that you are intentionally "opening yourself" on the right inner levels for receiving spiritual instructions from reliable and responsible sources.

This is why genuine Qabalah is still called the "received teaching." It is received not from books or even from words spoken by those who have studied the lore for many years. These will only tell you *how* to receive it. You have to receive instruction from inside yourself like everyone else who plods the Path. Everything else can only guide you up to the departure point where you must push forward on your own initiative and start learning inner realities from those who live with them. If what you learn seems to disagree with what others have taught, do not let this worry you unduly. You have to see everything with *your* eyes, and make sense of what *you* find. The best advice is not to take it for granted that what you see is necessarily accurate in that *form*. Appearances alter as experience extends.

Now that you have some ideas of how the Tree alphabet works, we can start progressing the principles involved to see how the idea of using an English alphabet instead of a Hebrew one works out. The first thing we come up against is that our modern alphabet consists of 26 letters or four too many. Either we have to add more Paths, reduce the alphabet, or double up on some letters. We cannot very well add Paths without wrecking the symmetry and significance of the whole Tree. To reduce letters would devalue the structure of our modern language. To double up on some of the letters like J and I would not really solve things and only add a lot of complications to everything. So what can we do?

Here is where the Hebrew alphabet comes to our help somewhat. Its main peculiarity was that it had no vowels like ours, but consisted of consonants. Vowels were pushed in afterwards as we have seen to make pronunciation possible and change the meaning of words. For instance, if we wrote in English *pns* and depended on subsequent vowels to determine the meaning, we might get *pans, pens, pins, pons,* and *puns,* to say nothing of *panes, pines,* and other combinations. Then we remember that our vowels are dedicated to the life-elements already, but if we take them away it leaves twenty-one letters or one too few for the Paths. A good final solution comes if we think that the Anglo-Saxon alphabet from which our modern one has evolved had, like the Hebrew, a last letter *Th,* since we use this combination so often in our language. This *Th* letter was called *Eth,* and was written Þ from whence the "y"

Figure 1.40. The English alphabet on the Tree (note Path numbering)

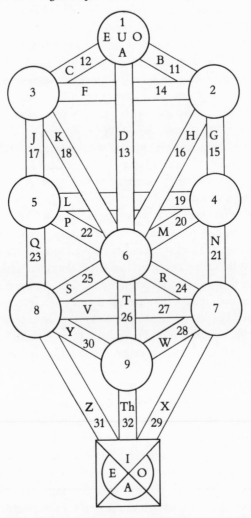

character derived. Hence the modern mistake of supposing that medieval English people went around saying "Ye this," or "Ye that." They never did. It was always "the." Restore this old letter to a vowel-less alphabet and we not only get our twenty-two letters, but also finish up on the same note as the first Tree-concept.

To convert the Tree of Life to our own alphabet, yet keep something of the spirit behind its original construction, we distribute the letters according to Figure 1.40, and from now on we shall continue to employ that interpretation. There is very little re-learning to do. If you want to start again with alphabet-rhyming to help you remember the combinations, here is one to begin with, or you can sit down and write your own as soon as you think of a better one.

The Tree Alphabet

A   is the Earth of which Adam began,
B   brings the Crowning by Wisdom of Man.
C   Crowns Understanding quite plainly to see,
D   denotes Beauty and Crown on the Tree.
E   is the Element thought of as Air,
F   finds Wise Understanding uncommonly rare.
G   gives Wisdom and Beauty, thrice blessed are they,
H   has Wisdom and Beauty, for which many pray.
I   is the Illumination of Fire,
J   Understands Justice, yet never knows ire.
K   keeps Understanding and Beauty as one,
L   links Mercy with Might, a good thing to be done.
M   makes Merciful Beauty a marvellous sight,
N   needs Mercy to make any Victory right.
O   is the Watery element pure,
P   provides Power to keep Beauty secure.
Q   questions connections of Glory with Fear,
R   regards Beauty and Victory both dear.
S   shows the sign linking Beauty and Glory,
T   tells a well-Founded and Beautiful story.
U   undulates round Elemental accord,
V   vouches Victory with Glory, but not by the Sword.
W   waits where true Victories are Founded,
X   explains how Victorious Kingdoms are grounded.
Y   yearns for the Glory of solid Foundations,
Z   is zest for all Glorious Kingdoms and nations.
Th   thinks Foundation and Kingdom must meet
     When this mystical alphabet is made complete.

From here on it is more or less a matter of learning aids and their applications. Possibly the most helpful is a small convenient sized card placed on desk or wherever the eye will meet it frequently. A copy of Figure 1.40 will do nicely, or for sheer simplicity, the table which follows can be quite useful. Anything at all which helps

List of English Letters connecting Paths on Tree between the Spheres.

Sphere	Letter	Sphere	Path
▽	A	▽	Earth
1	B	2	11
1	C	3	12
1	D	6	13
△	E	△	Air
2	F	3	14
2	G	4	15
2	H	6	16
△	I	△	Fire
3	J	5	17
3	K	6	18
4	L	5	19
4	M	6	20
4	N	7	21
▽	O	▽	Water
5	P	6	22
5	Q	8	23
6	R	7	24
6	S	8	25
6	T	9	26
•	U	•	Truth
7	V	8	27
7	W	9	28
7	X	10	29
8	Y	9	30
8	Z	10	31
9	Th	10	32

associate Paths with letters will do. A good trick is to get a set of solid letters such as are used to teach a small child the alphabet. Make a bag for these and keep them handy, or you can leave them loose in your pocket if you like. The idea is to put a hand inside, select a letter by touch alone, then place it mentally on the Tree. This is a useful idea because it helps connect the letters without sight or hearing.

The important part of this entire process is not merely learning the intellectual connections of Paths with letters, but attaching an actual sense of spiritual significance to each letter. It is no use thinking: "L goes between Spheres 5 and 6 of the Tree." The right way to think is: "L means a combination of Might and Mercy." In the end, every time you see, write, or think of any word with L in it, an inner impression of Might and Mercy should come with it for even the briefest fraction of a second needed to include it in your thinking.

A point to note is that you need not expect the Tree-connections of the letters to line up very closely with the usual meaning of the English words they form. Our words have been drawn from so many languages it would be impossible to correlate them with any system set up for one in particular. We should remember that this Tree-system is not specifically for unravelling spiritual meanings behind the literal words we use in everyday language, but for using that language so as to keep us in contact with the underlying spiritual realities of life itself. Let us take a few examples, in opposites. For convenience we shall use numbers to indicate Spheres, and put vowels in capitals.

WAR	= 8A6 9A8	Victory-Foundation, Earth, Beauty-Victory.
PEACE	= 5EA1E 6EA3E	Might-Beauty, Air, Earth, Crown-Understanding, Air.
GOD	= 301 406	Wisdom-Mercy, Water, Crown-Beauty.
DEVIL	= 1E714 5E815	Crown-Beauty, Air, Victory-Glory, Fire, Mercy-Might

These should be enough to show that there is no especial ideological connection between letters of our alphabet and specific words they spell, while at the same time there is a constant flow of spiritual awareness behind whatever was verbalized. If all we are thinking about consciously has been carefully conditioned so that every word evokes some kind of spiritual contact on inner levels of intelligence, this can scarcely fail to have a beneficial effect on our whole being. Nevertheless, there is a *quid pro quo* clause involved. Everything depends on the degree of spiritual reality you manage to make out of the Tree-concepts in the first place. Just how *real to you* are they? If they mean nothing to you except hypothetical states represented by words on paper then you cannot expect to learn anything from letters connected with them. First you have to make the concepts "come true" by experiencing each of them as conditions of your own self. You must have some idea of what it feels like to *be* each, any, or all of the Sphere-concepts of the Tree of Life.

You may have heard of a spiritual exercise known as "Path-working" which has been gaining in popularity among Western esoteric operatives. This consists of "working the Paths of the Tree" by meditating on one particular Path at a time while carefully confining the consciousness to associations connected with that Path alone. The exercise really lies in the conscious control and application of the various types of awareness involved. Many people, for instance, make quite an inner adventure out of this exercise, turning it into a sort of audio-visual and sensory experience projected into their inner fields of perception. However, the point we want to make here is that before any kind of Path-working becomes possible, it is *absolutely necessary* to solidify the Spheres in yourself by making them real to you through some kind of experiential exercises. Unless the Paths are able to relate these spiritual realities *in yourself,* they will never mean more to you than lettered lines on paper.

So how do you make *any* spiritual concept come true for yourself? First and most importantly by believing in it, but *with a flexible faith*. Never set up hard and immovable concepts incapable of altering without breaking apart altogether. Faith is a force, and a very potent one, but it should be a flowing and *living* force, able to alter as your inner awareness comes closer to truth. Realize that your faith concepts must be models or symbols by which you are gradually adapting yourself to life on higher than human levels. Faith should be something you fix yourself to life with, but it must always be totally free to change the shape of its hold according to necessity. Otherwise you may only strangle yourself with it. Always try to see the difference between fundamentals and forms. The first are relatively fixed, while the second shift around and change appearance.

Faith is essentially a relationship between yourself and a projection of your perceptions to some life level beyond your experience. It is a positive prerequisite of knowledge which is a result of the actual experience itself. Faith is to the soul what sight is to the body. It "sees ahead" and makes an equivalent contact long before later experience and knowledge catch up with its focus. In a way it is not unlike radar without which all modern aircraft would be blind. Faith may not always see accurately, but neither may sight. We spot something gold glittering in sunlit grass and go to examine it in case it may be valuable. When we come close enough to experience the thing it turns out to be nor more than a cigarette packet. Yet it might have been a lost piece of jewelry.

That should illustate the real use of faith. It is a guide, a sensor, a vital indicator of spiritual actualities we should search for, and without which we would never reach anywhere worth aiming for. Faith is an explorer, yet never an explainer. It puts us in touch with matters to examine, but by itself is no firm guarantee of anything being exactly what faith believes it might be. Faith is a contactor, not a creator. Believing in a God does not automatically make one. What it does is provide a Path along which we may travel in search of a God. Unless we had such a Path in the first place we could not even begin to look. That is how important faith is.

Faith is not something to tell you: "That is this, thus and so precisely." Its proper job is to say: "Such and such could be true and I think it would be good for us to go and find out." The only way of finding anything like the truth is to follow what faith brings to our attention and discover the rest by experience and judgement. As we learn how to condition faith by caution and discernment it becomes a lot more accurate and reliable. That is all part of living in this or any other world.

Faith may bring our first remote contact with the Tree-concepts, but it needs actual experience to bring them alive in us. How is this to be managed short of living long enough to find them factually? There is only one way left: by symbolic simulation. If you cannot achieve an experience by firsthand involvement, you can at least do so to some extent through synthetic substitutes which are much more readily available. That is why so many people glue themselves to TV in our times. It affords them an alternative imaginative living they are unable to make for themselves in their own minds to compensate for the unsatisfactory conditions of their "normal" mundane existence. Additionally, it offers them channels of consciousness they could not otherwise open on their own initiative. Here you will be expected to manage this and much more out of your maybe yet unopened store of inner resources.

What happened in the old days? Something of that very nature. You had pictures put into your mind by people who could paint with words, but it was *you* who had to make them come alive and move around on the screen of your inner vision. People used to say that some sermon, address, or other confrontation by concentrated consciousness was a *moving* one, and so it was. It made people move inside themselves and so gave them a sense of being alive in spiritual dimensions rather than remain living lumps of animated meat in merely mortal bodies. That is what you have to do here. Confront the concepts of the Tree in such a way that you will move yourself into sensations of inner life because you are admitting their actualities as essentials of existence.

Questions

1. What is the difference between words and thoughts?
2. How is the speech of the Tree constructed?
3. How are concepts associated with letters?

4. How can anything have a spiritual meaning?

5. Devise a Tree alphabet of your own.

6. What is the practical use of faith?

7. How do you associate ideas with letters?

8. How do you combine "letter-ideas" to make "word-ideas?"

9. Choose the ten most important sentences in this chapter.

10. Draw from memory the Tree-plan and write in the English alphabet letters on each Path.

· Part II ·

Qabalah Practices

·13·

Concerning Creativity

This is where you have to start really experiencing the Spheres on the Tree of Life so that you will know something of how they feel to *you* from the inside, as it were. So far as you are concerned there is only one Tree of Life, *that which you grow for yourself.* The Tree you are reading about in these pages or elsewhere is only a plan or model for you to construct your own with. You are being shown blueprints or designs, but *you* will have to supply your homegrown materials before you can begin raising any such Tree-structure.

To begin, let us take things from the very bottom: your kingdom in this world. What is it? Your home? Your job? Probably both and then some, but let us suppose it is your home. That is a kingdom of a very small kind even if it is a single room in somebody else's house. Whether you own it or just pay the rent, you are its "king," insofar as you are responsible for the place. Maybe you would prefer to call yourself "co-ruler" if you share with a consort, but that still does not exempt you from liability. If you have the slightest say in making any rules for your home then as a ruler you have some rights in your "kingdom." A king is one who rules, governs, and if necessary, sacrifices himself on behalf of his people. Take a look round your home. Surely you had to sacrifice *something* for the good of its people (who may be your family). Even if only money for the landlord or owners, your home must have cost you something. So far as this world is concerned you can think of your home as your tenth Sphere on your Tree, the Kingdom where you are a sort of "king."

There is a higher side to all this. You know you will have your home only for a limited period. Some day you will move on in this world or into another one. What happens to your kingdom then? You cannot take any of it with you, but you can have its equivalent *inside* you which goes wherever you do. Are you a king in your inner kingdom? Do you make rules that you keep yourself? Can you control and govern your own attributes, such as your temper, your impatience, your emotions and other impulses? How far do you ever sacrifice yourself for the good of anything or anyone connected with you? For instance, what would you sacrifice for the sake of your own health or happiness? Your family or those who love you? Your beliefs? Just how good, bad, or indifferent are you as a king in your tiny kingdom? Sit yourself down on your favorite throne and do a lot of thinking about this. How much are you kinglike in your life and living? Some kinds of behavior are called "regal" because they are typical of what a real king ought to do, like being generous, forgiving, or noble. Anybody can make a regal gesture, even a beggar. The Kingdom indicated on your Tree is not some faraway "Kingdom of God" in distant heavens, it is *your* kingdom right here in your own home and in yourself. If you are Christian you mention it every time you say the Lord's Prayer, but how much do you really think about it?

You can do one kingly thing right now. Make a small rule of conduct for yourself and determine to keep it. Don't attempt anything big, or anything you know is going to be difficult. Put a time limit on it for safety. Say to yourself something like: "Because I believe in my own kingship, I am making it a rule for myself to do so and so for the next week. Having heard, I will obey." Make it something very simple like saying a special prayer each day, but whatever it is *do it*. Real kings should abide by their own rulings. You may not think you have done anything especially regal, but you will have done so *if* you fulfil your own ruling.

Figure 2.1. The Tree as a "Wheel of Life"

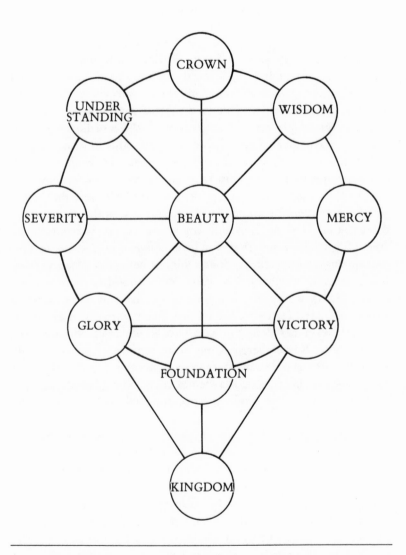

Do you get the idea? Take each concept on the Tree (see Figure 2.1) in turn, work out how it applies in your everyday life, then raise the whole ideology a fraction higher and see it from another angle. The concepts are not merely abstractions. They are *spiritual solidities* you have to experience just as when you encounter anything else on this old earth.

Now let us have a look at what you might do with the Foundation concept. From a purely worldly viewpoint this means what you base your life on—even if it is only food, money, social contacts, sports, work or the family you were born into, your ancestry, or nationality. This is the broad basis on which your present physical life rests. Think about all these ordinary facts of your life, your upbringing, education, your status in general, your marriage and children, if any, whatever you can think of which gives you ideas of citizenship or standing in your community.

Now look a little higher up the scale. All those things you have been considering are only yours for the rest of this incarnation. You can't take one of them with you when you go. So what do you have of greater value that you can convert into some sort of interdimensional currency? Your religious beliefs or whatever you base your faith in spirituality upon? Your confidence that you do have an existence apart from your body, and you will indeed be guided and cared for by a consciousness behind what you can see of creation? Yes, ideas along those lines are all bound up with the Tree concept here. Remember it is one stage removed from the purely material, and it should supply some thoughts and speculations about your non-material aspects. Maybe not very noble or inspiring ones, but still connected to slightly more spiritual topics than totally materialistic ones.

From this Sphere, most people get ideas of a Heaven resembling a kind of superworld with golden gates, harps and crowns, everlasting junketings and joy—everything they ever wanted on Earth and didn't have. None of it is really very convincing in spiritual terms, but at least it is a start away from this world towards images of a better one. What have you got in yourself on which to base any beliefs that life could be better for you beyond embodiment? Whatever it may be, dig it out of your depths and examine it in the light of clear consideration. Even if it is only hope, that is something to found beliefs upon. When you have found a solid enough hope or basis of belief to justify your words, say aloud to yourself something like: "I am founding my beliefs and hopes for a better type of life than we have in this world upon (whatever it may be). Let this be my first step up the Ladder leading to eternal *Light*."

The next branch of the Tree takes us up to the concept of Glory or Honor. Cynics may be tempted to think of all the honor scrapped for the sake of glory, but that was not quite the idea intended by this title at all. What is glory anyway? The Hebrew title Hod (HVD) also signifies renown or the praiseworthiness of God. It implies something worth acclaiming because it is admirable in the eyes of observers. From a worldly point of view, what have you done to make other humans admire you or think you glorious? What do you admire in others that you might cultivate in yourself?

Maybe you have made a lot of money, got a business going, or are famous in the arts or entertainment. You may never be certain that other humans truly admire you or if they just envy your position. People often admire what they intend to imitate or emulate, but they envy what they know they can't get without working for maybe more than a lifetime to achieve. If people admire you, it is because you inspired them somehow by what you have accomplished, or maybe just because of what you are. If they only envy you, they merely resent your having what they haven't. It isn't that they dislike you personally, but that you show them their own shortcomings and inadequacies by pure contrast, and nobody enjoys being reminded of their non-achievements.

So what have you done in this world to make you admired? Written or composed anything wonderful? Been noted for some benefaction? Stood out in any way? Never mind if the answer to all those questions is no. They were not really important. If your family and friends find something to admire in you, that is more than sufficient in life. You should look for your glory reflected in the eyes of someone who loves you. If you cannot find it there you will never meet it otherwise.

But why all this talk of *you* being glorious? Surely you can see and notice some glories in nature? A glorious sunset, for instance, or a splendid display of flowers. Glories all over the place, if you look for them. Have you never gloried because you felt in good health or high spirits? We hope you have because that is all part of this concept. The saying "Glory be to God!" meant that whoever said it appreciated the wonder and splendour of something attributed to the creative genius of the life spirit, a tribute and acknowledgement of authorship.

In old ideas of heavenly bliss, we were told we should spend all our time "praising and glorifying God." Nowadays this sounds like a revolting condemnation, to constantly be flattering a dictatorial and insecure deity who could not live a moment without such assurance from a sycophantic audience. No genuine God could possibly behave in such a way. It is we who need a sense of wonder at the glory of discovering the truly splendid secrets of creation. In fact it is that very wonder itself which leads us on to look for truth on constantly higher levels of life. Therefore, we "glorify God" for our own sakes and nobody else's. So if you do find anything in life that appears in the least glorious, be generous and fair-minded enough to give Cosmos credit for what it seems to have done and say: "Whoever You are that conceived Creation, I do think that (whatever it is) is a wonderful example of your work, and I would like to learn how I might contrive something of that nature in my own scale of time and space." You might also add: "For Thine is the Kingdom, the Power, and the Glory."

When you get to the next concept of Victory or Achievement, you will have to think very carefully about it, because it means so many different things to so many people and one man's victory could be another man's defeat. Can anybody really win anything without making somebody else lose? What is *your* idea of Victory in this world? Defeating social or business rivals? Winning championships in sports? Gaining from gambling and stock market dealings? Coming out on top in a lawsuit? Getting the sex partners you want? Gratifying any greed of the moment? Maybe you suppose you live victoriously because you have "won" your place in this world by fighting opposition fairly and squarely against heavy odds. After all, the very word, "victory" implies some kind of a struggle.

Yes, maybe you deserve what you have won in this world and possibly quite a lot more. No one is suggesting you don't. We all know that living here calls for continual struggle against all sorts of difficulties, ill health, poverty, and all other human disadvantages. It isn't the sort of war anyone "wins." Sheer survival is sometimes the nearest thing to victory that combatants can claim. Besides, your "winnings" will only be brief anyway. Death swallows all of it in a matter of seconds. The Sphere of Victory on the Tree is meant for something more permanent than that.

Then what about "enemies within the gates" already in yourself? These include all your faults, fallibilities and imperfections, to say nothing of any anti-human entities opposed to your making spiritual progress and, on a broader scale, the obvious evils existing all over this earth. How can you hope to fight against those while you cannot win your *own* internal battles? Soldiers are of no use until fully trained and those fighting on spiritual grounds must be trained by maneuvers against conflicts within their own consciousness. Remember the adage about a house being divided against itself, then look at your consciousness and ask if this applies to yourself.

Life is a struggle, a fight, a constant conflict. Every one of us realizes that. Against whom or what? Some would say "the Devil," others misfortune, others again fate or nature. All of these indicate external influences we are all up against. How many are enlightened enough to say: "My own divided being?" The real battle of life begins and must end in one's self. That is the Victory we must gain here before we expect even the slightest sign of Perfect Peace Profound.

Therefore make some recognition-signal in the direction of whatever deity you believe in and formulate your thinking in this manner: "I'll go on struggling for inner peace in my soul until I gain victory against all opposition. I've got to do this for the sake of my spiritual survival. However, I *would* appreciate some help if you really mean me to win in the end."

The next concept is going to be more difficult because it is Beauty and balanced Harmony. How many of us have actually experienced this condition for ourselves? For many, this concept can only be recognized as a missing factor one wishes with all one's heart were present. Because one knows what ugliness and discord are by experience, one senses what Beauty must be like by inference and contrast; for example, the balance of nature, if mankind didn't interfere with it, the harmony in your own life, if so many factors didn't disrupt and disturb it, the beauty of everything related rightly together, if that could last longer than moments. Beauty *is* a matter of relationships. Choose something beautiful—any common flower will do—and examine it closely. All its separate pieces are related harmoniously with each other, and that is what makes the beauty. Have you ever had a lot of things come together at the same point of your life and make it all beautiful for perhaps only a matter of seconds? If so, you may understand what we mean here, but the Beauty of the Tree concept should persist as a normal state of living.

Imagine, if you can, what life would be like living in an extended condition of beauty. No disharmony, no unbalance, no unhappiness or misery anywhere. As fast as any disturbance might begin, a compensatory factor would automatically come into action and stabilize everything. An automatic pilot does this mechanically on all aircraft, so why don't we have something like that in Cosmos? We do, but it takes a much longer time to work. Some call it karma, and others call it "the mills of God." At least this idea implies that Beauty isn't a static state, but one that has to be maintained by constant effort and expenditure of energy. Eventually everything has to balance out somehow, even if the process may be painful in order to produce peace.

Though Beauty may be a rare factor in your life (yet we hope it is not entirely absent), it is very important you should have some clear ideas about it in your consciousness. The Tree design should show you what Beauty is, a harmonious relationship of All with One. If the Tree were drawn differently so that the Spheres related equally, we would get Figure 2.1 which is more or less the same as the Buddhist "Wheel of Life" with its Eightfold Noble Path. That, however, is a very highly idealized picture. Our Tree does show up the imperfections of humanity with its "Fall" and so is more factual.

If you really want life to be beautiful for yourself and others in this world, think of this concept and say to the Conceiver of Everything in your own way: "If you intend to have Harmony and

Beauty as the controlling influence of our Cosmos, I'll do everything I can to help you make this come true, if you'll show me how to do the same for myself in my world. So long as I am imperfect, your creation can't be entirely beautiful, because I'm part of it, and true beauty must be faultless. Please help."

After Beauty, we come up against the concept of Severity and Might which was sometimes called *Pachad*—fear. Sadly enough, this will be a very familiar feature in the lives of so many human beings. Everybody is afraid of something one way or another, so you needn't be ashamed of admitting this to yourself, if to no one else. What are your special fears? Disease, poverty, starvation, and other major disasters? Let us take these for granted, together with world wars, famines, and other such horrible happenings. It is mostly that the little personal fears which nibble away at the structure of human souls do more damage than death could ever inflict by itself. What are yours? Do you know them consciously? They are part of your life like this concept on the Tree. Have you ever made someone else afraid of you in order to curb bad or unsocial behavior, like disciplining a child or training a pet because you really love them? In that case you should know why this concept is on the Tree and understand the well-known text: "The Lord chastiseth whom he loveth," and also "The fear of the Lord is the beginning of Wisdom."

There should be little difficulty with recognizing this Tree concept somewhere in your ordinary life. Have you ever sacked an employee because your firm could not afford to keep him? Then you should see how the economy factor comes into the construction of Cosmos. You know the rules; huge herds of animals eat up all the vegetation, so they starve to death till there are only a few left and the vegetation comes back slowly. This is the ecology of existence. Humanity is in a similar position today, no point arguing about that. We need this concept like a naughty boy needs a spanking, if that is the only thing to stop his tiresomeness.

Can you see, however, how this concept applies cosmically? It has nothing whatever to do with an angry and easily offended God punishing humans for "sins." It is no more than the action of an automatic pilot correcting the course of an errant aircraft, or the neuro-mechanism of your own body maintaining its position— a purely reflex action to keep Cosmos in control; no more, but not one whit less. Imagine a Cosmos *without* this concept built into its construction. Think of your own body with *no* antigens to oppose the invasion of loathesome diseases. Think of your car with *no* brakes when you need them to avoid a fatal accident. Think of yourself being beaten slowly to death by vicious muggers who are taking their time because there are *no* police to prevent them. Then you might get some idea of what this concept is doing on the Tree scheme, and thank Heaven for its presence there.

When you are doing so, perhaps you might arrange your thoughts along these lines: "I know I've got plenty of faults in me that need putting right, so just show me how to do this for myself and then you won't have to. Nevertheless, if my correction is going to hurt during the process, please let me find enough fortitude to bear it as bravely as I can."

Coming to the opposite concept of Mercy and Compassion, we shall find that human ideas of this quality vary a great deal. We hear people say: "It was a merciful release" when someone who has suffered a lot of pain dies. Or, "What a mercy we weren't there" when some disaster happens. To them it was what *didn't* happen that was merciful—pain or unpleasantness spared. Yet true mercy is a positive power, really, and never a weakness or only forbearance. You have heard of "errands of mercy," meaning that someone goes somewhere to do a kind or charitable act usually for the benefit of someone unable to help themselves. Maybe you have undertaken a few of these yourself, or perhaps had them done for you in an hour of need. It is human need which qualifies a response as merciful or compassionate. Needs, mark you, not *wants*. How merciful are you? I do not mean being foolishly generous or carelessly prodigal. That is not mercy of any kind—but rather a needless waste of resources which could be better applied elsewhere.

It is merciful, for instance, to spare people from pointless pain of body, mind or soul. Sometimes there might be good reasons for pain as an experience of life, but humans are seldom competent to judge this, and should not attempt to do so. If we can help fellow humans in distress it is best we should try without questioning the merits or demerits of specific cases. For instance, no doctor (we hope) would query whether or not a sick or injured person *deserved* medical attention, though he might ask if they *needed* it. Suppose your doctor refused to attend you because he thought you didn't deserve any help? He would soon be struck off the medical list.

How merciful are you? Do you at least try to prevent yourself from inflicting thoughtless and needless pain on others whether they are human or not? Remember that Mercy extends to all living creatures, and it means actually helping them in need quite apart from not inflicting injuries. There are many considerations and opinions involved with the practice of Mercy in this world, but maybe it was best summed up by the Rabbi Hillel a little before the time of Jesus when he said: "Do not unto others what you would not they did unto you."

Do bear in mind that Mercy, per se, is a quality which can only be passed *down* the Ladder of Life. Theoretically, humans cannot possibily be directly merciful to a God, because we cannot hurt or injure such a potency. Yet by being merciful to fellow mortals and lesser orders of life, we can indeed be merciful to that fraction of divinity which lives through us. That is what the Mercy concept should mean to us on our long climb back up the Tree. That is the significance here of the saying: "For as much as you have done it to the least of these my little ones, you have done it also unto me."

After you have put your thoughts on this Sphere together, you could frame them in this fashion: "I accept whatever Mercy you may offer me with thanks. Help me return it to you a bit at a time as I meet you among other creatures living on this planet or anywhere else."

To reach the next three concepts, we shall have to "cross the Abyss." This means we approach the realms of pure consciousness which are not actually in this world and are only represented here by extensions of energy rather than realities. Consider the concept of Understanding, for instance. How much real and genuine Understanding are we likely to meet with in this world? There are semblances of it, certainly. When anyone says they understand anything they usually mean they have experience of its construction, workings, and peculiarities. People say they understand their job when they really mean they know how to do it. Knowledge is not Understanding. Knowledge is brain-learning that ceases with death, but Understanding is a spiritual quality which is *in* you as an ability to experience the essentials of anything or anyone. There are degrees of Understanding as there are degrees of any quality. It is certainly possible to achieve some degree of it in this world even, though this is seldom a high one.

Its chief characteristic, we might notice here, is an intention or want to "understand" human or other life-forms by sheer empathy. This means to experience that other and external creation *from inside,* so to speak. To really understand another human, you would have to share their living as if you *were* that being. So you can only do that to a remote degree while you have separate bodies, however intimate you become. However, if you try to understand other souls by means of sympathy or some symbolic substitute, that is a great deal better than refusing to recognize their existence.

We usually think a mother should understand her children best because their physical beings are first formed from matter supplied from her own body, and she had a share in their souls before their minds began to evolve. Their consciousness and hers connect along ancestral lines of descent. That is why Understanding is a mother associated concept on the Tree. Do you think your mother tried to understand you, and if you think she didn't, was it because she lacked the ability or the interest? Do you ever try to understand your own children or fellow humans? That is to say, do you "put yourself in their place" and imagine what it would be like if you *were* them for a change?

From a theological viewpoint, it could be said that only a God really understands humans since he or it can actually live through our consciousness as all of us, whereas we can only achieve an infinitesimal comprehension of what God might be in return. Even to do that much, we would have to devote our *entire* awareness, consciousness, and *all that which was God in ourselves* to gain that distant degree of understanding. That is what is meant by: "Thou shalt love the Lord thy God with *all* thy heart, and *all* thy soul."

This time, when you are thinking about what Under-standing might mean, tell the life spirit in yourself: "You under-stand all I am or will ever be, while I can only understand the least of what I think you might be. I would like to understand life better than I do, and that means I must learn to see it through the eyes of other souls something like you do, but in my smaller way. Please help this Understanding between us."

Like Understanding, Wisdom, the penultimate concept when climbing the Holy Tree, is an extremely rare quality this side of the Abyss. Who dares say with authority that he or she is truly wise? Humans may be very clever, intelligent, knowledgeable, or cunning but those abilities are *not* Wisdom. The nearest thing to Wisdom we have in this world is an inherent faculty for adhering to "rightness," and that is virtually exceptional over a lengthy lifetime. An old proverb says: "No man is at all times wise." It was once said: "A thing is not right because God wills it, but God wills it because it is right." That is the principle of Wisdom in action, and why the Godhead is symbolically represented as an ancient in right profile, while Wisdom is heading the right hand Pillar of the Tree.

It is often supposed that Wisdom comes with age because of lessons learned by living a long time. That is really just experience, but it can and should bring humans a lot closer to Wisdom in each incarnation. Once they have access to Wisdom on a truly spiritual scale they need not incarnate any more, which explains why so few humans seem genuinely wise. We are here to learn by experience how not to live here any longer than we have to.

However, as in the case of Understanding, humans may indeed have occasional contacts with Wisdom and, as they advance in life, show some degrees of it in themselves through clarity of consciousness and individual enlightenment. Wisdom is something which shows up in the character of a human being. It is a quality so uniquely "Godlike" that even a mild degree of it seems to set someone apart from average humanity by sheer contrast alone. Do you know anyone like this? Can you think of anyone you honestly feel might be wise in this sense? Have you ever felt the influence of Wisdom in yourself when you suddenly realized what was exactly the right thing to do yet you couldn't explain how it reached you?

Although age is presumed to bring Wisdom with it, this is by no means a *sine qua non*. It is spiritual experience which counts. As you should see for yourself there are some very foolish old people in this world and signs of Wisdom among quite young ones. They are what was once called "Old Souls" who, after many incarnations, are bringing back traces of inherited Wisdom from former lives. Developments arising from this may yet deliver humanity from the fate its foolishness faces. Remember the Sacred King cycle, when the sacrificed Victim returns to life on earth as a Teacher of Truth.

If any ideas about Wisdom as placed on the Tree of Life reach you, it might be as well to acknowledge them by saying: "I know real Wisdom is something we have to work for until we become worthy of it. That is what I intend doing for as many lives as I need to attain it. Meanwhile, I rely on your Wisdom to teach me the way towards Truth."

As anyone might expect, it is very difficult in this world to detect a trace of the ultimate concept on the Tree—the Crown. Maybe the idea of a clear life-aim is representative. How many people have a definite and absolutely clear conception of what they intend to make of themselves in this incarnation, beyond which point they have nothing more in view? Some do. Some actually achieve it and then feel lost because they are faced with a vacuum they have no means of filling. The top of any tree can be a perilous place for a single soul unable to fly further. Ambitious and single-minded humans may set themselves some goal to achieve in earthly terms which they consider would be the crowning of their entire lives. They gain this, so what then? Back to the eternal question: "EH NA?" After the Crown concept, all the *Ain Soph Aur* awaits us.

From a loftier viewpoint, the Crown on the top of the Tree means the goal gained is the end of incarnate living but the beginning of existence as sentient energy beyond anything we can possibly imagine because it is outside the widest limit of our human consciousness. Therefore, when you reach this point of your contemplation on the concepts, there is not really much left to say except perhaps: "I *am*. You *are*. We *will*."

If you have gained anything out of these exercises, you might like to know that a stylized form of them exists as a booklet entitled *The Office of the Holy Tree of Life.* *This is a prayer-meditation series covering every Sphere and Path on the Tree. They are designed to be chanted, but may quite well be followed silently. All the major symbolism through the Four Worlds of Life is mentioned with each Sphere so that the whole invocation is a summative call to the mind of the esoteric essentials attributed to it. In the case of the Paths, the process is briefer but includes the Tarot Trump of each. We shall be dealing with these quite soon.

Presuming you intend to progress and make solid spiritual relationships with the ideals symbolized by the Holy Tree, you would be well advised to get a copy of this booklet which can be carried easily in your pocket or wallet. There is no reason why you should not write out favorite invocations or aphorisms of your own and include these wherever you feel it is appropriate.

Questions

1. What is your Kingdom in this world?
2. Translate Spheres (Sephiroth) 9, 8, and 7 in terms of your own life.
3. Translate Spheres 6, 5, and 4 in terms of your own life.
4. Translate Spheres 3, 2, and 1 in terms of your own life.
5. What is the true purpose or function of a King and how do you relate this with yourself?
6. Write a short invocation for each Sphere of the Tree.
7. Differentiate between the Spheres on each side of the Abyss.
8. What is *your* idea of Heaven?
9. Choose the eight most important sentences in this chapter.
10. In what way do you find the Tree concept helping you the most in your own life?

---

*This exercise is included in Wm. Gray's *Sangreal Ceremonies and Rituals*, published by Samuel Weiser.

·14·

Pathworking

Now we are going back to the Paths again. Have you got a little picture of them with the letters? If so, put it in position where you can see it easily; if not, make one up or use Figure 1.40 from Chapter 12. Think of anything at all you want to write, your own name and address if you like. With the picture to guide you, write it out slowly letter by letter concentrating on the meaning of the Spheres involved. You can type if you prefer. There will be a lot more mental effort required than you might suppose, so don't try anything too long the first time.

You will probably find the vowels are easiest because you only have to think of one element each. Try writing them over and over again while you think of their elements and see if you can speed up a bit. By cheating permissably, you could work a mnemonic of eArth, aEr, fIre, wOrter and trUth. Keep trying until you can write them fairly fast, AEIOU, while thinking as you write. Hard work at first, isn't it? Never mind, keep going. After that you might experiment with the well-worn sentence, The quick brown fox jumps over the lazy dogs, or anything else using all the letters of the alphabet.

When you get tired of this try a reading exercise. Pick up a book or some printed material near you. Open it at random and take the first sentence your eye falls on. Start reading, letter by letter, associating the Sphere significances with each. Go on till you feel the strain becoming too much, then stop. What is of fundamental importance is that you do not think of the letters simply as positions on a diagram or parts of a numbered series, but as symbols of *an actual experience of life* on each Path conditioned by two of its concepts. Unless you can see and understand this vital point quite clearly, there is not much purpose in going on.

It may seem absurd to ask: "What does N mean to you?" Apart from being a letter of our alphabet and a sonic unit of speech, it has got to mean the way you feel and are conscious while living in a state of existence caused by a combination of Mercy and Victory. Every time you employ a written or sonic N, the experience of those Spheres should go with it. Conversely each time you feel the Mercy-Victory combination *through the Tree code* the idea of N should come up in your mind. The same process, of course, applies to the other letters.

Granted the speed of normal thinking will make this a micro-experience in terms of our time sense, but this does not reduce the *quality* of its inner reality. As you may have heard somewhere, it is possible to "compress" sounds into high-speed transmissions when all a normal listener hears is a single sharp screech lasting only a second or two. When slowed down to a comprehensible rate every word is audible and there may be a couple of minutes of speech. Much the same can happen in spiritual terms, too. You might "receive" a spiritual contact in the flick of a millisecond which would take years to understand on our level, or it might need years to communicate something you would "get" in a matter of seconds. That is often what so-called "inspiration" amounts to, realizing rapidly what has been coming to you for a very long time without your conscious recognition of it. You might almost say you are spelling the story of your life at the rate of one letter per day, week, month, or even year. Only at the end will the whole tale be told.

When we are applying such principles to the Path-letters of the Tree, the question is, can you sum up a double Sphere concept as a single unit identified with a letter-symbol, or, conversely, can a letter-symbol evoke a double Sphere concept in you? Moreover, can you run a sequence changing series of these through your mind at more or less the same rate you normally read and write? Perhaps it would be better phrased if you were asked, would you be willing to try practicing this for a while to see what progress you make? The worst it can do is brighten your brain and liven up your mental processes, so there is nothing to lose and no mental exercise can ever be entirely wasted. Let us take the process step by step.

The first step is, obviously, to familiarize yourself with the ten concepts of the Tree and bring them to life in yourself. This you can only do by repeated meditations and practices you perform on your own. Your purpose throughout should be to compress each Sphere in your consciousness so that you can actually *be* in a simulated state of that Sphere, evoking it with a flash of your mind. This is not unlike an actor assuming a character part in less than seconds as a controlled condition of consciousness. This may sound terribly difficult, but is really no more than a matter of practice and usage.

The second step is an association of Paths with letters in terms of experiential inner energies, in other words, something you can actually feel for yourself and believe in because of your experiences. This is a much more difficult stage and calls for considerable discipline and devotion in order to condition consciousness and train your thinking along the lines required. Yet it is only a logical progression from the first set of exercises and a matter of putting yourself through the right hoops, so to speak.

The third step is only a question of improvement and extension of the previous two, so if they can be mastered with any degree of skill the hardest part is over. It looks as if the bottom rung of this particular ladder is the ability to characterize the Spheres as a state of being at very short notice, and experience some degree of identification with them for a moment or two. Therefore, we need to devise a simple exercise to feel our way up and down the Tree as rapidly as possible. This is best done mentally while sitting in an ordinary position at a desk or in a chair, since that is when the use of consciousness is most likely to communicate with inner intelligences. It is also one exercise which can comfortably be done lying in bed, because it tends to connect consciousness with spiritual levels where these concepts are more than merely symbolic.

Begin by looking round the "Kingdom" of your world, close the eyes and transfer this sense to your inner being. "Lift off" to a sense of stabilization between the Pillars. Then get a feeling of Glory followed by Victory because of something you have won or would want to win out of life. Stabilize yourself once again by a consciousness of Harmony or Beauty somewhere in the center of your soul. Then sober your thinking with a realization of discipline, duty, and Severity with which you will have to control your activities if they are to be productive, but comfort yourself by acknowledging the Mercy and Compassion your human failings will be met with by (here give a little mental hop across an imaginary Abyss) a "Cosmic Controller" who Understands with Wisdom your ultimate aim in living and will take you past it to *Perfect Peace Profound.*

Come down to earth the reverse way. Start with a sense of *I am,* then think as follows: "With Wisdom and Understanding I will leap across the Abyss into life where I will meet with Mercy and Might balanced by Beauty. Then I shall gain both Victory and Glory by stabilizing and Founding myself as ruler of my Kingdom upon Earth." Change your state of consciousness to match each concept. When you think them make yourself *feel* them at the same time.

Carry on with this type of exercise until you feel fairly confident that you can go up and down the Tree gaining a sense of positive contact with every concept and a feeling of "changeover" between them. When you can do this with rapidity and accuracy, you will be ready to begin filling in these "changeover" gaps by means of the Path-letter workings. Here it becomes a matter of teaching and learning techniques for idea association and so is largely an individual affair because some people learn quicker than others. We can suggest a few methods which may be useful, especially for those who have great difficulty in assimilating ideas and responding to symbols.

The first obvious system is to write out the letters with Sphere associations on each side and study them in turn. They can also be put on tape and listened to in the form of an alphabet-rhyme or other arrangement. Here is another alphabet attribution identifying the Paths with a single word commencing with the appropriate letter. This is necessarily farfetched here and there, but the meanings are within the bounds of imaginative reason.

Path	Concept-Combination	Creates		Letter	
11	Crown-Wisdom	the Path of	B	elieving
12	Crown-Understanding	the Path of	C	onceiving
13	Crown-Beauty	the Path of	D	edication
14	Wisdom-Understanding	the Path of	F	aculties
15	Wisdom-Mercy	the Path of	G	oodness
16	Wisdom-Beauty	the Path of	H	appiness
17	Understanding-Severity	the Path of	J	eopardy
18	Understanding-Beauty	the Path of	K	arma
19	Mercy-Severity	the Path of	L	egality
20	Mercy-Beauty	the Path of	M	agnanimity
21	Mercy-Victory	the Path of	N	iceness
22	Severity-Beauty	the Path of	P	erils
23	Severity-Glory	the Path of	Q	uerying
24	Beauty-Victory	the Path of	R	omance
25	Beauty-Glory	the Path of	S	earching
26	Beauty-Foundation	the Path of	T	enacity
27	Victory-Glory	the Path of	V	ariety
28	Victory-Foundation	the Path of	W	inning
29	Victory-Kingdom	the Path of	eX	periencing
30	Glory-Foundation	the Path of	Y	ielding
31	Glory-Kingdom	the Path of	Z	estfulness
32	Foundation-Kingdom	the Path of	Th	oughtfulness

Another useful idea is to make a set of cards in a handy size with just the letter on one side and the Sphere meanings on the other

Figure 2.2. Path Cards

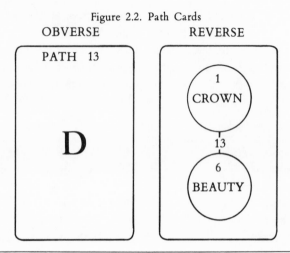

(see Figure 2.2). You can then view them from the letter side and try to attach the meanings mentally, or go through them the other way looking at meanings to which you have to try visualizing the connected letter. Don't forget you have to make yourself *feel* the Sphere meanings while looking at the letter. Failing any of these methods, you could try reciting the list aloud the way children used to learn the alphabet years ago, in a sing-song fashion. The trouble with this is that it tends to become very mechanical and purely repetitive with no particular feeling or sense of importance in the background. The whole object of this exercise is the attachment of spiritual significance to ordinary letters of the alphabet.

Anyone with handicraft abilities might make a rosary for letter-learning which could convey a suggestion of spirituality by its very name and purpose. Instead of a crucifix there would be a small Tree of Life at the end followed by twenty-six beads in alphabetical order. Large beads would be the vowel-elements and smaller beads the Path-consonants. Even beads are not really necessary. Early rosaries were no more than knots tied in cords, large knots for major meanings, small ones for standard repetitive significances. It is customary for prayers or pious utterances to be made as beads or knots slip through the fingers during rosary devotions. Originally, rosaries were only meant as prayer-counters when it was believed that a specific number of prayers would accomplish a definite spiritual aim. The Christian use of them as backing for meditation was a later development. Here we are suggesting that an alphabet-rosary as described might have a very brief minimum formula attached to it, something like the following which could also be used as a litany with its response phrase:

Invocation		*Response*
A	Earthly Life-Element	Means this to me.
B	Crowning Wisdom	Means this to me.
C	Crown Understanding	Means this to me.
D	Crowning Beauty	Means this to me.
E	Airy Life Element	Means this to me.
F	Wise Understanding	Means this to me.
G	Wisdom and Mercy	Mean this to me.
H	Wisdom and Beauty	Mean this to me.
I	Fiery Life-Element	Means this to me.
J	Understanding Severity	Means this to me.
K	Understanding and Beauty	Mean this to me.
L	Merciful Mightiness	Means this to me.
M	Merciful Harmony	Means this to me.
N	Merciful Victory	Means this to me.
O	Water Life Element	Means this to me.
P	Mighteous Harmony	Means this to me.
Q	Mighty and Glorious	Mean this to me.
R	Beautiful Victory	Means this to me.
S	Harmonious Glory	Means this to me.
T	Beauteous Foundation	Means this to me.
U	Truthful Life Element	Means this to me.
V	Victorious Glory	Means this to me.
W	Victorious Foundation	Means this to me.
X	Victorious Kingdom	Means this to me.
Y	Glorious Foundation	Means this to me.
Z	Glorious Kingdom	Means this to me.
Th	Foundation and Kingdom	Mean this to me.

Note how the concept combinations have been adapted to allow rhythmic chanting, and the four-beat "Mean this to me" response after each invocation gives time to adjust consciousness accordingly. This rosary system can be altered by re-positioning the Spheres and letters so as to read:

Earthly Life Element	Means	A	to me.
Crowning and Wisdom	Mean	B	to me.
Crown Understanding	Means	C	to me.
Crowning of Beauty	Means	D	to me.
Airy Life Element	Means	E	to me.

And so on all down the Paths in sequence.

Those interested in the devotional aspect of the Tree system may be pleased to hear that a regular rosary scheme for prayer meditation practice does exist. The preparatory prayer while the Tree symbol is being considered goes:

O Supreme Life-Spirit, Thou alone are cause and Crown of Cosmos with Thy Wisdom and Thine Understanding. Grant us avoidance of the Great Abyss in our Experience of Thine existence.

Extend Thy Mercy unto us with all thy Might, that we may realize the Beauty of Thy being.

Let us lovingly Achieve the Glory of Establishing ourselves immortally in Thy most Holy Kingdom evermore. Amen.

If the Sphere concepts are being meditated on, the invocation and response is:

I. Blessed unto us upon the Holy Tree of Life be thou the principle and Power of ... (here the concept concerned is named).

R. Permit and prosper Thou we pray our present purpose with the Perfect Plan.

In the case of the Paths the formula is:

I. Blessed be the Path of. . .(Path named) upon the Holy Tree of Life that links the Principles of (Sphere) and (Sphere).

R. May this and every way within the Perfect Pattern lead us toward enlightenment in living evermore.

Lastly, there is a prayer of thanksgiving which might well be used on other occasions:

> Gratitude to Thee, O greatest Sovereign Spirit of Supernal Wisdom and Omniscient Understanding, since we are enlightened by Experience of Thine existence.

> Thanks be for Mercifully tempered Might, and blessed be the Beauty of Achieving Glory by Establishing our living entities within Thine ever-lasting Kingdom.

(Note how the concepts are all linked and inclusive of DAATh as *Experience*.)

There is quite a lot to be gained from rosary practice in accomplished hands, so never despise it because of sectarian associations. Hindus, Buddhists, and Muslims have been using rosaries for centuries to regulate devotional rhythms, and there is no real reason why they should not be used to mark off any kind of invocation. You could employ the same principle by cutting notches on a stick, tying knots in string or transferring small stones from one hand to the other. All things considered, a rosary seems neatest and most practical. Why should it not serve the Tree system as well as any other mystical method?

When modern esotericists talk about "Path-working" they refer to meditational practices often carried out by small groups meeting especially for the purpose. The general idea is to specify a Path and then confine consciousness entirely to those specifications sometimes for quite a long period. If any mental impressions arrive which do not seem consistent with that Path, they are supposed to be solemnly "banished" by an act of will, excluding them from the mind, sometimes accompanied by a specifically worded formula or gesture. Various groups usually evolve their own methods which are seldom superior to those of any others, so there is no reason why you should not invent your personal version if you want to. The only difference between working with groups and alone is that shared consciousness *can* give "extra uplift" (though by no means necessarily) and at the end of an exercise a group discussion on results obtained individually (if permitted) is often quite interesting.

The procedure is generally to make one member responsible for conducting the exercise from start to finish. His job is to read or recite what is called the "induction narrative" for that particular Path while the others settle down in meditational postures and concentrate their minds in conformity. An induction narrative is a suggestive and semi-hypnotic story calling up all the associated symbology with the subject of meditation, so that the narrator needs the right kind of voice and the ability to use it effectively. Otherwise it is liable to irritate, annoy, or just plain bore and antagonize hearers. The idea should be to capture their interest, put stimulating thoughts into their minds, and persuade them to begin looking into themselves along the lines indicated. Once they seem ready for this inner journey, the narrator may sink his tones to softer and quieter levels followed by silence, or he may stop suddenly with a command, or else bring in a suitable musical background at correct level. Other sensory stimuli such as incense may be used.

There is usually some kind of "go" signal for the Path to be entered. Sometimes this is described as a door in the appropriate color for the Path concerned, usually a blend of those of the Spheres which are shown as Pillars between which the door hangs. On the door is the number and letter of the Path itself. While the narrator is depicting these details, his listeners have to put themselves in a proper frame of mind. In some groups there is an understanding that once anyone achieves this state of readiness, they will silently indicate this by some minor hand signal such as finger positions on knees. This is so that the narrator will then know when all are ready and get them started as soon as possible. He also has to get them back either at the end of an agreed period, or if he notices that all finger positions are indicating completion of mission.

At the end of this period there is usually a general discussion and comparison of inner experiences. Though these will naturally vary, it is not unusual to find that a great deal of consciousness has been shared in common and everyone's experience has enriched that of the others. Sometimes, however, there are groups which do not believe that inner encounters should be shared objectively by open discussion, because they think this might "devalue" the spiritual content of the experience. So everyone either speaks of other matters or goes home in silence. This is entirely a matter of opinion and up to the people concerned. Some are able to cope with their inner activities capably and rationally while others are not. In the case of group-workings, nobody except the leader can really decide who falls into which category and then sort them out accordingly. On the whole, it is probably best to commence Pathworking by yourself and get some practice at it first before taking part in any group activities.

There is no reason at all why you should not outline and put your own induction narrative on tape, then listen to it as you settle down to meditational work. Either you can switch this off at the end, or leave the tape running for a set period of, say, ten to fifteen mintues with background music or sound effects and then a "wake-up" call to complete the exercise. Otherwise you can do the whole thing in complete silence. The general idea is to approach the Path along a visual inner angle and then deliberately enter it through a door having the symbol of the Sphere concepts at its sides, and the Path letter or special signs displayed on the door itself. The reason for this standard approach is to facilitate future Path-workings and also to implant the idea in our collective consciousness so that it becomes as real inwardly as any physical building on earth.

Once the visualized door opens, a scene should appear which is symbolic of both concepts. Some viewers choose the Tarot card attached to the Path. You are then supposed to "enter" by imaginatively experiencing what that symbol is *doing* and your own reactions therewith. You are not meant to be a mere observer of what goes on so much as a *participator* in the action. Each symbol of the Path should hand you on to another one in sequence so that everything makes a composite and *intelligible* experience arising from your inner consciousness. Yet, if and when obviously alien or inappropriate impressions intrude, you must firmly "banish" these with an effort of will associated with a word or gesture. There is no real need for elaborate "Magical Banishing Rituals." A dismissive hand gesture and the instruction "Get out!" or simply "Out!" should be sufficient. To illustrate, if your visualized scene is the deck of a ship and suddenly an express train starts thundering across, you will have to remove the invader mentally and restore the scene to order. An experienced Path-worker would do more. He would re-direct the train image to another Path where it would be more appropriate, such as the twenty-fifth Path.

One of the main objectives behind these Path-working practices is to comb out consciousness, as it were, into several streams so that *everything of which we can be conscious becomes graded into classifications of spiritual significance.* This has the advantage of arranging and organizing our inner awareness so that it makes sense and conveys meanings to the human minds it meets with. It makes the difference between a library where all the books are muddled on shelves haphazardly without regard to subject or authorship and another where they are all categorized and classified. In other words, it enables you to know where everything in your consciousness is and how to find it when you need it in a hurry. This is much more than a mere memory-system, because it amounts to a facility for making contacts with other minds than your own through a commonly shared "fund" or "collection" of consciousness itself. At this point you should try a Path-working for yourself and see how you get on with it. Let us take the nineteenth Path between Mercy and Might. You could write your induction narrative as follows:

Are you sitting comfortably? Good. Then settle down and close your eyes. Breathe regularly and evenly, in...out...in... out. That's the rhythm. Now concentrate your inner gaze right at the back of your physical eyes, at the root of your nose, but don't *strain.* Ease off tension and relax. Yes, relax...relax. Now we are going to visit the nineteenth Path on the Holy Tree of Life between Spheres four and five, Mercy and Might. That's halfway up the Tree, but we shall get there by elevator. You are sitting in one at the moment. Can you hear the doors slide shut? There they go. Press the button marked 19. Up she goes. Up, up, and still up. Ah, it's stopped. Did you feel that little hitch under your feet as the movement ceased? There's the elevator door opening with its usual gliding sound and we can see another door immediately opposite the opening. An odd kind of door between two Pillars, the left one red, and the right one deep blue. The door itself is a sort of purple. Its red Pillar has a sign which says, "I am Mighty," and the blue one says, "I am Merciful." The door has number 19 on it. Keep looking at that. It is an illuminated number which glows quietly with a pulsating light. Now the light is getting brighter, and brighter, and brighter still, becoming brilliant while keeping up its steady pulse. Flick, stop, flick, flick, flick, flick, flick, flick, flick, flick, flick, pause, then it begins again. One nine, it is going, nineteen. Can you hear anything? A sort of humming beep keeping time with the light? Be conscious of it. Keep looking at the light and listening to the note.

What are you expecting to see behind that door when it opens? Something connected with justice and fair play certainly. This is where wrongs get righted, and you will find whatever you deserve because of what you have done with your life. It will show how you ought to behave if you intend to remain in balance without being too sentimental or over-severe. You will meet some fair-minded people here who believe in keeping a balanced viewpoint in life. They will be interested to meet you as well since you are calling on them. You had better let them know you are here. Just knock on the door with the numbers of the Spheres. Four taps, then five. Go on. That's right. The door will only open a mere crack, and then you will have to give your name and say exactly why you have come. Are you ready? The door is opening now. Speak quietly and they will hear you. There you are, now the door is really opening to admit you. Go in and learn. Go in and learn. Learn...learn...earn ...rn...nnnnnnn.

Do you see the idea? A sort of auto-hypnotic introduction to each Path, something to put your mind in the right mood and advance a few suggestions about how to arrange your awareness before entering. Once you do enter, the rest is entirely up to you, and nobody else can possibly tell you what is likely to happen. You are not a slave to obey orders, but an adventurer going to map out your own inner life. Do remember, though, that all you see or hear is *symbolic* rather than actual, and you will have to intepret your truths on that level. This is why it makes good practice to work with the Tarot cards, because that is entirely a matter of making comprehensible meanings out of pure symbology.

Questions

1. How clearly can you associate vowels with life-elements?
2. Write a short meditation of each Path.
3. Try making your own Path-letter mnemonics.
4. Design a Path-working which can be adopted for each Path.
5. Which Path (if any) do you find easiest and why?
6. Which Path (if any) do you find hardest and why?
7. What do you think is the greatest value of Path-working?
8. Describe *your* favorite method of Path-working.
9. Choose the seven most important sentences in this chapter.
10. What do you find the best aid to Path conception?

· 15 ·

Tree and Tarot

You may know something of the Tarot cards already, so we will not waste time and space covering their better known aspects. What we are mainly concerned with here is the precise connection of the twenty-two Trump cards, better known as the Major Arcana, with the 22 Paths of the Holy Tree of Life. This has always been a controversial question among Western occultists, uneasily settled during the last century by attributing the cards to the Paths according to their sequential numbers regardless of their ideology. The results gave what looks like a very peculiar association indeed—see the table on page 214.

Now take a good look at those associations but ignore the card numbers. Does it begin to remind you of those old child-puzzlers entitled "What is wrong with this picture?" They were a kind of intelligence test to discover how quickly the child's mind recognizes incongruities? At the same time this reveals the youngster's aptitude for clear and ordered thinking and ability to "put things in their proper place" with a minimum of confusion.

It surely seems obvious that many of the associations on this list are so strained and unlikely that it would take a very convoluted mind to make out any convincing relationships. Take the Beauty-Victory connection with Death, for instance. What is really

Path Number	Conjoining Spheres	Tarot Trumps	Card Number
11	Crown-Wisdom	The Fool	0
12	Crown-Understanding	Magician	1
13	Crown-Beauty	Priestess	2
14	Wisdom-Understanding	Empress	3
15	Wisdom-Beauty	Emperor	4
16	Wisdom-Mercy	Hierophant	5
17	Understanding-Beauty	The Lovers	6
18	Understanding-Might	Chariot	7
19	Mercy-Might	Strength	8
20	Mercy-Beauty	Hermit	9
21	Mercy-Victory	Wheel of Fortune	10
22	Might-Beauty	Justice	11
23	Might-Glory	Hanged Man	12
24	Beauty-Victory	Death	13
25	Beauty-Foundation	Temperance	14
26	Beauty-Glory	The Devil	15
27	Victory-Glory	Blasted Tower	16
28	Victory-Foundation	The Star	17
29	Victory-Kingdom	Moon	18
30	Glory-Foundation	Sun	19
31	Glory-Kingdom	Judgment	20
32	Foundation-Kingdom	The World	21

(Please note the Path-numbers are old style ones.)

---

beautiful or victorious about death unless you are a masochistic mystic? Then Victory and Glory linked with the Blasted Tower. Whose victory does this represent? Is the Devil glorious or beautiful? He may be thought so by his followers and supporters but surely not by anyone with a spark of human kindness in their souls. Then what is mighty or glorious about the Hanged Man? There are a lot of things that just don't match in the concepts of the Tree as connected with the concepts of the Tarot.

Suppose we start sorting out the Tarot Trumps into sets of homogenous ideas entirely apart from their official numbering. For instance, the Sun, Moon, and Star would go together as astronomical or cosmic phenomena. So would the Emperor, Empress and Hierophant as external rulers of temporality and religion. Justice, Judgement, and the Wheel of Fortune seem to connect as the workings of karmic laws of compensation and balance. Let us set up a skeleton of the Tree and see if any of these ought to fit anywhere quite naturally. Two sets actually form the backbone of the Tree. Looking out into space we have the Moon nearest to our world, then the Sun centrally in our solar system, and after that stars (which are other suns) far away towards infinity. So we put them up the central Pillar in that order. Then Judgement is a faculty taking all our combined Wisdom and Understanding to handle, therefore its card symbol is place on that Path. Justice is a fair combination of Might and Mercy in proper proportions and there is no doubt of its placement. Nor can we deny there is an element of chance in our lives symbolized by the Wheel of Fortune, and the Victory-Glory Path is a good place for that because these are the factors we risk our lives very often to gain, ephemeral as they are.

This produces Figure 2.3, on page 216, which is more or less a figurative display of the space-time elements of Cosmos. Now what about the event factor? This should run around the perimeter of the Tree connecting the concepts in descending and ascending order of importance. We need eight cards to do this. Starting at the top we proceed clockwise. First, we need something to join our ideas of an ultimate with wisdom. The archetype figure of the Hierophant, who is supposed to symbolize the height of our spirituality and initiated Wisdom certainly fits here. Then for a junction between Wisdom and Mercy let us choose the Emperor as sign of a "good governor" to show that our lives should be ruled by those truly kingly qualities. Let him be followed by his Empress whose rule it is that Mercy shall determine whatever victories we may gain in this life. To connect her with our Foundation, the Priestess (or female Pope) is a fitting counterpart of the Hierophant and symbolizes that all victories worth having are best based on

Figure 2.3. Tarot Trumps backbone of Tree

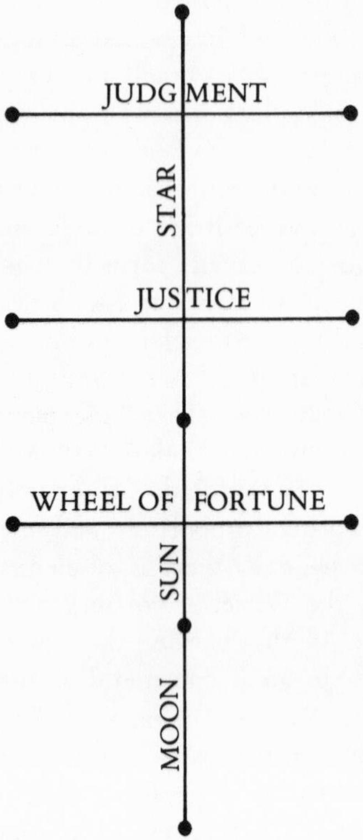

prayers and sincere spiritual devotions. She also symbolizes the Orphic Path.

Going up the other side of the Tree, we rise from Foundation to Glory by the masculine equivalent of the Priestess—the Magician. He is well placed here, commencing the Hermetic Path. As the Priestess represented a devotional and religious side to living, so the Magician symbolizes the intellectual and scientific approach to the mysteries of life. But Glory meets the check of Severity next, and we come up against all the oppositions and hindrances we are almost bound to meet in the course of any incarnation. What else in the Tarot could symbolize these problems and annoyances except the Devil, the Tempter, Adversary,

Falsifier? He symbolizes all the things that go wrong in life that we have to contend with and overcome in the end. We all have our devils, and there he sits in the Tree waiting to bother us. But if we are adequately backed by the Magician we should push past the worst the Devil can do. Can there be anything worse than the Devil? This depends on whether you consider Death as the great necessity of life and the executive economist of existence. Life *needs* death which in turn demands life and so the cycle of creation continues. Past Death, what do we find as a symbol to join it with the summit or Crown of Consciousness so that Understanding completes the circuit on the Tree? What else but contemplative or intuitive awareness symbolized by the Hermit or Solitary, who may be male, female, or both. Here it can also mean a waiting in the womb (or the Great Unconsciousness) prior to proceeding back to life by the birth process. We have now constructed Figure 2.4 (see page 218) and used up 14 of the Trumps.

If you look at this last circuit, you should see that it roughly represents the spiritual sequence of our average incarnations. First, there is our entry across the Abyss with all the genetic wisdom we have earned in past lives, symbolized by the Hierophant. We are then born by the relationship of our father (the Emperor) and our mother (the Empress). After that, the relative innocence and idealism of our youth (the Priestess) becomes converted to the cunning and skill of the Magician, which we shall need to deal with the difficulties and "devilishness" of living as human beings. Eventually, we have to face the re-crossing of the Abyss by experience of Death, and afterwards our solitary souls contemplate Cosmos and consciousness like the Hermit awaiting the call to creation once more. The complete combination of these symbols makes a tremendous amount of spiritual sense.

Now we might manage to sort out the complements among the Tree concepts. Two that stand out are Temperance and the Hanged Man. Both are balance cards. Temperance appears to balance from one side to the others, and the Hanged Man is suspended or balanced between Heaven and Earth. The two together form an idealistic cross. Since their common factor is poise, they must connect with Harmony in the center and Wisdom,

Figure 2.4. Tarot Trump cycle of Tree

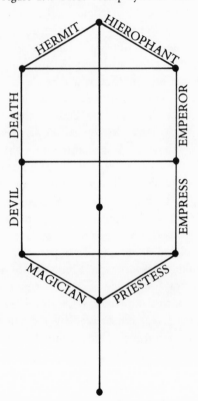

giving meaning to Temperance on the right, and Understanding, denoting the karmic ties of the Hanged Man on the left. Another pair remaining are the World and the Fool—our world, and all of us foolish enough to be here (a cosmic joke). The Fool is also the innocent, or "one without Wisdom," a neophyte, so its path lies at the bottom of the Tree beginning the ascent. Seeing that the life-circuit is sunwise, let us put him between the Kingdom and Glory (which attracts his attention) while the World is between the Kingdom and Victory (which is needed in some degree before humans can survive here at all). See Figure 2.5.

This leaves us with only four Trumps to fit in appropriately. We can place one—the Blasted Tower—straight away. Clearly it

Figure 2.5. Tarot Trump ascents of Tree

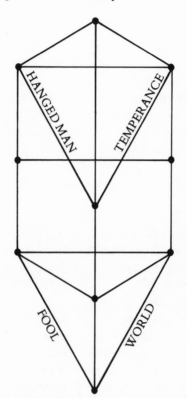

must go between Severity and Beauty as does anything upsetting balance and harmony in our universe. No question of that, and no denying that there *are* such aspects of life as we know it. This is where they are shown on the Tree scheme. Next, the Chariot, or travel, seeking and questing after experience in life. It plainly connects with the Hermetic factor of Glory and the solar symbol of Harmony in the center. There are only two Trumps left. Of these, the Lovers seems to fit nicely between Beauty and Victory because real love is surely the great triumph of life and certainly its most beautiful manifestation. That leaves us with the last one, Strength. This joins Mercy with Beauty very appropriately. Remember what Shakespeare made Portia say about Mercy? "It is mighty in the

mightiest, and it becomes the throned monarch better than his crown." Remember, too, that Mercy can only be shown by the strong to the weak. If we make the quality of beautiful Mercy the strength of our lives, we shall not go very far wrong. Now have a good look at Figure 2.6, then read down the list below and see what you think about it.

Go over the list carefully and contrast it with the list on page 214. Then decide which makes the best sense of the Tarot symbols. There can scarcely be a great deal of doubt, can there? Now it may well be that you have already been familiar with the

Path Number	Concepts Joining	Tarot Trump	Letter
11	Crown-Wisdom	Hierophant	B
12	Crown-Understanding	Hermit	C
13	Crown-Beauty	Star	D
14	Wisdom-Understanding	Judgment	F
15	Wisdom-Mercy	Emperor	G
16	Wisdom-Beauty	Temperance	H
17	Understanding-Might	Death	J
18	Understanding-Beauty	Hanged Man	K
19	Mercy-Might	Justice	L
20	Mercy-Beauty	Strength	M
21	Mercy-Victory	Empress	N
22	Might-Beauty	Blasted Tower	P
23	Might-Glory	Devil	Q
24	Beauty-Victory	Lovers	R
25	Beauty-Glory	Chariot	S
26	Beauty-Foundation	Sun	T
27	Victory-Glory	Wheel of Fortune	V
28	Victory-Foundation	Priestess	W
29	Victory-Kingdom	World	X
30	Glory-Foundation	Magician	Y
31	Glory-Kingdom	Fool	Z
32	Foundation-Kingdom	Moon	Th

Figure 2.6. Tarot Trump lower diagonals

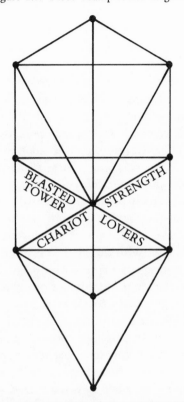

Tarots under the earlier attributions and may not want to face the trouble of re-considering them now. If this is so, we shall understand if you will be honest enough to face yourself in a mirror and say aloud: "I just can't be bothered to alter my ideas about the Tarot Trumps now after all the work I went to in the first place." You have the perfect right of refusing to learn anything in life, providing you realize that only your refusal prevents you from making any form of progress. Nobody is telling you that you must, or ought to accept this system rather than another, but once you refuse to consider it, the onus is on you to say why and to point out exactly where it is fallacious in representing the Tree concepts concerned. This implies that you are also in a position to

222 • CONCEPTS OF QABALAH

demonstrate the accuracy or superiority of other systems. Remember we are nor referring to the interpretation of the Tarot Trumps themselves as symbols, but only to their connections with the Paths on the Tree of Life. Figure 2.7 shows the place of all the Tarot Trumps on the Tree of Life.

Granted there could be cases made for many different ways of linking the Tarot Trumps with the Paths of the Tree but it would be difficult to find a more convincing distribution of symbolism than the one we have been working out here. Commonsense alone should tell you that much, if nothing else does. If it doesn't, then try to work out a better way for yourself and then build up an unbreakable theory in support of your system.

There can scarcely be any argument about the minor arcana of the Tarot, about the four suits and decade of each in sequence. They can hardly do anything else except fit the concepts by numbers corresponding with the Four Worlds, elements, quarters, and so on. Each concept is expressed as a quarternity in Cosmic Cross significance. The four suits are our old magical instruments of Rods (Wands) for Fire, Cups for Water, Swords (or Arrows) for Air, and Shields (Pentacles or Coins) for Earth. The Cord is not represented except as an invisible connection between them all. What is of most interest is why those particular symbols should have been chosen in the first place.

Legend says that when it was realized among the cognoscenti that our old, and by that time, secret inner tradition in the West was being rapidly lost, a brilliant idea for preserving it for posterity was born. What was the least likely thing to die out among mankind? Apart from sex, the obvious and cynical answer was the gambling instinct, or devotion to games of chance in hopes of winning money or some other gain. Dice were several thousands of years old then and are with us yet. If some means could be found of synthesizing the essentials of our esoteric lore as a set of symbols usable for gambling and gaming, they were very likely to be handed from one generation to another. This meant that anyone recognizing the key symbology could reconstruct the whole theme with an effort of imaginative ideology.

Figure 2.7. The Tarot Trumps on the Tree of Life

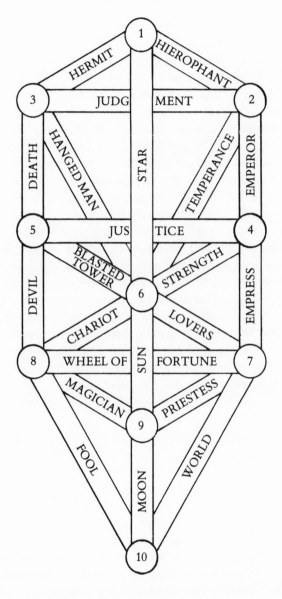

If it was going to be based on a decade (which is why a pack of cards is called a "deck" for short) that meant ten cards multiplied four ways, or forty altogether. If the values indicated the concepts of the Tree, and the suits signified the angle from which that concept should be considered, that should give coverage to consciouness reaching from one end of life to the other. It was realized, however, that this would hardly be enough. Those represented events and aspects of living, but where were the people who constituted human life and made it meaningful on Earth? So human beings had to be represented and symbolized by a "people-pack" of its own, showing four sorts of people four ways; two males and two females per suit—the ideal family, Father, Mother, Son and Daughter, or human generations replacing each other. These became the King, Queen, Prince (Knight) and Princess (Page). They also made up a special magical square corresponding with the "Letters of the Name" or numerals adding up to ten in each direction. Thus they made a theoretical forty to equal the scheme of ten concepts with four cards each. The four suits corresponded with the "Four Worlds" idea of creation on the Tree of Life: Rods (Fire) representing the world of archetypes or origins; Cups (Water) representing the creative world; Swords (Air) representing the formative world; and Shields or Coins (Earth) representing the expressive world of matter. Here is how the "People of the Tarot" combine as a quarternity.

Letters of Name	Numbers	Tarot People
I H V H	1 2 3 4	F M S D
H I H V	2 1 4 3	M F D S
V H I H	3 4 1 2	S D F M
H V H I	4 3 2 1	D S M F

From these combinations it should be possible to choose something to represent almost any type of human worth considering. It was likely that early packs were limited to the forty basic plus sixteen people making fifty-six cards in all. No one knows for certain by whom or when the extra twenty-two for the Paths of the

Tree were introduced and termed the Trumps or Major Arcana, thus bringing the pack to seventy-eight cards. It is clear that whoever conceived this arrangement certainly knew what they were doing! It was supposed the Trumps were given their present numerical value purely for gambling reasons. That is to say, when games were played so as to make up specific sets of figures and you had a Trump in your hand of some needed value, you could produce it and win. This would account for Death (the unlucky) being numbered 13. The Fool (Zero) could be whatever number you needed (hence the Joker in modern packs), but of course you could only "play the Fool" once. Hence the saying "Don't play the Fool," meaning don't chuck your chances away.

So when you handle a Tarot pack, you are looking at the recorded remains of our inner tradition codified in symbols, and if you knew how to put them together and interpret them, you would find the essentials of our Western Inner Way all there to be understood and appreciated. It is only a question of going in and digging them out. The Tarots were not intentionally designed as symbols only meant to foretell the future, but they became popular when put to that use as their name indicates from its Hebrew roots, ThAR OTh, to mark out or delineate happenings to come. They were really meant to interpret the spiritual significance of any given situation so that you would know what to do if and when it happened.

Maybe you know a lot of Tarot attributions already, but it won't hurt you to hear of another system which is both interesting and reasonable. First of all, the suits were classified as four main factors encountered by most people in the course of their human lives, like this:

Gladness	Sadness	Earning	Learning
CUPS	SWORDS	COINS	RODS
Water	Air	Earth	Fire

These represented the Good (CUPS), the Bad (SWORDS), Obligations (COINS) and Opportunities (RODS). Then the Court (PEOPLE) cards were classified into four as:

Cups   = Tolerant
Swords = Exacting
Coins   = Industrious
Rods   = Sociable

The Kings and Queens were seniors of their type, and the Princes and Princesses were juniors, or those of less importance. So this covered all types of humans except the moronic, insane, or others one might exclude from normal society.

According to this system we react with life gladly or sadly, while we learn and earn our way through it. A fair enough assessment of average living. Linking these with the Tree-concepts, we shall get enough meanings to interpret a considerable amount of Tarot significance as follows:

Concept 1: Crown

CUPS	Gladness in Life	Heavenly hopes	Pleasure
COINS	Effort in Life	Willing work	Profit
RODS	Interest in Life	Alert attention	Purpose
SWORDS	Sadness in Life	Constraining care	Pain

Concept 2: Wisdom

CUPS	Glad Wisdom	Enjoyable experience	Happy choice
COINS	Earned Wisdom	Rewarding experience	Careful choice
RODS	Learned Wisdom	Grasp of intelligence	Determined decision
SWORDS	Sad Wisdom	Sadder but wiser	Difficult decision

Concept 3: Understanding

CUPS	Glad Understanding	Cheerful concord	Pleasing encounter
COINS	Earned Understanding	Deserved discovery	Dedicated design
RODS	Learned Understanding	Acquired knowledge	Widening outlook
SWORDS	Sad Understanding	Bitter experience	Unhappy affliction

Concept 4: Mercy

CUPS	Glad Mercy	Welcome benevolence	Kindly idea
COINS	Earned Mercy	Rightful rewards	Appreciated affluence
RODS	Learned Mercy	Thankful thoughts	Festive feelings
SWORDS	Sad Mercy	Suffering spared	Peace after pain

Concept 5: Severity

CUPS	Glad Severity	Sacrificed happiness	Lost illusions
COINS	Earned Severity	Distressing deprival	Poor prospects
RODS	Learned Severity	Salutary lesson	Taught through trouble
SWORDS	Sad Severity	Defeated schemes	Abandoned struggle

Concept 6: Beauty

CUPS	Glad Harmony	Blessed Beauty	Sweet sympathy
COINS	Earned Harmony	Patience repaid	Deserved delight
RODS	Learned Harmony	Cultivated control	Dignity displayed
SWORDS	Sad Harmony	Tranquility in trouble	Protection in peril

Concept 7: Victory

CUPS	Glad Victory	Alluring ambitions	Seeming success
COINS	Earned Victory	Patient progress	Worthwhile work
RODS	Learned Victory	Opposition overcome	Situationary skill
SWORDS	Sad Victory	Empty triumph	Dangers delayed

Concept 8: Honor, Glory

CUPS	Glad Honor	Search for satisfaction	Quest for Glory
COINS	Earned Honor	Honest achievement	Admirable activity
RODS	Learned Honor	Effort in transit	Good attempt
SWORDS	Sad Honor	Bounden duty	Precarious position

Concept 9: Foundation, Basis

CUPS	Glad Basis	Heart's Desire	Wish won
COINS	Earned Basis	Social success	Pleasure provided
RODS	Learned Basis	Lesson learned	Warning and worry
SWORDS	Sad Basis	Rueful regret	Fear of failure

Concept 10: Kingdom, World

CUPS	Glad World	Benign brightness	Happiness ahead
COINS	Earned World	Advantageous affairs	Prosperous proceedings
RODS	Learned World	Information gathered	Facts found
SWORDS	Sad World	Bloody betrayal	Ruin and wreckage

So there is another set of meanings for you to assimilate. It is useful to keep a "Tarot Book" with loose leaf pages so that the meanings of each card can be extended by thinking and meditation as you gain fresh ideas of them. Possibly the Court cards could be compared with real people you know personally or have heard of. The Trumps might be linked with actual incidents which have happened in your own life or other people's. In that way the cards could interpret living in terms familiar to you.

The meanings of the Tarots do not lie so much in their designs as in the images they evoke from your deep subconsciousness. To some extent they are like Rorschach blots which suggest different things to different people yet have specific lists of rational interpretations with each. For instance, if an intelligent person were asked to classify all the gladness of life into ten stages of importance and give a symbolic example of each, we should have that person's concept of the Tarot suit of Cups. The same could be done with the other suits, and the Trumps identified by twenty-two key ideas concerning life, death, fate, and the universe. In other words, *every thinking individual has a Tarot already in them*. The various packs are no more than different artists' conceptions of a common ideology relating humans with their shared state of existence from a Western viewpoint.

Theoretically, a Tarot pack need be no more than seventy-eight cards with nothing on them except identification figures. For instance, the symbol "C 10" should be enough by itself to evoke many ideas about the ten of Cups to a skilled Tarot reader. It is the mental images, impressions, and connected ideas in the consciousness of the interpreter which is the *real* Tarot. The actual symbol-cards are nothing more than call-up signs for those inner realities. Nevertheless, different packs suit different people, so the thing to do is find a pack which works best with your type of mentality and stick to it. Possibly one of the most evocative packs for modern Westerners is the Waite-Rider one drawn by Pamela Coleman-Smith. However, mention should be made of the Regardie & Wang pack based on Golden Dawn ideas. This pack is clinically clear and links in with most of the advanced studies covering human psychology. Some prefer the Case Tarot but it is a matter of finding which pack gets the most out of *you*. Maybe you will have to design your own before you will have one to satisfy your requirements. Meantime, if you like quick lists for reference, here is a "one card-one word" summary of the Minor Arcana which might be useful:

Court Cards

	RODS	CUPS	SWORDS	SHIELDS
King	Incisive	Magnanimous	Severe	Reliable
Queen	Capable	Affectionate	Serious	Practical
Knight	Astute	Idealistic	Aggressive	Ambitious
Page	Diligent	Cheerful	Troublesome	Amenable

Suits

	RODS	CUPS	SWORDS	SHIELDS
1	Fire	Water	Air	Earth
2	Choice	Liberty	Uncertainty	Change
3	Intention	Affection	Suffering	Effort
4	Celebration	Hope	Truce	Reward
5	Retribution	Grief	Defeat	Adversity
6	Balance	Happiness	Safety	Benefit
7	Ability	Amusement	Deceit	Attention
8	Expediency	Enthusiasm	Danger	Skill
9	Endurance	Satisfaction	Misfortune	Means
10	Responsibility	Friendship	Disaster	Opportunity

It is not proposed during this part of the present course to branch into techniques of using the Tarot for fortune-telling purposes, since there are so many existing works dealing with that topic alone and it is a separate study in itself. What is important is that you should see and understand its connection with the Tree of Life scheme and realize how to relate it therewith. On more advanced Path-workings, you might try confronting the Tarot symbol of the Path concerned as soon as the door is opened, and mention its name at the end of your induction narrative. Then you should be able to make a more complete picture of any Path on the Tree.

As an aid to Tarot learning, you may find it helps to make a set of blank cards and then fill in details on each of what the cards mean to you. For instance you could head a card 4S, for four of Swords, then list anything you know connected with it neatly underneath. The same with the Major Arcana. Head the card with the name of the Trump then add underneath details like Path attribution, Sphere contacts, letter symbol, and anything else you have space for. Handle and read these cards as often as convenient and *try to build you own picture in your mind* of what all these items suggest to you as connected units of consciousness. A Tarot you construct *in yourself* is worth a lot more than all you could buy in any shop. When you come to the Court cards, you might write them out as descriptions of people you think correspond with their meanings, and then perhaps find pictures in papers of people typifying them. Cut the faces out of unwanted papers and stick them on your specimen cards. That will help your visualizations.

Questions

1. In what way can you see a connection between the Tarot cards and the Paths of the Tree of Life?

2. Can you see the sense behind the latest layout of the Tarot in relation to the Tree?

3. What is the real purpose of the Tarot cards?

4. What do the four suits of the Tarot represent?

5. Do you see the reason for keeping a "Tarot Book" and how are you making entries into yours?

6. Discuss the Tarot Court cards.

7. Make a "one word-one card" summary of your own for the Tarot pack.

8. Which is your favorite Tarot pack and why?

9. Choose the ten most important sentences in this chapter.

10. Do you have your own conception of what an "ideal" Tarot pack should look like? If so, describe it.

•16•

Associations and Ideas

It may seem repetitious to you that we are still with the Paths of the Tree and their alphabetic Tarot associations, but it is highly important that you should conceptualize everything as clearly as possible, because these associations form the standard "consciousness code" through which the "Inner Wardens of the Western Way" communicate with those seeking to keep our secret spiritual tradition alive and active. With this code, you will be in touch with invisible yet intelligent agencies attempting to safeguard and stabilize the forces and future of West-working souls. Without it (unless you have access to alternatives) you will have to fall back on much less reliable means of making contact through your waking consciousness.

Remember that our "inner intelligences" can only communicate with those whose minds are working on the same wavelength. That is only reasonable. Most people respond best to their native language. Take any international airport. An announcement is made in English, and the English-speakers respond, in German and the Germans follow, because people have to be addressed in whatever word-system their thinking minds react with. Here we are dealing with a spiritual *lingua franca* common to souls seeking communication with each other along inner lines of life. This is the "language" which has been developed among

Western esoteric workers and "speaks from soul to soul" in order to maintain conscious continuity among those concerned with the survival of our Holy Heritage from one generation to another. If you are one of those souls (or want to be), then study on.

You should realize that you cannot very well comprehend the inner language of Western consciousness until each unit (or letter) of it can be activated through your own life-experience. Since this would take an impossibly long time in terms of incarnate living, the only other method is by simulated or *symbolic* experience by ritualized or otherwise mediated methods. For example, if you cannot go and live in a country physically, the next best thing is to read about it, study pictures and films, hear tapes of its spoken language, and so forth. That is, live it vicariously through other people's findings.

That is what you should be doing with your Path-working practices: seeking symbolized experiences of life when its influence is polarized by spiritual forces represented by the Sphere concepts of the Tree. In other words, in taking a short cut to something it may require many years and considerable resources to experience in the ordinary course of events. You intentionally create conditions in your own mind which would probably cost fortunes and take ages if they were external physical encounters. The accent here is on the word *create*. You have to *make* those inner experience for yourself with *real* effort. However visionary your impressions might be, the energy you constructed them with is definitely real, and that is what matters in the long run.

Now, to *create* an inner experience is not exactly an easy matter. If you think of it carefully, it is really a reversal of the process by which you experience life through outer activities. Say something happens to you. You encounter *people* in various *places*, where different *things* appear for one reason or another. Those externals cause changes in your consciousness which result in experience for you because they came from outside to inside, as it were. What you are asked to do here is this: *Originate your own experience from inside to outside yourself and let it become part of your life because you have authorized it to do so.*

Put as a bare statement that way, you could miss the vital significance of what it implies. Let us phrase the problem a bit differently. What percentage of your life experience reaches you from purely external factors originating on this earth outside of your control and apart from your sphere of influence? While it is impossible to give an exact figure, you will have to admit the percentage must be fairly high. All the media you encounter, the people you listen to, the books you read, the happenings of everyday living are external influences. Yes, you are reacting with these in many ways, mostly automatic, and that is largely a matter of conditioned reflexes. This is really not so much *your* life, but a life with which you are involved because of circumstances. Even if you were able to alter them entirely they would still *be* circumstances external or environmental to yourself. That is the same in principle even if changed in practice. Your life is not so much your own as you supposed, is it?

Then what is *your* life and what does it amount to? Strictly speaking, it is the existence you actually make for yourself *out* of yourself in much the same way as the fourfold process we dealt with in earlier lessons: by origination, creation, formation, and expression. From the *Ain Soph Aur* of your non-being, you have to originate an idea, then create it, formulate it, and lastly, express it, in that order. This is the life you *need* in order to exist as an authoritative entity instead of being content to drift along comfortably and in conformity as a sort of automatic answering machine to stimuli sent from everywhere else except your own seat of inner authority.

As an interesting illustration of what this means, you may have heard of what was called "dream deprival." That was a psychological experiment in which volunteer subjects were deliberately deprived of their dreaming faculties by means of drugs and electro-narcosis. Though they were allowed normal periods of unconsciousness, it was *dreamless* unconsciousness. After a while, their health began to suffer and their mental functioning deteriorated. They became irritable, unstable, and eventually the experiment was terminated because it had proved its point beyond argument. Our dreams are a very important part of our life experiences because we *invent them for ourselves on our own initiative.* They are manifestations of an inner existence we *need* in order to live with any sense of conscious continuity. Their quality and content may be poor, but their *actuality* is essential to our well-being as creatures capable of more than merely mortal levels of awareness.

If the suppression of dreams on the lowest levels of inner life produces negative effects on waking consciousness, how much more so does a *lack* of spiritual awareness from higher sources? People who are incapable of directing their lives in this world by any form of conscious control derived from superior states of existence are very sad specimens indeed. We may know quite well that the total direction of our earth lives by purely spiritual means is an impracticality, but what is needed is a *reasonably proportioned rulership* of our mortal manifestations by a spiritual directorate stemming from our "True Selves" which can make conscious contact with divinity, whatever we call that Supreme Spirit of Life.

That is the real value of meditative and mediative exercises such as Path-workings or other spiritual activities. They afford opportunities for conscious contacts between the inner identity and its incarnate end on this earth living for the sake of experience in these conditions of existence. Mystics of all kinds have known this for many centuries. It is only a question of contemporary methodology. Path-working happens to be a modern Western one in our era, therefore compatible with our ways of living. After all, if you want your incarnate life to become self-governed from the very top, as it were, you will have to open up practical pathways of communication from the bottom until one end of you manages to reach the other somewhere higher up the road. What is more, you will have to keep those paths open by sufficient usage of them, or they are liable to clog up and may prove difficult to re-negotiate.

The proper use of the Paths will create an inner life for yourself which is capable of acting on your outer life so that both will complement each other in a helpful way along your life path to *Perfect Peace Profound.* Your living should be a reciprocal affair between your inner and outer condition of consciousness which is determined by the percentage balance of each. You will live best with a relatively even distribution on either side or with a slight preponderance in favor of the inner direction. Just as shareholdings depend on more than fifty per cent for controlling interest, so does the tempro-spiritual directorship of lives on earth. Far too many humans allow their temporal interests to outvote the spiritual side of their lives, while some few are incapable of coping with temporal existence because they cannot convert its experiences to spiritual equivalents. This is where you have to learn how to hold both sides of your life in balance and ascend the Middle Way between them. Surely that is the only sensible thing to do.

Difficult? Of course it's difficult, at first. So is everything else worth doing in life. No reasonable person could expect otherwise. On the other hand, no reasonable person would deny that life should be a fair exchange between energies originating from outside and inside yourself. If you haven't been putting enough of yourself *out* to counterbalance what has been coming *in,* then it is time you began *living back at life* for a change. The only way you can do this is by making a spiritual life of your own initiative inside yourself and "beaming it back" into your ordinary areas of earthly living. You are probably doing this to some extent already, otherwise you would scarcely be reading these lessons, but it could help to study a systematic layout of inner life in alphabetical order according to the Holy Tree of Life.

As you have seen, the idea is to categorize the conscious eventualities of life under the headings of the Sphere-Paths, so that the spiritual content of living may be associated with all its material counterparts. As a result, you tend to live with increasingly conscious contacts operating through the spiritual side of yourself, and so both spiritual and material aspects of your existence tend to balance out beneficially. Then you realize your own relationship with each and live in harmony between them.

Your ordinary physical consciousness deals mostly with input received through your five senses, and this input can be broadly classifiable as coming from people, places, and things. Suppose we set up a framework of these factors correlated with the Paths. It will only be possible to outline this very roughly, but that should be enough to give you general ideas of how you can fill in details for yourself with individual workings and findings. Let us start by going back again to the vowels and life elements for the five senses, and then consider the Paths of the Tree as related with people, places and things. From those fundamentals you should find assembled quite a good stock of standards from which to construct your own symbolic rituals and meditations sufficiently for all the inner consciousness you will need to maintain touch with our secret spiritual tradition of the west.

A: The Earth, Life-Element

Touch: Anything imparting feelings of weight and solidity. Earth itself, heavy stones. A thick heavy cloak with hood to match. Roughness, coolness.

Taste: Fresh raw mushrooms, or whatever stimulates Earth ideas. Roots of some kind maybe.

Smell: New dug earth if possible. Farm and field smells. Heavy incense such as poppy or dittany.

Hearing: Silence. Slow, dragging, thudding sounds. Cavernous echos. Very deep slow drumbeats and low notes. Stones being struck with other stones. Digging noises.

Sight: Darkness and very dim lighting without visible sources. Caves or vaults. Tunnels or graves, symbols purely connected with earth. Shovels. The letter A suitably displayed. Earth colors like dark brown. Nighttime, without stars.

Action: Slow, regular-rhythm shuffle-stamp dancing. Deep and low chanting. Invocation of Earth-Mother. Prostrations. Accentuation of "Ah" sonics. Silent meditation. Mimetics of digging, planting, and cultivation. Striking staff on earth. Burying talismans. Lying listening with ear to earth or against standing stone. Setting up standing stone.

E: The Air, Life-Element.

Touch: Anything very light and insubstantial. Loose, delicate, and very free gauzy clothing. Feathery ornamentation. Feel of breeze blowing with varying intensity.

Taste: Effervescent and "fresh flavors." Aerated drinks like soda-water or sherbet.

Smell: Any fresh natural breeze-borne scent or incense suggesting the same. Pine forest, meadows, or flower-perfumes.

Hearing: Rushing wind across moors or through trees. Whistles and all wind-instruments suitably orchestrated. Aeolian harps. Birdsong, especially dawn-chorus.

Sight: Sky-blue colors. Symbols of Air. Birds in flight. The letter E shown in appropriate style and colors. Dawn or morning light. Sunrise effects.

Action: Graceful "flying" dance motions imitative of birds. Whistling in a high key. Accentuation of "Eeee" sonics. Invocation of Air-archetypes. Leaping and jumping. Swordwhirling exercises. Archery. Fanning or winnowing. Imitation of birdcalls. Scattering flower-petals, horn blowing.

I: The Fire, Life-Element

Touch: Warm-feeling yet light garments. Place must be well-heated. Dryness and sweating encouraged. Air can circulate but it must be hot air *not* steam. Nudity permissible, if high temperatures employed. All precautions against fire-risks or burning injuries to be taken.

Taste: Hot spices, curries, ginger wine or hot drinks. Peppermint.

Smell: Woodsmoke. Pleasant cooking or roasting smells. Frankincense.

Hearing: Crackling flames. Any "Fire" music especially orchestrated for strings.

Sight: Bright lighting, wavering for "Fire" effect. Smoke clouds. Symbols for Fire. Brilliant letter I displayed like flame. Candles, lamps, full noon illumination, and colors to match, especially yellow. Solar glare.

Action: Swaying, semi-static dancing varying from "brisk flame" to "glowing ember" effects. Invocations of Fire-archetypes. Accentuation of "I" theme. Torchlight processions. Lighting of candles or lamps and incense offered. Fireworks ignited.

Food cooked. Great care must be taken at all times to emphasize *only* the beneficial aspects of Fire to humans.

O: The Water, Life-Element

Touch: Theoretically should be water, but practical difficulties impose problems. A compromise might be made with a basin of water in which hands are dipped and face laved. Enthusiasts might swim in pool or dance in rain with wet garments. Anything reasonable to convey water ideas.

Taste: Plain water, preferably from a spring or uncontaminated source apart from household supply. *Make sure it is fit to drink first.*

Smell: Seaside. Seaweed and ozone. Lily perfume or similar scent.

Hearing: All water-sounds and appropriate orchestrations. Rain pattering. Sistrum shaking. Splashings. Rivers and waterfalls.

Sight: Green-blue lighting, wave effects. The letter O shown as water symbol. All Water signs. Evening illumination. Sea-sunset. Fishes or dolphins. Underwater scenery.

Action: Swimming dance-movements, including floating. Invocation of Water-archetypes, accentuation of the "Oh" sonics. Meditation while rocking gently as if moved by waves or in boat. Washing hands or paddling with feet in water. Lustrating with Cup. Watering plants.

U: The Truth, Life-Element

Touch: Normal sensation of comfortable vesture at pleasant temperature. Nothing restrictive or awkward. Everything smooth and easy.

Taste: Changes from bland through sharp, hot, bitter, sweet, etc, and finishes with something leaving a taste of satisfaction to suit individual concerned.

Smell: Any scent that stimulates sense of investigation or encourages the mind to seek its source.

Hearing: Natural background of combined effects. Wind, sea, shingle, and beach-fire, plus indeterminate sounds of human

conversation. Organ music. Chanting. Orchestral composi-
tions. Animal sounds.

Sight: Daylight effects and colors of all sorts. Symbols of all
elements. Letter U centrally or in motion anywhere.
All details to be very sharp and clear.

Action: Comprehensive. Walk, run, dance, hop, stand, sit or lie.
Move as inspired. Invoke universal element of Truth in life
under whichever archetype this is recognized. Exercise
with Cord. Tie and loosen knots.

Note that all these connections are as near "natural" as
possible, insofar as no humans or artifacts apart from basic ritual
instruments are introduced, and consciousness is kept to sensations
or "feelings" rather than intellectual levels. The accent is on "soul"
more than mind. We shall encounter mental approaches to inner life
with the Paths next. These cover the people, places and things
category of consciousness.

Bear in mind that the first four Paths of the Tree (B, C, D,
F) connect with the Supernal concepts above the Abyss. They are
concerned with pure consciousness in three distinct streams. If we
consider consciousness as a spectrum of energy, B would be the top
end, C the bottom, D the middle, and F as a link between top and
bottom. They are best color-coded by B being silver for the white
Pillar side of the Tree, C being bronze for the black Pillar, and D
being pure gold for the Middle Pillar. Remember the symbolism:
"Between the two extremes of life, always choose the golden mean
in the center." F is half silver, half bronze. Remember that Sphere 1,
the Crown, is brilliant white, Sphere 2, Wisdom, light grey, and
Sphere 3, Understanding, very dark grey indeed. It is a mistake to
show 3 as black. Black only occurs at the very bottom of the Tree as
the winter tint in Sphere 10, where it balances the brilliancy of
Sphere 1 very nicely. The real colors of the Tree only appear
beneath the Abyss, where silver becomes blue, bronze becomes red,
and gold becomes yellow.

It is good to try to make your concepts above the Abyss
relatively outside the limitations of human history insofar as you
can. That is to say, details like costume, accessories, and sonic

effects should be as timeless and "otherworldy" as you can manage without reducing them to science fiction levels. The lower down the Tree you get the more contemporary you may become. Nor should you forget your own appearance and personification. If you like you can change this to suit every Sphere and Path, or keep it just vague and general. This is an important consideration. You may not be able to do much with your physical body, but in your spiritual selfhood you can look the way you like *within reason,* though you must specify *why* you need to adopt any particular appearance. For instance, it is wrong to think: "I wonder what I should be like as such-and-such? I'll try it and see." The correct approach is: "In order to fully appreciate such-and-such an experience, I need to view it through the consciousness of this particular type of being. I will therefore endeavor to confine myself thereto." Then alter your outlook accordingly. You have to change your view from *inside.* There is nothing to be gained by masking your external looks and remaining the same behind them.

Unless you are fairly good at character acting, it is not really advisable to try "shape-shifting" to a great extent when exploring inner life through the Tree system or any other magical approach to existence. You may have read of this practice in fairy tales and especially Celtic legends when people changed themselves from one creature into another in rapid succession, or incarnated as a different being in each life. This was indeed regarded as a magical practice, but was not meant to be taken literally. What it meant was they were supposed to change their *consciousness* in attempts to face life from entirely different angles, even to something other than human. It was a sort of "method acting" in old times, and it is still a very valuable exercise in mind control and creative imagination, as well as being a poetic form of art. It is probably best to begin your Pathworking investigations in your own present person, and then you can graduate to more exotic characterizations as you gain expertise.

Now we are going to consider a list of "possibles" for each Path which you might come into contact with as you go down the Tree, Path by Path. There will not be room for all in this lesson, but we might as well start now. The important thing is that you should add your own findings to each Path but *know why* in each case. It is not enough to "put something on a Path" because you may "have a feeling" about it or like the look of it being there. You must know (or believe you know) just *why* the association is justified before you finally classify anything, and even then, if you subsequently find it should be moved, *move* the thing once you discover *why*. Remember this is *your* Life-Tree you are making—not anybody else's. All you need to know is why you believe that particular person, place or thing should be where you intend to put it. Let us begin with:

Path B: Crown—Wisdom

People: Here they are likely to be Father figures and archetypes of the all-wise kind, seniors and superiors of a very high order, those you automatically know are a long way ahead of you on the path of life, yet in no sense do they make you feel inferior. They are only ahead of you in time and experience, and are trying to help you make your own way ahead, and hoping you will avoid the mistakes they made when they were in the present position. They are no mere instructors, but actual *imparters* of Wisdom by conscious contact alone. They do not so much look ancient as ageless, and you feel you can trust them with perfect confidence.

Places: Very probably magnificent vistas on a grand scale as if from mountain tops. Well lit and sharply clear. The phallic symbol of a mountain peak may be seen. There could be a Temple with nine Pillars supporting its cupola, since this is 10-1 on the descending Tree. Hence the "Nine Pillars of Wisdom." Or two upright monoliths with a lintel across them as at Stonehenge, because this is the 1 + 2 path. There is always a sense of altitude and purity here. Another impression is sometimes a mountain monastery or retreat of "Masters in the Mysteries" where the Ancient Wisdom is safeguarded from worldly desecration and passed on from one generation of teachers to another. The topmost turret-chamber of the Grail Castle would be appropriate here. An odd feature of this Path is that the traveller never seems to be alone yet cannot see his immediate companion whom he senses as slightly behind or above him.

Things: It is seldom wise to overburden the Supernal Paths in particular with a plethora of attributed articles. It is better to let things make their own appearance than question their appositeness. Scrolls of Wisdom would certainly apply here, a common sort being the Scroll of the Law presented as a single roll for the sake of phallic Father-significance. The Grail Hallow of the Lance is also valid for the same reason. So is the Torch of Wisdom illuminating the doubtful passages of life. There is a possibility you may find yourself personifying the Tarot symbol of the Hierophant or be conscious of approaching such a figure with reverence. There are many other symbols associated with pure spirit and the principle of Wisdom.

Path C: Crown—Understanding

People: Here we find Mother figures from every pantheon, though in sympathetic and Understanding aspects. The Sophia ideal. People on this Path may seem very quiet and serious, and there is not much prospect of actual laughter, though there could be mysterious and meaningful smiles. There is sometimes a somber note here and there as warnings are given or admonitions made, yet there is never oppressive sadness or grief. Only thoughtful and "pregnant" silence accompanied by suitable gestures, much as a mother would control children firmly but very quietly. People on the whole are darkly clothed with only occasional glints of ornamentation like stars at night.

Places: Often nocturnal or heavily shaded backgrounds. Soft light and dignified surroundings. Could be a seashore with a very calm sea or simply the ocean alone. Womb conditions symbolized. A comfortable chamber with soft cushiony chairs and thick deep carpet to muffle footfalls, nothing rushed or hurried, all very orderly and controlled. Environments suggestive of timelessness, such as a sheltered hermitage. Sometimes dark pools of water reflecting a spot of light will appear, or deep wells with a star reflected therein. Flat polished stones, usually deep grey. Occasionally a cavern or temple. The night vigil in the Grail Chapel.

Things: Womb symbols of every sort. The Grail-Hallow of the Cup. The Cauldron of inspiration. Sanctuary lamps with red glass. The female breast and emblems thereof. An Ark as a chest to contain the phallic Scroll of the Law from Path B. An ibis or crane is sometimes seen standing in water here, because it suggests contemplation while patiently waiting to catch a fish. This symbolizes finding food from the ocean of thought, hence a Fisherman image could belong with this Path. No Path is exclusively male or female. It is simply a question of proportional relationship between the sexes. The Hermit figure here could be either, and there is often a sensation of being wrapped in a heavy hooded cloak as a womb-suggestion.

Path D: Crown—Beauty

People: This Path crosses the Abyss so the only sort of beings we are likely to encounter here as it passes the Abyss by the Middle Way of Knowledge (Daath) are radiantly beautiful souls much too bright for us to identify, but we realize somehow that they are Avatar figures passing in and out of incarnation for the sake of human salvation. Christians might sense a "Christ presence" here. We might also meet with advanced humans of transcendent appearance radiating a type of energy unknown on earth producing a harmonious happiness so intense it can be quite unbearable to ordinary mortals. Here, people appear as they are in their highest spiritual form closest to absorption in the Absolute. Travellers on this Path may be aware of a bittersweet sadness because of a comparison between their state and that of the others thereon.

Places: There are really no standards to describe situations on this Path. They might be likened to the most wonderful environments imaginable to the Pathworker and extrapolated from these. Every human idea of "Heaven" applies. There is a brilliance and intensity about everything here which can only be termed a condition of pristine purity and near perfection.

Things: These too are difficult here, but generally whatever might be associated with harmonious and perfectly poised being. Musical instruments capable of the most magnificent sonics. We have to remember the Apollo connection here as patron of music and medicine. Since no disease can cross the Abyss, all healing aspects have to be kept to the lower end of the Path. Splendid jewelry and gold ornamentation are seen here. This is the Path where all the visions of "Golden Gates," and apocalyptic notions of "Cities of God" appear, and the "Grail in Glory" is seen surrounded by its Hallows and supported by all its Champions.

We shall carry on with the Path association ideas in the next Chapter. Meanwhile you should be making out your own ideas of what ought to go on the Tree. Never mind if they disagree with ours or anyone else's. It is *your* Tree which you are making, but do remember there has to be a good and sufficient reason why everything is where you put it. That is the important part of the process. Making reasonable and rational relationships with all the various aspects of your consciousness so that everything you are aware of aligns with the "Plan of Perfection" as outlined by the Holy Tree of Life.

Always bear in mind the aim of this work you are doing with the Tree: to align *every part* of your consciousness, whether objective or otherwise, to focus on your own ultimate identity in union with divinity, not just a scattered thought here and there, but *all* of yourself on every level of existence. Think of the analogy of a huge airliner with several hundred passengers and crew aboard. When the small auto-control compass is set to a bearing, the entire ship and every soul on it is pointing in the same direction relative to this world regardless of which way they are facing on board. So should you set your Tree that every bit of you is pointing the same way inwardly no matter how you are angled otherwise. The Tree *is* a compass in one important sense. Wherever you are in this world it will always indicate the same direction—the most direct line between you and divinity.

Questions

1. Define "consciousness-code."
2. How do you create an inner experience?
3. Why are our dreams important to us?
4. Make up a list of your own life-element associations.
5. How do the colors of the Tree change across the Abyss?
6. What people and places would you associate with Path 9?
7. Write an experience of any Path above the Abyss.
8. How do you "live back at life"?
9. Choose the seven most important sentences in this chapter.
10. If you found yourself suddenly on any Path, how would you tell which it was?

·17·

Paths, People and Places

It is our inner lives which make our outer
lives worth living. Our outer lives have the value of experiences
they contribute to inner living which enables this to become more
effective. In other words, we normally live between two worlds,
one the purely physical and material existence of so-called
"civilized" humanity, and the other an internal state of consciousness wherein we are aware of an existence apart from this world in
different, though inter-related dimensions of being. Ideally, these
conditions of consciousness should harmonize with each other and
between them lead to better living in both. As we know very well,
this is seldom the case, and that is why we are working along these
present lines of practice.

With oriental types of mystical practice, the accent is on
rejection of; our material world as being inferior, "illusory," and
misleading; therefore humans should concentrate on the "high, pure,
spiritual" factors of life alone for the salvation of any soul. The
tendency is to denigrate materialism as unworthy of notice by a
truly spiritual entity entrapped in a mortal body. In Western eyes,
this attitude may look ultra-idealistic, but it does seem impractical
for the average human in the midst of incarnate problems
attempting to cope with the complexities of our "civilization"

while attempting to "balance the books" between inner and outer living. We who look at inner life with somewhat awakened sight are just as anxious to live beyond the boundaries of human bodies as the highest Himalayan sage on earth. However, we believe this to be a process of evolution and progression which cannot be accomplished simply by the denial of mundane necessities and a refusal to accept responsibility for involvement with incarnate affairs.

On the other hand, we cannot concur with the ultra-materialist who says dogmatically: "Your bodily life is the only real one you will have. Your so-called inner life is nothing but your imaginative fancy, wishful thinking, and a load of rubbish anyway. Forget it and don't bother with anything beyond your bodily being." Insofar as *anything* is "real," both your outer and inner connections with living consciousness are real in their respective ways. What matters most is your ability to relate these rightly with each other and direct yourself on the path to peace between them. That is why the Western system of esoteric working is not purely meditating on some vague and nebulous "nirvana," but includes active inner living along paths of life which can only be pursued by expenditure of spiritual energy in terms of this world transmuted into inner experience. We believe in "spiritualizing matter" to the equivalent degree with which we "materialize spirit" through one and the same life action in opposite directions. Hence our use of the hexagram symbol and the meaning of our Hermetic adage: "As Above, so Below."

That is why the inner living of the Path associations we are following does *not* include the worst and nastiest things which can be encountered in this world, such as brutalities, sicknessess, wars, injustices, malice, and all the myriad evils and wrongs which everyone knows exist on earth as behaviors among human and other creatures. Oh yes, they exist all right, but do you want them to exist in *you*? If so, then put them in by all means, providing you don't expect others to share them with you. On the other hand, if you hope they might diminish and eventually disappear from this world altogether, then start excluding them from *your* inner being *now*. You will not be denying their "reality," no one with the least powers of observation can do that, but you will be denying them access to your inner life where only *you* hold the admitting key. Because they may happen in your outer experience is no reason why they should be allowed inside you.

Let us take up the threads of where we left off with the Paths and see how inner life lower down the Tree is likely to be encountered. We have to start with the last of the Supernals on the other side of the Abyss. After that, we begin our "back to earth" descent.

Path F: Wisdom—Understanding

People: Mixed male and female figures of great ability and acumen. They are gifted with exceptional accuracy in summing up life situations on all levels. They are mostly people of mature appearance with an authoritative nature giving complete confidence in their powers of perception, intuition, and insight. You realize at a glance they can be trusted. It is here on the Tree that we have to make "life-altering" decisions at very deep levels, and this is where to meet Inner Guides who can help us formulate them.

Places: Halls of Judgement. Anywhere that calm deliberation is possible. Courts presided over by wise and understanding judges. Conference rooms. Consulting chambers. The Grail Castle chapter house. Outdoors in any favorable environment for furthering the purpose of this Path. Possibly a pleasant garden or impressive vistas with a view of sea and mountains.

Things: Anything calculated to aid faculties of judgement. Reference books, instruments, often with male-female symbolism such as the phallic pen and the feminine inkwell, or the masculine seal being impressed on virgin parchment or wax. Judgement scales with level pans holding a man and a woman or other sex symbols. Everything here suggests combinations of consciousness between sexes resulting in correct courses of action and procedure. Spiritual sex—equality is an essential keynote of this Path.

Path G: Wisdom—Mercy

People: This Path is another Abyss-crosser by what is sometimes called the "Royal Way" to birth, because souls are sent in to learn of life how to govern themselves. So here we meet with magnanimous monarchs and rightful rulers. Archetype figures showing us how to control and direct ourselves by the rules of Wisdom and Mercy. There is a senior masculine preponderance here, and Father figures are not uncommon. They are all kindly and compassionate.

Places: Throne rooms. The Round Table scene with King and his court around him. The "Good King Wenceslas" story. Almost any setting showing a kindly King being wisely generous to his subjects. There could well be a lot of laughter and happiness on this Path. Outdoor events might be the announcement of an amnesty or public proclamation of some benefit. Crowds and heralds would fit in here, and so would reprieves or remissions of punishments.

Things: Symbols of Wisdom and Mercy. Sheathed swords, open purses. Royal regalias such as scepters and orbs, but not crowns since these associate with sphere 1. Rulers seen here should wear circlets or caps of maintenance only. A Royal birth would be appropriate here, with peals of bells in celebration.

Path H: Wisdom—Beauty

People: Another Abyss-crossing Path, this time the "Angelic Gateway" by which guiding spirits are supposed to be sent from Heaven Earthwards to help struggling humans. So here we encounter "Guardian Angel" types which counsel reason and restraint against rash or hasty behavior. The "faithful friend" who always seems available in times of trouble or difficulty. Dependable and reliable companions of either sex whom we consider trustworthy. Whoever shows the beauty of Wisdom, and how to find this in balanced temperate living.

Places: Any scene suitable for thinking things out or talking them over. Possibly a library, cloisters, or a lovely garden, especially that of the Grail Castle. There is always a bright and hopeful atmosphere and the sun shines pleasingly without too much heat.

Things: Symbols of moderation and tolerance. A calming hand over a clenched fist or to prevent a weapon being drawn. Water in wine, a storm abating, hot iron being tempered. Masonic trowel smoothing rough plaster. Creases being flattened out. Shaken poise restored. Rocking Pillars steadied. Ragged rhythm made regular, or discord turned to harmony.

Path J: Understanding—Severity

People: This Path is an Abyss-crosser by the "Gate of Death." Possibly an "Angel of Death" figure might be seen in some very kindly guise such as a "Dark Mother" who hushes us to sleep on her breast. She might wear a deep grey cloak lined with very dark red. Here we might meet heros who gave their lives to save others, those who understand death and try and help others through its difficult gateways. We might also meet some of those who supervise the process of purification by directing rubbish down the Abyss for disintegrative reconstitution while the worthwhile re-mainder is sent on to the Supernals for incorporation into divine identity. The cleanliness of Cosmos depends a lot on its "Sanitation Department" and this is one Path where the workers are always fully employed.

Places: The dangerous Bridge before the Grail Castle, or the "Siege Perilous." Avenues of tall cypresses. The edge of the Abyss. Elysian fields. A dark ocean meeting a sky of equal color imperceptibly. Anything to suggest serious thought and facing change or a journey into the unknown. A waiting room for some very important life-altering interview. On the lower part of the Path only, perhaps deathbeds, or scenes associated with necessary severity for the sake of restoring a state of ruin.

Things: Symbols of death and change. Hourglass and scythes etc, but must include symbols of resurrection too. Christians might see an Easter tomb here, or just an empty cross. Any actual death scenes should be seen as *past* experiences. Nothing here is to be viewed as unhappy in the least, only needful and entirely necessary.

Path K: Understanding—Beauty

People: This is the last Abyss-crossing Path by the "Gate of Fate." Here are encountered those whose lives are to some degree "fated" from pre-birth causes. They often alternate between serious and sunny outlooks, and nearly always have a sense of "mission." They are deeply concerned with some major and particular purpose behind their lives, and have a strong devotion to "duty" on behalf of their religions, countries, families, or wherever their loyalties lie. They will help you find yours if you ask them.

Places: Wherever some particular cause for the advancement of humanity towards divinity is being upheld. Possibly a temple, or could be a laboratory dedicated to research of humanitarian benefit. Perhaps a vessel cruising through days and nights on a questing voyage. Many places are possible providing they do not contradict the purpose of this Path.

Things: Here is a Solar-Saturnine conjunction, gold cased in lead. Valuables in dull and protective packaging. Portia's lead casket. Dark cloaks with gold linings, silver lined clouds. Most alchemical symbology and items suggesting transmutation of base human nature into pure spiritual gold. Remember screening effect of lead on radiations harmful to human lives. Note also significance of Masonic symbolism of plumbline (Hanged Man Tarot Trump) for ensuring uprightness and truth.

Path L: Mercy—Severity

People: Those concerned with the process of Justice in the sense of righting wrongs. Knights of the Holy Grail. Peace-keeping controllers of human conduct. Surgeons and doctors trying to compensate for ravages of sickness and injuries. Defenders of the weak and helpless.

Places: Justice Hall of the Grail Castle. Courts of Justice anywhere, providing the element of compensation is always present. Opposite places of action which must always be seen in pairs. Deserts and gardens for instance. Any contrasting locations varying between pain and pleasure, but the result must always be peace.

Things: Scales of Justice and blunt Sword thereof. Thunderbolt and Cornucopia. Anything bittersweet. Fire and Water. Iron and Tin. Salt and sugar. Sharp and sweet scents like ammonia and cedar. Any complementary opposite.

Path M: Mercy—Beauty

People: Those with quiet strength which prevails against all evil in the end. People who overcome opposition by sheer endurance and fortitude. The "strong, silent types" who make no boasts but just perform almost incredible feats of "effortless energy" with slight smiles at your astonishment. They never hurt anybody or anything; they only restrain violence with compassion.

Places: Wherever we meet instances of patient and peaceful applications of power for performance of purpose. That covers an enormous area. Examples could be construction sites, dams, power houses, engine rooms, waterfalls and so on. Intellectually this might be studies, reading rooms, meditation chambers, oratories, anywhere allowing concentrations of conscious energy.

Things: Tin and gold ornamentation. Could be motors or solar-power plants (not nuclear). The Masonic ashlar and hoist. Protective clothing apart from military armor. Gymnastic or physical training equipment. The rod as a lever. Stores and provisions intended for charitable purposes. Some new form of energy not yet known on earth.

Path N: Mercy—Victory

People: Rulers of their feelings and emotional impulses. No puritans or prudes, but sensible souls who do not let their emotions run away with them. Here we meet artists, musicians, writers, dramatists, and others concerned with affairs of heart and soul. Especially those who do so in a grand or regal manner.

Places: Studios, theaters, gardens, temples, places of pageantry for the sake of joy and emotional expression under controlled circumstances. Sports stadiums sometimes. Could also be love-making environments. Anywhere a sense of cultural achievement seems possible.

Things: Whatever supplies a feeling of comfort and satisfaction in living. Nice clothes. Good furniture, pictures, sculptures, well tended gardens. Pleasant food and drink. Laughter and welcome company. Luxury items with aesthetic rather than practical value.

Path P: Severity—Beauty

People: Here we meet those that may seem a curse to others they disturb, but may be necessary to the ecology of existence. Sometimes they could be revolutionaries against utterly corrupt and oppressive regimes which resist all other attempts at reformation. They are demolitionists, yet never wreckers simply for the sake of destruction. Exposers of evil. Attackers of untruth. Could be those that have to force themselves out of bad habits or harmful situations. Grail Knights in action.

Places: Wherever circumstances demanding drastic reactions might apply. A fire to be extinguished for instance, or a dangerous ruin to blow up. An undersea wreck to be cleared by blasting. Tangle of weeds to be burned out. Intellectual equivalents of these. Surgical removal of growths. Burning off fields.

Things: Iron and gold. Sharp swords or scalpels. Antiseptics. Cauteries. Excavators. All rubbish-clearing equipment. Disinfectants and chemical cleaners. Bonfires. Lightning-flashes. Anything connected with destroying debris in order to restore harmony and beauty which became defaced or damaged.

Path Q: Severity—Glory

People: What Carl Jung would have called "Trickster" figures. The sort who in old time initiations would have acted as testers of character by contrived situations meant to fool candidates if possible. Yet they always had to provide clues to arouse suspicion leading to discovery of truth later. They were sometimes called "provokers of perception." Their real job is alerting you to frauds, lies, and deceptions you are so likely to meet with in life.

Places: Could be anywhere at all where trying and deceptive circumstances might be encountered. Homes, offices, public places, everywhere humans are likely to impose on or deceive each other. Ancient initiation caverns. Old-time Masonic Lodges. Universities. Political gatherings. There is almost no end of likelihoods on this Path.

Things: Anything of false appearance. Artificial limbs, teeth, etc. Masks, make-up, forged papers and money. Practical jokes. Unfulfilled promises. Blind alleys. Bogus schemes. Fake jewelry. Inaccurate instruments. Anything to annoy and hinder yet not seriously hurt.

Path R: Beauty—Victory

People: Lover-archetypes from Adam and Eve down to Abelard and Heloise. Beautiful and lovely beings rejoicing in their attachment to each other, and happy if you can emulate their example. Also those who truly love life in one form or another. Musicians, dancers, and those loving in the Orphic Tradition. Romanticists.

Places: Beautiful gardens and parks. Lagoons and soft sandy beaches. This is another luxury path, so everything should be seen as pleasingly as possible. Richly furnished bedrooms and other apartments. Art galleries, concert halls, anywhere that one might imagine being accompanied by a beloved life-partner. A first-class restaurant, maybe. A medieval court of love.

Things: Gold and copper. Lamps and girdles. Palm branches. Anything associated with romantic settings. Playgrounds. Soft and beautiful clothing of a sensuous nature. Jewels. Perfumes. Intimate whispers. Accessories of the amatory arts. Aphrodisiacs.

Path S: Beauty—Glory

People: Seekers of intelligence. Questers of the Grail. Agents of inner authorities. Time-space travellers. Telepaths. All concerned with communications. Detectives. Transport specialists. Possibly telekineticists. A few Qabalists engaged on "The Work of the Chariot."

Places: Too varied to specify. Might be too blurred to focus properly, but could be impressions of vehicle interiors. Traffic terminals. Roads, rails, vapor trails in sky. Anything suggestive of travel and motivated movements.

Things: Gold and mercury. Alchemical gear. Scientific scenes, spacecraft, flying carpets, golden horses with wings, chariots. All forms of transport. Balloons, flying gear, kites. Could be sub-aqua too. Anything to do with mind-mobility and questing.

Path T: Beauty—Foundation

People: Avatars and supersouls seeming to link humanity and divinity by sacrifice of self-interests. A few ordinary humans attempting the way of At-One-Ment and offering themselves as oblations for the sake of fellow human-beings.

Places: There is certainly a sense of environment, but as a condition rather than an actual location of any kind. It is probably best to work with the idea of a Heaven-state on sub-eternal levels. A sort of paradisical place of limited extensions between incarnations. Everything is very bright here and strongly sunlit.

Things: Gold and silver ornamentation, topaz and yellow jewelry, solar and lunar discs. Highly polished brass. Ritual breast-plates. Sundials. Burning glasses.

Path V: Victory—Glory

People: All kinds of folk taking chances with life. Rich and poor changing places. alternating gladness and sadness everywhere. Show-biz people of every kind, witty and winsome types in contrast and combination. Gamblers, fortune-tellers. Hermes being patron of thieves, and Aphrodite of prostitutes could produce odd yet interesting characters on this Path.

Places: Wherever fortunes change. Stockmarkets, racetracks, etc. Also wherever love life may alter drastically, and that is open to wide interpretation. Circumstances have to fit the place as indicated.

Things: Anything associated with chance. Dice, cards, roulette, lottery tickets. Race horses, bonds or shares. All symbols of love and luck such as horseshoes, true-lovers-knots, wedding rings, and so forth.

Path W: Victory—Foundation

People: Nuns, nurses, priestesses, devotees to religion or beliefs. Introspective types. Religious artists and designers. Embroiderers, flower arrangers, idealistic dreamers.

Places: Temples, cathedrals, cloisters, chapels and oratories. Nurseries or institutions administered by females which care for disadvantaged humans or animals. Gardens or natural scenery in quiet surroundings very likely. So is moonlight reflected from peaceful pools or lakes.

Things: Copper and silver ornaments. Pleasing devotional objects such as illuminated prayer books, embroidery, rosaries. Rich vestments and soft fabrics. Artwork of all religious kinds. Childrens' toys, especially those of nursery types. Flowers and potted plants. Pet animals.

Path X: Victory—Kingdom

People: Those we love, admire, or want to know. Companionable folk of an ordinary kind in whose company we can feel happy and relaxed. Good friends and nice neighbors.

Perhaps not on a permanent basis, but definitely welcome as associates during an incarnation. Nice, normal fellow-humans.

Places: Anywhere that ordinary happy relationships between humans may be made. Pleasure places, social scenes, outdoors, yet nowhere evoking sad or bitter feelings. Try to make a pleasing place of your inner world, while remaining realistic enough to admit that it cannot very well be perfect on these lower levels. Here are familiar environs like homes, workplaces, shops, entertainment areas, yet having something a little "special" about each.

Things: Anything in keeping with human living with friendly and family conditions. Home gear of all kinds. Clothes, fashions, amusements, hobbies, the sort of things humans of your own kind employ during earth life.

Path Y: Glory—Foundation

People: Ceremonialists of all sorts. Priests, magicians, members of occult or secret "orders." Freemasons. Also psychiatrists, doctors, actors, scientists, all brilliant thinkers or speakers. Writers of occult and fantasy literature. Composers of classical music connected with such themes. Those associated with the inner arts.

Places: Occult temples, lodges, etc. stages, consulting rooms, laboratories. Anywhere action is going on concerning the mindworkings or investigation of psychic happenings.

Things: Hermetic apparatus or magical equipment. Ceremonial robes or lodge regalia. Ritual or scientific books. Electrical gear. Musical or mathematical instruments.

Path Z: Glory—Kingdom

People: Average mortals of all types, especially those aiming for some kind of distinction in life. Business people, commercial and technical or agriculturally minded folk who are not very spiritual at all. They are more interested in material living, but they seem to have an instinct they feel may be more foolish which inclines them to wonder if there is something more to Life than just jobs and social activities.

Places: Anywhere in this world ordinary people live, work, play and exist from cradle to grave. Perhaps especially in odd situations which evoke feelings of wonder and speculation on possibilities of life beyond bodily boundaries. Circumstances which afterwards make people admit: "I felt a bit of a fool."

Things: Just about everything we come across in this world, but particularly things which unexpectedly or even awkwardly distract attention from material matters towards higher possibilities. For instance a loose page from a Bible found while sweeping a factory floor. Oddities and incongruities which tend to awaken dormant wonderings about life outside this world.

Path Th: Foundation—Kingdom

People: Religious, mystical, and idealistic enthusiasts of all kinds. Occultists and followers of all creeds however peculiar. Most of them "have a go" at this Path at some time in their lives and then fall to one side or other of the Tree. In our times, Neo-Pagans, Spiritualists, Christians, and virtually everyone looking for even a glimmer of reflected light above earthly levels of living.

Places: Churches, temples, lodges, or wherever people are likely to look for spiritual guidance away from this world. Somewhere, they are seeking a start, however shaky, up the ladder leading towards light. Nothing may seem very clear or definite here, but at least it seems better than sitting on the ground and grumbling.

Things: Any kind of artifact connected with the slightest interest in some sort of spiritual existence. Mirrors, crystals, divining pendulums, the whole of the "Outer Court" in fact, with all its toys, trappings, and contrivances. Whatever you might expect to find at the bottom rung of the Ladder or the very foot of the Tree.

262 • CONCEPTS OF QABALAH

Questions

1. Make up a list of people and places for Path R.
2. How do you keep a balance between material and spiritual life?
3. Differentiate between Eastern and Western life approaches.
4. Arrange an excursion along Path Y.
5. Do you enjoy Pathworking? Why?
6. What is your main objective in Pathworking?
7. Describe a journey along Path Q.
8. Do you encounter anything that was not previously known in your Pathworkings? If so, what are they?
9. Choose the nine most important sentences in this chapter.
10. Does Pathworking help you in your everyday life? If so, how do you believe this happens?

·18·

Coding Consciousness

If you have been doing your homework properly you should now be in a position to approach the "inner teachers" of the Western Tradition for yourself and start learning from source rather than from reading material. This does not mean that external material reaching you through print or spoken language is valueless, far from it. Everything you learn from anywhere is useful, if only to specific degrees. But do try to distinguish between *information* and *implantation*. You can get information from almost anywhere, but for genuine spiritual implantation of true teaching in your mind and soul, you have to make contact with "instructors" *inside yourself,* and obtain it from thence directly. There *is* no other access available for anyone.

People usually evolve their own styles of approach to inner intelligence by sheer practice and experimentation. We suggest you try a standard approach until you "pick up your contacts" for yourself and learn from them directly how to continue working. At first, you will need to arrange some meditative sessions for yourself and be reasonably sure you are unlikely to be disturbed. Don't forget all the routine procedures which should be a matter commonsense by now, but there is no harm in reminding you. Have your notebook or tape recorder handy. Do not have a heavy meal just before the session, or an entirely empty stomach either. Make sure neither bladder nor bowels are going to interfere. Don't attempt a session if you have a persistant cough, snuffly cold, or other irritating physical problem. Also don't try these "contact" sessions if you are suffering from severe mental or emotional strain. You must be in a calm and normal state of mind. Check that the room temperature is not too warm or cold. Optimum temperature is about 65–68°F. Select a chair with a firm straight back and padded (but not sprung) seat so that thighs and legs make a right angle when sitting. An ordinary dining chair is suitable. Sit in the usual position, hands loose on knees, backbone straight, head slightly inclined forward, with subdued lighting sufficient to write by if you need to. Incense is optional.

Remember you are *not* trying to put yourself into a trance or lose complete touch with this world, only to distract your attention from it a while so that your consciousness can make contact with intelligence originating elsewhere. If you think there is any possibility of "passing out," take the precaution of setting a "pinger" for the time period you have chosen, and say firmly when you set it something like: "The moment this rings, I will return to normal consciousness quite naturally and happily." Though it is very long odds indeed against your losing consciousness unless you really want to, it might be a good idea to ensure that nothing is near your chair on which you could knock your head if you fell off it on to the floor, and that such hazards as electric fires or oil heaters are well in the clear. If you have any misgivings at all, you could have a companion in the room with you if you know anyone who could be trusted to keep absolutely quiet unless emergency demanded action.

When you are settled, "make yourself into a Tree" by imagining the Spheres roughly aligned with the salient points of your body as shown in Chapter 9. In case you have forgotten them (which you shouldn't have done!) or feel the need for rediscussion, this is how you ought to do it: First, try not to think of the Spheres as colored circles of definite size, but as *energies* reaching you in specific frequencies for each type invoked. Do you remember a make of radio set which you tuned simply by pressing buttons marked with names of whichever station you wanted? Well, think of yourself as such a set with the buttons arranged around you so that each separate energy will "turn on" as you press its control. Unlike the radio, however, each control is not cancelled by pressing another one. As the frequencies are brought in, they enhance each other's action to the utmost. If you like, you can think of yourself as being like a conductor bringing in one type of instrument after another to play its part in a great symphony, the greatest of all in fact—the symphony of life.

You could slightly ritualize the procedure by touching the air above your head with your right hand and visualizing Sphere 1 activating, then above your left shoulder feeling Sphere 2 come in. Follow this with Sphere 3, left hand over right shoulder, and so on. Remember you are *in* the Tree looking out of it, so the Spheres will be on opposite sides to those on paper. Here left is the white Pillar, and right the black one. Thus you will grip the left arm with the right hand to bring in Sphere 4, and the right arm with the left hand to connect Sphere 5. Both hands (left over right) will press just below the heart to summon 6, but each hand may grip a knee on its own side to call up 7 and 8. Sphere 9 is brought in by pressure on the pubic area with both hands again but right over left this time. Finally, Sphere 10 is realized by pressing the feet firmly on the floor or giving each foot a very slight stamping movement.

If you can do all this mentally without the gestures so much the better. Ritual gestures are not obligatory but only meant to help those who find them useful. You may notice we have mentioned *feeling* the Spheres here rather than *seeing* them. This is because you should now be treating them as parts of your "internal spiritual economy" similarly to the way you consider your internal physical organs as parts of your bodily being. You do not see those objectively, but you experience them as a state of well or ill-being depending on how they are functioning. You do not see other peoples' internal organs in normal life either, but you assume they have the same as yours, though for all you know, some may have been removed surgically. You can check to some extent on the working of your own organs by the pulse beat of your heart, the breathing of your lungs, and the excretion of your bowels and kidneys. If those are functioning without pain or stress, you presume your innards are in reasonable condition.

Here, you are doing the equivalent of a "function check" on the workings of your spiritual system by *feeling* your major "spiritual organs" operating as you think about them. You know quite well, for instance, that the quality of mercy is not limited to your left arm, nor does it originate there, but nevertheless your left arm *symbolizes* it in action, just as the heart symbolizes love and tenderness as well as courage. So as you direct your conscious attention around your body either by physical or mental indications, you should feel the force of each acting throughout your entire inner being. Granted it has to be a *simulated* experience induced by yourself, but this is all part of the exercise. As you "press the buttons" around yourself, you should feel the influence of the Sphere concerned surge right through you and mingle with the others already invoked. It is not a case of "switching on and off," but of switching on and *leaving* on. It will switch off by itself eventually.

The next thing you will need is a sense of "lift" slightly above normal physical plane levels. You can do this quite well without any form of drugs, alcohol, or hallucinogenic agents whatever. Controlled breathing will do this adequately, though it needs to be treated with almost as much care as artificial consciousness-alterers, because it affects brain chemistry by variation of oxygen supply. A useful method to begin with follows.

Take a good inhalation with no particular effort at all. Just let the air flow into your lungs like a sponge absorbs water by its own springiness. Now concentrate *hard* on the root of the nose right behind and between the eyes, which should be shut and turned inwards. Expel the breath with firm pressure as if you were directing its stream with focussed force at the point of your concentration like wringing water out of a sponge by squeezing it strongly. Breathe out through your mouth with the lips very slightly closed so that an effort has to be made pushing the breath through them. The overall rule is: "Easy in—hard out." The breath has to be taken in as loosely as possible, then *pressed* out relatively slowly with a sort of contraction of the nervous system all focussing on that one spot. Relaxation—tension, in rhythmic repetition.

You will probably find your eyes are automatically following this inner direction and there may be a sense of strain afterwards. It is also possible the exercise may produce some giddiness and mild nausea if persisted with too long. *Do not continue past the point when you feel the onset of such symptoms.* There is nothing to be gained by so doing. Just continue long enough to give the needed "lift." If the practice is done properly, each exhalation should produce a sensation of "power residue" left behind at the focal point, so that the impression of "otherness" begins to mount in the forefront of the brain a little more with each breath-cycle. It is almost as if a leaky tire or balloon were being pumped up. Pressure is being pushed in, and before the next stroke is possible a lot of it has subsided but a little remains to be implemented by the next addition. Eventually it will all leak to nothing, but in the meantime there may be just enough holding to accomplish a short-term purpose. Some have said this exercise gives the sensation of climbing a tiny bit higher inside one's body with every breath until it seems as if one is looking down on the top of the head from about a couple of feet above. In any event, it serves the purpose of producing a "psychic" condition of consciousness to an adequate degree for the purpose intended here.

It may be as well to point out that persons with known lung or heart complaints or those who suffer from gross obesity are advised *not* to practice breath control exercises without approval from a physician. The same applies to epileptics or asthmatics. It could be that such exercises might be most helpful to their complaint, but there are contra-indications in certain cases, and it is always advisable to check. About the worst that could happen with the exercise given here is a temporary loss of consciousness which does no harm in itself, but it is what one hits on the way down to the floor that does damage.

Once a sense of communion with your "internal intelligence" seems likely after a few mintues, *begin sending out your own name in Tree-code quite deliberately and carefully.* Again, try not to think of the spelling as letters printed on a diagram, but as *"wave-changes"* *in yourself as you react with each.* This is very important. It is not the little pictures in your brain which transmit signals recognizable by "inner intelligences" but the energy variations of mind which you make while conceptualizing them. That is to say, it is not just thought alone which reaches anywhere beyond your brain but it depends on *how* you think and the energy you are able to put behind it as to the extent you can contact other than human minds.

You have to distinguish between "brain thinking" and "mind thinking." The former is limited to the more or less mechanical thinking confined to a physical brain, while the latter involves your actual "life awareness" and perceptiveness as a conscious creature partaking in the act of life itself. That is to say, "mind action" is much more than memory retrieval from the stored tapes among the cells of the physical brain. It is the activity of consciousness enabling you to experience anything as an item or integral of existence relative to yourself, however remote from your present point in the scale of time, space, or events. It is thus an activity of the non-material part of yourself which survives the death of your physical body for an indefinite time, yet is not immortal in the true sense. Only Pure Spirit is immortal. What we are trying to say here is simply that the "mind" part of you has existence apart from your body, and it is the faculties of your mind and soul which need to develop with these exercises.

The nature of the Spheres of the Tree are not appreciable to the human brain by itself. It will take in the diagrams, wording, and all the mechanical details perfectly well, and there it stops. To realize the meaning and full significance of those Spheres, "soul consciousness" is needed. How can anything without a soul comprehend concepts of Mercy, Harmony, and so forth? Your faculty of mind may follow them theoretically and intellectually to quite an extent. It may see their necessity and agree with all the reasons for their existence, but there again it is limited as regards actual life experience. Where the mind comes into its own is with the Paths and their blending of objectified awareness into focussed fields of symbolism and allied associations. So a good general rule to make is: "Explore Spheres with soul, and Paths with mind." That is very much of a generalization, of course, since all types of consciousness link with each other down the long chain of life.

Here you are in the position of working with mind consciousness which is conditioned by two distinct aspects of soul consciousness. That is how your thinking becomes operative in spiritual dimensions. It is no longer confined to purely mental realms, but projects past them into what might be called "spiritual space" where it then becomes readable by intelligences on the alert for such communications. That is what you are supposed to be doing by "sending" your own name in "Tree-code," trying to attract attention on higher than human levels of living, and seeking communicative contact with the right type of inner intelligence.

If you have a special or "magical" name which you habitually use, then send out your "call sign" by that one. If not, just transmit your full normal human name for about five minutes. Then stop, concentrating on "being a Tree," and see if you can sense any kind of a response from inside you. Whatever you do, don't expect any long answers crammed with platitudes, advice, or elaborate messages of an intensely personal nature. Should you suppose such a thing, then suspect interference from some part of yourself, "switch off," and try again on another occasion. At first, you are most unlikely to get more than perhaps a sense of "acknowledgement" from some unknown recipient without further comment or explanation. If you start to become importunate or to demand immediate extensions of contact, it is likely to break off altogether and prove more than diffiuclt to re-establish. Slowly, steadily, and cautiously, is the only way to proceed.

Whatever you believe you get through these "Tree contact" sessions, note it down carefully and study it in the light of further developments later. On no account worry if you are not receiving miles and miles of "spirit messages" from well meaning but garrulous and insipid astral entities. Be thankful instead if your consciousness remains uncluttered by such intrusions. Under no circumstances should you treat this system like a ouija or planchette during a "let's try it for fun" sort of seance with its questioning and answering. The purpose of this practice is not gratification of curiosity by discarnates of any kind, but conscious contact with the inner intelligences of our Western Tradition who have helped evolve codes of this sort for reasons connected with our spiritual survival.

If anyone imagines these inner sources are only too anxious to pour out endless streams of information, intelligence, and "instant enlightenment" merely on demand by anyone clever enough to learn the Tree-code, then please be assured they are *not.* They will respond surely enough, and through the Tree, but invariably in their own terms, times, and standard of values. It may take a lot of patience and tolerance on your part to adjust with this, but at least it should be an interesting experience and open up many formerly closed ways of inner life for your exploration. At the same time *you will learn nothing you are not entitled to know.* Yet most humans are entitled to know a great deal about the inner workings of the universe, but few bother to enquire because of lack of sufficient interest or utter indifference. Your guideline should be: "Let me learn what I need for making progress on my path to peace."

Here are one or two more guidelines you would be well advised to consider. When beginning this type of exercise, do not be tempted to overdo it in frequency or length. Twice a week for ten to fifteen minutes will do nicely for a start. Send your name in Tree-code, wait for some kind of response, note this down, and leave things at that for the time being. There is no reason why you shouldn't think it all out afterwards, or go over the coding in your mind as often as you like when engaged in routine work during the day. In fact it is sometimes during these ruminative self-sessions that the answer which evaded you previously comes through with startling clarity. Eventually you will find that inner communications may begin arriving at almost any time, and you will grow quite accustomed to them.

It is usually only during the first few sessions you will need to start by sending out your name in Tree-code. After that you will probably find a sense of inner contact will "pick up" shortly after you begin operating. You may even evolve (or be told) your own special call-sign to identify yourself with, something like a radio transmitting station on earth. If this does happen, you must on no account reveal it to another soul in this world. Nor should you write it down unless very carefully concealed. What passes between you and your "Inner Guides" must always be kept confidential unless you are expressly asked to "pass it on" for some good purpose.

The exact form by which you might receive your replies varies a great deal according to your reactions. Some people tend to see words as if written before their eyes in various characters. Others hear them spoken in different dialects or voices. Others again only sense the gist of them, or get the idea more or less instinctively. Everything depends on how you translate subconsciously received intelligence into terms understandable by ordinary awareness. This is actually the case with normal human conversation. Our ears do not hear words as such. They hear noises which we translate into words with meanings because they are already in our stock of mental understanding, computerized into categories to be matched against anything our ears bring to our brains. Our ears only bring us sounds our minds have to make meanings with. It is the same in this case, except that our minds have to make meanings out of inner signals received by our souls.

Some workers with this Tree system will first of all suppose they are getting no replies at all, but as they persist it will gradually dawn on them that they are in fact receiving responses on deep levels which "drift up" to their focal consciousness a lot later due to time lag. There is not a great deal which can be done about this other than accept the situation and continue with it until conditions change. There will actually be no loss of real contact, but only delay in response for which there could be very good reasons. The main thing is not to worry or fidget around, but just carry on with the program at the same pace. Remember you have plenty of things to do apart from these contact sessions.

A very great deal depends on the discipline with which you conduct your sessions. They should be as regular as possible, but never prolonged beyond the few minutes or so while they are effective. These are *not* meditations, nor should they ever be allowed to drift into dreamy reveries or imaginative inner journeys. That has its proper place in esoteric practice, but not during direct contact periods. The best way of beginning these is as if they were very expensive, long distance calls which have to be kept at a minimum while meaning is put over at maximum, to be thought over at leisure later on when the call is finished.

For instance, say you received such a call in connection with some personal matter. Your caller would first identify himself, then wait your acknowledgement and after that deal with the specific subject of the call as concisely as possible. He may have spent quite a time choosing the right words to convey the message as clearly and plainly as possible in a few moments. If it is purely a business call, much of it could be in commercial codewords like acronyms which put whole sentences into syllables. This is sometimes called "telegraphese." Anyway, you would be keyed up on your toes to get the message as soon as you could, respond as rapidly and sensibly as possible, then break off the call as soon as you could so as to minimize expenses. You would certainly not ramble on with irrelevant conversation, remarks about weather, and long hesitant silences while you wondered what to say next. Most people would establish the contact quickly, get the sense rapidly, then acknowledge and close fast. That is the way to start working with the inner intelligences behind the Western Way of Light. Once they realize you are not just fooling around, they are likely to be more forthcoming.

It must be heavily emphasized that the intelligences you are liable to contact through the Tree-code system are *not* to be confused with the "Spirit Guide" who might be interested in the trivia of your mundane living except insofar as something in that area could seriously impede your spiritual progress as an individual soul seeking its own liberation and ultimate identity. They are not trying to make you live their way or *anybody else's but your own*. What they are chiefly concerned with is that you (and all others) should find your proper path and place within our spiritual tradition and rule your life along it beneficially for all involved. Remember it is in their interests as much as your own that this should be so, therefore they will help you as far as they can, but they are subject to the same laws of life that you are, though in a different way.

This is not the occasion to go into the possibilities of how far such intelligences may intervene with human affairs on earth, or to what degree they are able to heal, help or hurt human beings living on ordinary levels. That is something you will have to find out for yourself as you go along, and if you are wise you will keep quiet about your discoveries. In fact, you would be best advised to treat *all* your personal contacts confidentially if you want them to develop, except where they are specifically intended for other minds than yours (which is quite rare.).

Years ago, in old-time mystery lodges, new initiates were often given considerable amounts of material they were told to keep secret at all costs. Some of it might have appeared quite important, but the fact was that none of it mattered very much. It could have been published on bill-posters without revealing anything very vital. The whole thing was a test to see how far individuals might be trusted and how they would behave in given circumstances. Most of their experiences during probationary periods were tests of this nature to determine their deep characteristics and help bring out the hidden side of themselves to play its part in their active living. Nowadays this has to be done in much more subtle ways. You may well find that the inner contacts you make might possibly communicate something just to discover what you will do with it or if you are able to interpret the sense of special symbolism. In other words, *you* are liable to be offered "intelligence tests" or spiritual stimuli to note your reactions therewith.

If *you* are seeking something above your life levels in reaching beyond them hoping to make contact with more intelligent minds than those of average humans, you may be certain that *they* are equally looking for people like you. Why would they be doing this? Because they are entrusted with the spiritual safety and integrity of the Western Inner Way of life in this world, and are trying to fulfil an obligation they regard as sacred on account of the life level from whence such responsibility derives. Put in a nutshell, they are looking for those capable of taking their places when they "move up one notch" in the scale of spiritual evolution. That is how their interest in you should eventually help them.

You do not *have* to tackle such a thankless job before you will be fit to mount the Ladder of Life beyond human incarnation. It is thankless partly due to human nature itself, and the inevitable opposition of forces antithetic to our evolution. God itself would not compel you to take active part in this work, because that would automatically make you totally unfit for the task. It is something which can *only* be accomplished by truly compassionate and *competent* souls. Furthermore, gaining such competence could take not only one, but several incarnations. You (or anyone else) can only develop in spiritual safety at a rate within the tolerance of your Self. Human history is full of examples illustrative of what happens when the spiritual safety factors are dangerously exceeded. They supply sad and terrible lessons. So no matter how much you might be willing to make a useless martyr of yourself, no truly responsible inner initiation (for that is what your contacts should amount to in the end) would ever insist on your pushing past your safety margin, though you might be shown how to widen its limits.

In the Middle Ages, you would have encountered all this inner training under the description of "The Knowledge of, and Conversation with your Holy Guardian Angel."* The fundamental idea was to gain some sort of conscious contact with intelligent agencies on inner life levels who were willing to help humans ascend towards ultimate attainment along their own lines of life. Yet such assistance was in no way intended to create dependency upon it. To the contrary, it was meant to foster emancipation from such a need. That was essential to the process.

For example, we all (or we all *should*) recognize the dangers of drug dependency. At the same time we are all of us dependent on *something* in order to stay alive here and now. We are *air* dependent, *food* dependent, *water* dependent creatures. We are even beginning to breed a species who are TV dependent! Psychiatrists love playing around with the words "deprived" and "underprivileged" as though lack of dependencies was the cause of many human troubles. They are very close to the problems of drug dependence, and might prefer it to be replaced by "psychiatrist dependence," but there are

*See *Western Inner Workings*, also by William Gray.

worse destroyers of the human psyche than chemical compounds which damage a body. Addiction to spiritual stimuli beyond rationality can be just as much of a danger as anything and a lot more than many.

As instances, we could point to the extreme cases of those who dare not do anything without first "asking the spirits" or consulting some favorite oracle. People have been known to telephone their pet astrologer and enquire if the aspects are favorable for having their hair done that day. Now this is the very sort of absurdity which genuine guardians of the Western Inner Way would discourage most strongly. The whole point is that we are in this world to learn or achieve the ability of making decisions for ourselves. Even when we take the trouble to obtain advice from experts in various fields, right thinking people realize that responsibility for acting on such advice lies entirely in their own hands in the last analysis. It is to be entirely understood that no Guardian Angel (no matter how Holy) could claim infallibility on worldly affairs or *compel* anyone to take any spiritual action at all. If they are genuine (and imitations have been known to exist), they will only communicate (or "converse") on the strict understanding that their hearers must react on their own responsibility alone. Otherwise they prefer staying silent and letting people learn by themselves the hard way.

So now you may have some idea of what you are up against when you seek spiritual support from inner initiators. They are emphatically *not* of the sweetness-and-light brigade associated with "spirit summerlands" and "heavenly habitats" so beloved by wishful thinking sentimentalists. Nor are they about to shower abundance and prosperity into undeserving and unprepared hands. If anything, they are fair traders offering help for help in a mutal scheme for spiritual progression. They can help you by leading you to understand and persevere with the problems on your particular path, sometimes managing to open up opportunities for solutions along material lines. You can help them in return by assisting their actions in this world and developing the capabilities of working from higher levels later on. Whether or not you are willing to participate in this plan for perfection of the species must remain absolutely and entirely your own uninfluenced decision, and this decision must not be made in a hurry. It has to be something you *grow into naturally,* and cannot be decided on the spur of the moment. That is more than important—it is *vital.*

If you think things over carefully, you will surely agree that we all owe some kind of debt to life itself. We have become what we are at the moment because of what our ancestors were in the past. But who *were* our ancestors? Only ourselves on other bodies. And who will our descendents in the future be? Us again, except those who have earned their way out of this human rat-race. So if we want to do anything which might improve our spiritual stock in the future (and who doubts we and the whole world needs this?) we shall only be working for ourselves in the long run. That is what an inner tradition really means; carrying on the spiritual progression of our species beyond our bodily limits, so that from one generation to another we evolve steadily towards a state of perfection outlined by our genetic patterns.

You should now be in a position to see and appreciate that you have been given the symbolic keys to our secret spiritual tradition of the Western Inner Way, and it remains with you to put them in the right locks to open doors for yourself. It may take you the rest of your present incarnation to do this little by little and you will never get to the end of such an exploration, but what a worthwhile experience it is sure to be! Probing, planning and, best of all, *participating* in the flow of life force which makes the Holy Mysteries in the West a truly sacred charge laid on us many lives ago for the sake of a future we *dare* not fail.

Continue with your Tree-contact sessions, but do not be tempted to try forcing them or continuing them beyond brevity and impact. Slowly but surely, you will become aware of a new guidance coming into your life. It was always there, in fact, but your awareness of it may be new. Let it declare itself in its own way and time. Make sure that whatever you write down or record in connection with your contact-sessions is not read by other humans. It may not look important to *you,* but it is *the act of your confidentiality which is important in itself.* That is a symbol of mutual respect and acknowledgement between yourself and those "Inner Guides" whose cooperation you are seeking with your life work. Since all communication is carried out through symbols of some kind, let the symbolism of how you treat "received teaching" (which *is* Qabalah in itself) be a mute message from you to whatever inner source you obtain it from.

We shall be branching out from the Holy Tree for a while with the next few chapters, but always keep in mind that it is the Tree-code which should give you an intelligent comprehension of its contents and enable you to follow its implications leading you towards inner dimensions of life. Remember that though you may now be able to read and enjoy the finest literature in this world, *it was your first faltering steps in alphabet learning which made this possible over the years.* Without those, you would be illiterate. The spiritual world has parallels. So don't expect too much in mere moments. Keep faith and continue. That is the most any soul can do no matter how highly advanced it may be.

Questions

1. How clearly can you feel the Spheres around you?
2. Do you experience any sort of sensations from your Spheres? If so, what are these feelings?
3. Differentiate between brain thought and mind thought.
4. Have you found a magical name for yourself yet?
5. Do you feel you are getting replies from inner levels of life?
6. What are your relationships with inner life?
7. How do you translate the Spheres in terms of your physical senses?
8. What debt, if any, do you think you owe to life?
9. Choose the ten most important sentences in this chapter.
10. State your ideas on "occult secrecy."

· 19 ·

Sexual Symbology

Had you ever thought of the Tree of Life as a sex symbol? Its originators did. To them, it was a mathematical glyph of the supreme sex act between God and God which created life in the first place. Not an act between a God and Goddess, but between the masculine and feminine polarities of one and the same being. They did not suppose that God did this exactly as man would have to, but the fundamental principles would be the same if man truly were "in the image and likeness" of his Creator. Humans, however, were twofold, man and woman, each of a double nature. So God was seen as an androgynous being, combining both sexes in itself yet superior to either as a pure spirit of life in which all living creatures existed.

So far as we know, the earliest human concepts of a God were matriarchal. God was the Great Universal Mother bringing all life out of her inexhaustible womb. As male supremacy began to take over tribal management, the concept of Father-God gradually grew in importance until it first overshadowed and then finally supplanted original Mother worship in many cultures, particularly in the Middle East and among Semites whose religious codes have been inherited by official Christianity. How God could produce a human son out of the Virgin Mary without some form of sexual intercourse is a mystery the Church has never fully faced since it first thought of the idea. Virgin birth, or parthenogenesis, is a biological possiblity and involves reproduction by the development of a single cell (as an ovum or ovule) without fertilization by union with the opposite sex. An instance is recorded of one male twin developing inside the other, but this was plain mutation with no miracles involved.

Exactly why the official Church should maintain such silence on the subject of temple impregnation or artificial insemination by selected God-fathers is a bigger mystery than the act itself. Humans supplied the seed, but it was God himself who decided on the individual one which fertilized the female, therefore the child was truly God's. Such was the honest belief. Though the priests could not have know the biological factors involved, they could work out simple arithmetic. If seed from ten chosen men were injected into a willing female, then one of this lot must be the physical father, but which? Only God knew. Hence the custom of counting the bloodline through mothers, and the need for ten males to "make a minyan" or minimum number for divine worship in the temple. Some supposed that all ten were the father, and good qualities from each entered the child at conception.

Orthodox Semitism could accept the idea of God creating a human woman out of Adam by the curious method of cloning a rib, but they only saw a kind of secondhand creation in this in which woman was not made directly in God's image but in Adam's, by reflection. So it was considered a blasphemy among them to impute any feminine aspects to God, and in banning images from their temples, the Semites included mental images in that injunction as well. God must not be seen as a living *form*, yet might be spoken of in the masculine sense, except in the odd instance of the word *Elohim*, a feminine word with a masculine plural suffix which has caused so much argument among scriptural scholars.

None of this pleased mystically-minded people who could not agree that any supreme spirit of life must be purely masculine in nature. Commonsense alone made this an anomaly. They were apt to view the Father-God concept in a somewhat suspicious light as being a "policy decision" which put males in secure seats of government and control of tribal affairs, in other words as a male-organized "takeover" which had succeeded from political and allied angles in their spheres of culture if nowhere else. So if this *fait accompli* could not be out-fought, it could certainly be out-thought.

That is exactly what happened. Behind the external male-oriented official religion presented to the people as the will of their rulers attributed to a God image of a nationalistic and political kind, there grew up another sort of faith devoted to a God which could be found by the people for themselves and *in* themselves, neither a masculine nor feminine deity but both in one capable of conceiving itself in the hearts and souls of those offering themselves to its spirit. It was a God which could be equally invoked from a masculine, feminine, or neutral approach. Hence the three Pillars of the Tree, and a virtual return to a pantheon wherein all gods and goddesses were only regarded as different aspects of the nameless spirit behind all of them. Now it had been given a name—*love*.

Everyone must surely be familiar with the saying "God is Love." The original word used for love in that instance was AHVH (Ah-Vah), "a breathing after." You "breathed after" someone you loved in the sexual sense. It was meant to be a poetic and idealistic description of the quickened breathing during sexual excitement where you "met your mate" in the true sense of mating for life. You encountered your "other Pillar," and between you, raised the third. When you wanted God with the same intensity as when you needed a sex partner, then that God would be with you, because you would *have* to find that God or perish in the attempt. This was the significance of the text. God itself must be your sex partner found through the mediatorship of another human. This was the way early mystics understood it. Their love affair with God was sexual in every implication except physical, and some would have included that as well.

To many minds conditioned by conventional Western ideology, any association of God with sex might seem shocking, irreverent, or maybe only incongruous. Yet there is no real reason why it should be any of these things apart from such conditioning. Sex is a plain fact of life, and if God *is* life, how can you possibily separate them as if God were some prudish old woman or another kind of easily offended human being. That would be an insult to common intelligence, let alone a divine one. Mystical systems in general may have some strange notions about God and sex, but at least they have mostly tried to relate one with the other and make sense or inspiration out of their findings. The designers of the Tree of Life obviously tackled the same problem in their mathematical way and offered their solution in the formula they constructed.

To follow their thesis, we have only to trace the Spheres sequentially downwards, reading each as a specialized stage of the entire generative action during sexual congress. This naturally starts with the *nil* state of *Ain Soph Aur* as a condition of "potential power" preparatory to being directed as willed. So an energy emerges from that origin and finds its way to the first Sphere, which is:

1. *Kether,* The Crown or "initiating intention" where "nothing" becomes "something." At this point it says something like: "I will find and fulfil myself through sexual experience." Just that imperative alone, nothing more at this stage. To maintain that intention as specified, successive factors must eventuate this way. The energy stream passes next to:

2. *Chockmah,* Wisdom or creative male-motivated consciousness. This supplies an outgoing drive which has to find its complementary acceptance from:

3. *Binah,* Understanding or creative female fertile consciousness which must afford mutual accomodation for the preceding principle so that together they offer an opportunity for:

4. *Chesed,* or the Merciful Grace of giving. To reach this point the Abyss has to be crossed beyond any possibility of recalling the intention to its origin. Once it has arrived here, it amounts to the "outgiving" during a sex act considered as compassion or "feeling together." This is counterbalanced by:

5. *Geburah,* Severity or the "terms of taking." This means whatever controls and disciplines may be necessary to make the act effective and ecstatic. If both these last two Spheres have been mediated properly they should result in:

6. *Tiphereth,* Beauty or held harmony. The central climax itself as all energy equates in a perfectly poised orgasm wherein man

and God meet for one brief moment. Subsequently comes the "climb-down" through:

7. *Netzach,* Victory or awareness of achievement. The sense of satisfaction which should follow naturally upon spiritually successful creative climaxes.

8. *Hod,* Glory or beatific brilliance. Otherwise an intimation of increased intelligence on earth through whatever extra entity has been invoked into existence. This should arouse a sense of:

9. *Yesod,* Foundation or evidence of establishment. For example, someone might say: "I have founded a family" or felt "solidity" in spiritual things worthy of founding faith or beliefs upon. Lastly comes the conclusion:

10. *Malkuth,* the Kingdom or concretion of consciousness. The end-product of effort, or "coming down to earth" which closes any cycle of creation.

It should be noted that all this is actually a continuum of conscious experience leading from light into life. Here it has been outlined as a very idealized sequence of human sexual realizations mainly for the sake of comprehension within a familiar frame of reference. Granted we are looking at it from a rather lofty angle, but such are the fundamental basics behind creativity per se. That is to say, we are taking sex purely as an act of *creation,* within the normal laws of life without considering any of the side issues involved. These may make a fascinating study on their own, but here we have to keep within mainstream limits. At the same time it should be seen clearly that the sex sequence of the Tree does apply in principle to all cycles of creative consciousness along every level of life.

The whole of this process is far more than merely biological. It takes place in us every time we use our living energies auto-creatively. We are all intrinsically male-female creatures, with a polarized bias which determines the external sex of the body and dominant sex of the soul. This still leaves masculine aspects to every female and feminine aspect to every male. Everything depends on the correct balance and proportion of these polarities in each single soul. As individuals, sex relationships are constantly taking place within us between the male and female sides of our natures, and it is of extreme spiritual importance that these should be as perfect as possible. Only when and if one's own internal polarities become properly balanced together can sound spiritual health be maintained.

This particular point is of very great significance. It means that most of our sexual troubles and difficulties which we blame on others are in fact due to faulty or inadequate functioning inside ourselves. The Tree of Life provides a plan of auto-sexual arrangement for relating the bisexual natures of individuals in a harmonious and sensible way. It also operates along similar lines conjoining separate souls with one another so that each compensates for the other's deficiences, making a balanced whole between them. One might almost say that for those able to respond with its sophisticated symbolism, that the Tree of Life is the sexiest of all symbols. To study this in detail would take a large volume, but if we reduce it here to the briefest review of the process, we might get an overall glimpse of the picture.

0: We are in a normally negative state of unauthorized life acceptance. Nothing in particular is intended or willed by the Self in control of the consciousness concerned.

1: An imperative emerges as an authorized concentration of consciousness. This has to come from the highest level of entity as a positive *I Will*, derived directly from the Self-source. For continuance into existence past this point, it has to divide in two and split between—

2: The male side of consciousness which works with calculation (Wisdom) and—

3: The female side of consciousness which works by intuition (Understanding). The resultant equation of this must now cross the Abyss between further action or re-negation. This is the point of no recall. Either it goes on past the Abyss and subsequently develops into something, or it "goes down the drain" of the Abyss and eventually back to the zero it started from. This is the "To be, or not to be" position. If it is "To *be*" it crosses the Abyss on the male side to—

4: Which deals with all the "pros" which processes the original intention and considers everything in favor of it. On the female side it becomes—

5: All the "contras" connected with the original intention and all considerations against it, or reasons why it should be changed, modified, curtailed, or otherwise adapted in any way. Both these "pros" and "cons" have to react with each other in rhythmical conscious activity relatable with a sex act until a central climax is reached which decides the issue with an approving "go forth" ultimatum or "fiat," which culminates at—

6: A peak of poised power at which the polarized energy resolves itself into a single outcome of the previous process. At this point there is a decisive impact from the Self-source along a direct line of centrally connecting consciousness. This brings a "purpose-plus" factor into focus. If this were a physical sex act, it would be an impregnation inviting another human being into incarnation by the emission of mixed male-female seeds towards a neutral egg awaiting their arrival. Subsequent to this, the initiating consciousness polarizes again into—

7: A realization of accomplishment amounting to a sense of victory and achievement, a triumphant awareness of "I've done it!" This announces the success of the enterprise so far, and encourages further projections towards eventual emergence into existence on more limited levels. This is the equivalent of a male reaction immediately after orgasm. It is complemented by—

8: A sense of being "glorified" by fulfilment of purpose so far and a hope of being able to develop it further still by intelligent care and work. If this were a human sex act, it would amount to the female reaction after orgasm with her natural thoughts that her womb may indeed have fulfilled its function and could carry its contents to some splendid fruition. Both these last stages should now combine at—

9: The basic conclusion, or arriving at a certainty that everything has indeed been well-founded and has been brought within reach of actual manifestation after one final effort. If this were a physical sex act, it would be a mutual feeling between both parties concerning their shared responsibility towards a welcome and gladly awaited offspring. It would also be the point where that emerging entity itself began to establish links of connecting consciousness with life along its projected lines of progression. To complete the creative cycle, only one final stage of manifestion is needed, which is—

10: Arrival at actuality in the sense that the concept now enters its intended life-level as an individualized item. This birth-entry is pushed through by a combination of the polarized powers behind it together with its own impetus along a central line of direction from its original source. Once out into the world, it continues with its career according to circumstances, and the story goes on from there.

These are the stages or Spheres by which creative conscious-ness ought to operate through us according to the Tree of Life plan of reaching matter through spirit. Whether the outcome is another living being, or just an idea focussed into materialization in this world, the principles involved are just the same. Brain children or body children are born by a parallel process, and both male and female types of consciousness are needed to create them.

What is so important about all this should be the realization it affords of the spiritual sex system possible within one's own microcosmos. We do not have to see ourselves as exclusively male or female creatures entirely dependent on external entitites for our sexual fulfilments. Each individual may consider itself as potentially bisexual, capable of creative processes inside the Self, initiated by a Self-source equating all sex polarity as its own entity. The Tree of Life plan points out how to work this principle in practice.

The implications of this are almost beyond calculation. Imagine, if possible, a state of freedom from any sex stress because sexual needs would be fulfilled and equated *inside* the cosmic circuitry of the individual. We humans suffer sex frustrations and their consequences because we are unable to find any fulfilment from our own internal resources and cannot meet or mate with other humans who are able and willing to supply our deficiencies. Suppose it is possible to control the process creatively through a series of adjustments along spiritual lines laid down within one's own microcosmos? That is precisely what the Tree of Life is about, and why it is of such intense importance to everyone seeking individuation into what was once termed "eternal life."

Satisfactory sexual stability is essential to living in a cosmically balanced condition of being. The Tree of Life amounts to a circuit diagram showing how to connect and control conscious energies so that this may produce such an end. Perhaps correct interpretation of this may not be easy, but once the idea stirs faculties of imagination and these are used the right way, a lot of very interesting thoughts are bound to arrive from inner levels. The chief thing to bear in mind while investigating this issue is to see the whole subject of sex as something reaching far beyond biological spheres of life. It must be recognized as a basically spiritual polarizing energy capable of being pushed or projected into physical manifestation, yet not necessarily compelled to reach that level of reality. At the same time it should be realized that this is a cyclic process which can be continued along return paths, all of which are indicated on the Tree. Once this become clear things will start making sound sense and the Tree of Life will speak in its unique way to those understanding its language.

All branches of occultism advocate various ways of dealing with sex problems, from the extreme of pretending there are none to the most bizarre practices possible for a body and mind to combine. Codes of conduct differ anywhere from advocating total abstention, to an almost compulsory sex act as often as posssible. The Tree of Life tells only of Middle Pillar practice. It does not moralize or lay down any hard and fast rules concerning sex conduct. All it says in effect is: "Does the male part of you match the female, and if not, why not?" It does no more than try to show people how to become balanced souls in their own rights.

Here, however, we have to note the need for extreme care not to overbalance too strongly and induce homosexuality as a consequence. All this does is short circuit energies within the individual leaving a very unstable state which renders him or her quite unsuitable for working in groups of correctly polarized people. As a rule, most occult or mystical associations will not admit homosexuals into active membership for that reason. Long experience has shown that they upset and unbalance any close combination of both sexes working associatively together for spiritual reasons. There is no question of animosity, criticism, or any kind of prejudice whatever. It is no more than commonsense and concern for the well-being of their carefully constructed circle. This would be as badly thrown out of gear by a homosexual as by the introduction of an ultra-masculine male or an ultra-feminine female. The balancing of sexual polarities within constituted circles of the Western Holy Mysteries is an extremely delicate and arduous operation, and once it has been achieved can only be maintained by replacing vacancies with correctly polarized people of the same potential.

A sexually stabilized person is one who is able to mate both masculine and feminine currents of creative consciousness in him or her self and produce a condition of harmonious poise from which it is possible to radiate power equably. One might say a *fulfilled* soul with a surplus to distribute, someone capable of reaching a state of spiritual orgasm and *sustaining it to a controlled degree* sufficient for some intended purpose. As most people should know, a physical orgasm is only a momentary affair, but for its brief duration a maximum of personal potency is experienced. It is about the closest an ordinary person ever feels to "becoming a God." Hence the attraction of sex activity for the average man. He might suppose that he is doing it purely for the tension relief and physical satisfaction it brings him, but underneath those natural reasons there is a far deeper and more subtle purpose which his normal consciousness might not comprehend at all.

Even the crudest and most inarticulate or illiterate humans feel instinctively that by prolonging the life of the human race they must necessarily prolong their own. They might not realize the reality of reincanation if it were put to them as an intellectual concept. All they know for certain is that they have to make more human bodies with the means they have been given to do this. They could not tell *why*, or give any rational explanation for their sexual compulsions, but the basic drive is their own survival through a long chain of life they would not even be conscious of, though life in them is urging them along to promote possibilities for future generations. They do so blindly so far as they are concerned, but life itself knows very well what it is aiming at—a sufficiency of bodies for housing souls willing to risk the results of evolution regardless of consequences.

As someone has said, Nature always prefers the shotgun to the rifle. This means that to make one live birth, millions of seeds are aimed and "fired" at only *one* egg. The same with plant growth. All fight to survive and most die off except the toughest or the luckiest. Adapt or die is the law of life on this planet. In the original scheme of things, humans hung on to their lives literally by their teeth and claws like other creatures. Of endless humans born, how many ever lived to grow up and propagate the species? Their only hope was to breed all they possibly could, and that instinct is *still in human nature,* particularly among the less spiritually advanced souls on earth. The more spiritually developed people become, the more they realize their tremendous responsibility towards other souls, especially those of their own category. This makes them very careful about providing bodies for others unless there is very good and sufficient reason for incarnation.

In other words, initiates of the Holy Mysteries *do not* breed carelessly and indiscriminately, purely for the sake of momentary pleasure. They are not anxious to breed at all unless they can secure an adequate foothold in this world for souls of equal or perhaps superior status to themselves who may want to incarnate on some mission likely to benefit the human race and particularly our branch of it. Members of the Mysteries should never have children merely for the sake of having them, but only if they are fully prepared to sponsor other souls with the same care as they would admit a candidate into their most confidential circles of companionship.

In ancient times, there were many customs connected with systems of selective breeding mostly administered by temples of various kinds. This is why they had temple virgins specially dedicated and trained for that purpose, who were only allowed to breed on special occasions with most carefully chosen males. The sex act then was a ceremonial affair with special prayers and chanting going on while the act was in progress, often in the center of a consecrated circle. Almost up to the Middle Ages, in the case of anointed kings, the nuptial bed would be attended by bishops and others who witnessed the deflowering of the bride by her royal groom after they had been solemnly blessed. Even in modern times, mostly in Middle Eastern countries, it was the custom among respectable peasantry for the bridegroom's mother (or some similar person) to exhibit a bloodstained sheet before the wedding guests as supposed proof of the bride's virginity.

Old temples also provided prostitutes for those needing no more than sex tension relief, and no one considered this abnormal or in the least shameful, providing the purpose was clearly understood. The money the girls made went into the temple funds, and some of it at least went to charitable uses such as care of orphans or old and sick people with no other support. The girls themselves were cared for by the temple authorities, and what they did was regarded as a necessity of human nature catered for by the Goddess concerned. In fact it was the task of the girls to mediate that Goddess for the benefit of their clients so that in the very act of sex intercourse the men would be made conscious of deity and therefore be guided in some divine direction. One cannot help wondering what would happen if a modern prostitute suggested prayers before practice. In some countries it is still possible to find a crucifix or devotional image with a lamp before it in Catholic prostitutes' bedrooms.

So the Tree of Life system sets no inflexible criteria on human sex conduct beyond insisting on balanced behavior and acceptance of responsibility for individual reactions. What really matters is fulfilling all the conditions of consciousness or "putting the process through the Paths" before "earthing" or making any physical manifestations. In other words, raise sex above the blind instinct level and conceive of it as being something of spiritual significance within the conscious control of those concerned. Do not practice any sort of sex act merely as a sort of automatic response to animal instincts, but as an authorized activity intended and willed by the Self or Selves involved, which takes place in their own time, space, and events. There must be absolutely mutual agreement and conscious cooperation throughout the whole proceedings.

In the East, a calculated combination of physical sex with spiritual associations has been worked out in what is called the Tantric system of yoga. The West kept its ideas in this area within very restricted limits mainly confined to oral instructions imparted individually, and sometimes only through symbolism. The Tree of Life as we have seen is such a sex glyph. We can also read it upward as:

10: A purely physical approach begins. The foreplay stage. Male and female mate polarities and rise together into:

9: A conjunctive point of mingled fantasy and intensified imagination during which they polarize apart toward:

8: Where the female reaches the Glory state, and

7: Where the male achieves a sense of Victory. Their poles change again and they are drawn to mutual attraction together at:

6: An orgasmic condition of beautiful Harmony held only momentarily before poles alter and they drift apart again into:

5: A female contemplation of life from the constrictive angle, and

4: The male contemplation of life from an expansive viewpoint. Here they need to cross the Abyss beyond bodily consciousness, the female making herself into a condition of:

3: Understanding it all by intuition, while the male converts himself to:

2: Wisdom by comprehension of what it means. After this polarity alters again, and both conjoin finally in the unifying spirit of:

1: The Crown of consciousness where everything is whole at last. They cannot go beyond this point and continue existing, so if they want to stay in being, they will have to descend the Tree and begin again.

If you want to picture this from a theoretical viewpoint, you can do this quite nicely with two bar magnets by moving them

Figure 2.8. Sexual attraction and separation on the Tree of Life shown by bar magnets. Move magnets as shown from bottom to top changing polarities where necessary. Plus (+) = North Pole, Minus (−) = South Pole. F = Female, M = Male. *Like* poles *repel, unlike* poles *attract*. All humans are bi-polar creatures. Note the seven stages of sexual heavens.

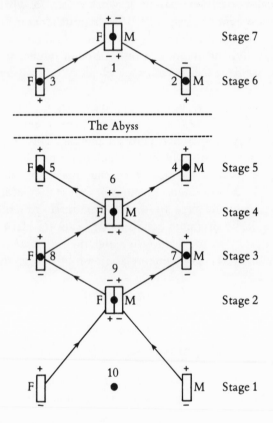

Magnets change polarities by rotating on axis thus

around on a diagram of the Tree, as illustrated in Figure 2.8. This whole process of course would represent a very highly disciplined sex act on the part of two trained and practiced people, but it can also stand for an equivalent action between the male and female parts of your own psyche. As you should now see, there is a lot more to learn about sex than commercial instruction books ever tell you.

Questions

1. Can you define God in sexual terms? If so, how?
2. Can you see a Father-God without a Mother equivalent?
3. Explain the expression "God is Love."
4. Can you feel your own bisexuality and if so, how?
5. Can you sense your place in a chain-of-life and if so, how?
6. Describe the sex-cycle of the Tree.
7. Why do bloodlines count through mothers rather than through fathers?
8. Explain the expression "Nature prefers the shotgun to the rifle."
9. Choose the ten most significant sentences in this chapter.
10. Can you conceive a state of self-sexual stability? If so, how?

· 20 ·

Esoteric Excretion

Here we come to a particularly recondite teaching concerning the Tree of Life which is not to be found in any orthodox reference book or hinted at with any clarity in scriptures or commentaries. The subject was regarded as far too delicate for discussion and almost blasphemous to think about. It is strange today when so few of us are shocked or offended by body functions that this topic still remains on what might be called the "secret list" of occult philosophy, yet it is simple enough in essence. Assuming that Man the Microcosm is made in the likeness of God the Macrocosm, does that God have the equivalent of a digestive and excretory system? If so, how does it work and affect the Universe? Put crudely, does deity produce dung?

The association of deity with excrement was anathema to Semitic and subsequently Christian scholars and literary mystical exegicists. The very idea filled their minds with revulsion, so they expunged or put the whole concept as far away from their awareness as possible. They feared that God might be offended by such a notion and punish them for their shameful thinking. It was the Devil they associated with dung and all other dirt. God had to remain utterly pure and radiant, but the filthy Devil was often caricatured as excrement-smeared and surrounded by attendant stenches. There is even a classic tale of Martin Luther being attacked by the Devil in his "house of easement."

An example of this "delicacy" is the strange reference made reputedly by Jesus to the Devil during the temptation in the wilderness. It is translated as: "Get thee behind me, Satan," but was an euphemism for a common crudity of those and modern times which we would now interpret quite plainly as: "I shit upon you," one of the oldest forms of expressing utter contempt and the lowest possible opinion of anyone. However, it did not look very nice to put such an earthy and forthright saying in the mouth of an idealized Jesus, so it got softened to its present puerility. An old Hebrew word, ShThN, from whence the name Satan could be derived, meant "to piss against a wall." So the very title of the Devil indicates a bodily waste product unfit for retention in a human frame. In other words, something which would make you ill unless you got it out of your system. An altogether apt analogy.

Another odd association with excremental shame was the traditional execution of criminals by hanging if they came from the "lower orders," but by decapitation if they were of noble birth. According to old beliefs, the soul left the body at physical death either by the mouth or nostrils. That is why we still speak of people "expiring," or "breathing their last." The theory was that in the case of strangulation the soul would be unable to quit its carcass by the normal route, and would thus be forced to leave by what was then called the "dung gate" or the anus. It is fairly normal anyway in the event of violent death for the bowels to evacuate forcibly, but in old-time thought if the soul were expelled with the excrement it would have a bad start in the next life.

Nobles, on the other hand, had the privilege of dying by effusion of blood—a warrior's death—and a soul outpoured through blood had a right to enter the afterlife with a certain amount of respect. Death by bloodshed was, after all, the ritual end of a traditional Sacred King. Jesus was always said to have shed his precious blood for us even though crucifixion was once considered a shameful end reserved for slaves and common criminals because victims were bound to their crosses by ropes and left to die of exhaustion and exposure. Nailing to the cross was said to have originated by Crassus who crushed the Spartacus rebellion of the slaves and gladiators. He was supposed to have introduced it as a humane measure to kill more quickly. Stories of the crucifixion of Jesus always lay heavy emphasis on the shedding of blood involved, even though this was not fatal by itself. The scourging, crowning with thorns, and nailing through the wrists and feet were non-lethal, even though they contributed greatly. A last thrust with a lance by Longinus was said to have been made after death into a lung where it released pleural fluid with some blood. So by maximizing the blood loss sustained by Jesus, his followers hoped to divert attention away from the fact that he died the official death of a rebellious slave under Roman, not Jewish, law.

No reference whatever was made to the excrement which would naturally have been shed by a crucified victim, because the mere mention of it would have linked a synonym of the Devil with the dying Jesus, and that was unthinkable. Besides, if he had been connected with the Essenes, it would have been considered disgraceful to perform such an act in public despite its unavoidability. Essenes had very strict rules about toilet behavior and each was provided with a small wooden shovel for disposal of excreta in the sand which had to be done quite privately. There were penalties for doing this within view of others, which was unusual for those days. An euphemism for defecation used occasionally in the Bible was "to cover the feet." This is only understandable by those who have seen robed Middle Easterners squatting on desert sands with the back of the robe hauled up to expose their posteriors, and the front of it dangling over their feet. Not all biblical authors were so nice-minded, but by the time the New Testament was written, conventions of speech and writing had become well established, and no references could be made to the natural functions of Jesus as a human being, certainly nothing which might detract from his image as a God.

When it came to designing the Tree of Life, this problem arose for its planners. How were they to work out a scheme for showing what was virtually a mathematical symbol for life on every level, without any open references to excretory systems common to all living creatures? In the end they compromised with the Abyss concept. Down into this mysterious gulf went everything and everyone meant to "get lost" in life because it was unfit for continuing in cosmic circulation. Only absolutely pure and spiritual sorts of souls could possibly pass this point and unite with the Understanding Wisdom of an omniscient God. To this day it is an ill-meant saying when anyone is told to "get lost." It means to become extinct by falling into the great Abyss and so lose all chances of attaining the status of being an immortal identity. Though it may sound harmless enough to moderns who have missed its original meaning, it is certainly not a wish which should be invoked by anyone comprehending its true significance. If you are in the habit of using it under the impression it is no more than an idle expression, then please realize now that it means much worse than any folk-obscenity and try to drop it from your customary curses.

Though the Abyss was certainly an inlet, where, if anywhere, did it come out? As things stood, it was the entrance to what seemed like a blind sewer with no exit. What actually happened to whatever "went down the drain?" How could the Tree system account for it all? Eventually the idea arose that the Abyss was really a *mouth* through which God swallowed up the surplus of life and then digested it with an inner system comparable to a human body. It was easy then to conceive that all which was good could be absorbed into divine life, becoming part of the Body and Blood of God, but what became of the remainder which might be classed as bad since it was unfit for such a fate? There had to be something to account for its disposal in a sensible fashion.

The idea of humans being "eaten up" by their gods is a very old one. In India, the black goddess Kali is shown in one aspect as having a huge open mouth with extended tongue, into which she is stuffing human beings with evident enjoyment. In Christian systems of thought, damned souls are depicted as being driven into the "mouth of Hell," and in old mystery plays this "mouth" was a mechanical device always on the left of the stage, into which the "baddies" were driven by acrobatic demons with fiendish yells before enthusiastic audiences. Christ was sometimes shown as holding these jaws apart during his harrowing of Hell to release the souls held in Hell since Adam, who is easily recognized by his lack of a navel, since he was the only human not born of woman.

Primitive people sometimes believed that the animals they ate had souls like themselves yet not so advanced, and as a reward for keeping humans alive by the mortal deaths of their bodies, these souls might be promoted to higher states of being, and eventually incarnate as humans in their turn. Similarly, humans helped to keep God alive by the mortal deaths of their bodies, so that they too might hope for Godhood in the end. Life fed on life like that forever. There is a legend that Gautama Buddha in one incarnation deliberately fed his body to a starving tigress with no milk to give her cubs because he was so compassionate and knew he could easily get another body again. In Semitic circles however, there was a terrible fear of one's body being eaten by pigs or dogs which left large lumps of excreta lying around. The thought of being converted into animal manure was not an attractive one to hygenic Hebrews.

Faced with the problem of "What goes in must come out somewhere," the Tree-makers went over their plan again and again until they discovered that there was indeed quite a reasonable outlet. To follow what they found, you will have to see how the Tree divisions are worked out in Figure 2.9 shown on page 300. They are based on calculating the Tree as being on evenly spaced levels so that the Spheres are exactly in the center of each. It is best if you draw this out yourself with very careful measurements so that you will appreciate how it was done in the first place. What you need to realize is that in addition to the space where there is *no* Sphere which represents the Abyss position and the shadowy Daath point, there is *another* unoccupied level at the bottom of the Tree between Yesod and Malkuth, the Foundation and Kingdom. In other words, *this could be regarded as the anus-exit for which divinity has passed through its system and reduced to excretory refuse for recycling through creation.* No specific name was given to this level, nor were any direct references made of it by official commentators. The only way to trace its presence is by this form of measurement.

Theoretically, it explains so much. For one thing it shows the economy of nature wherein nothing is wasted, and all is

Figure 2.9. The "other" Abyss on the Tree of Life

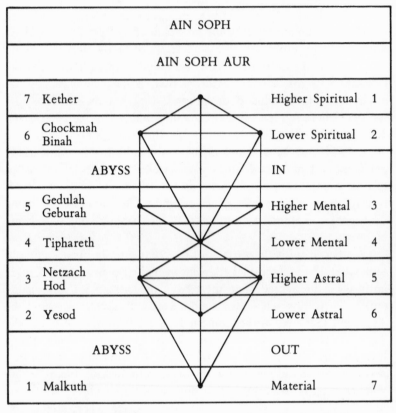

The Spheres — The 7 Levels of Life

converted up and down the scale of life, used and re-used endlessly in the same scheme of existence. Metaphysically, it means that whatever God cannot conveniently make into something good enough to incorporate in its "cosmic corpus" gets reduced to an equivalent of "divine dung" and returns for breakdown into humus capable of fertilizing the Tree of Life at its roots placed at the bottom of the plan. It also might explain a great deal of low quality behavior and inferior spiritual standards noticeable on this earth.

People so often wonder why if God is supposed to be essentially good, He (or It) seemingly permits so much wrong and evil in human nature. If it can be seen that this arises from the excrement factor in the process of re-conversion back into something a lot better, such a realization might help us to be more tolerant.

It may be that this would not elevate our opinions of deity very much, but it does enable us to appreciate that we ourselves are part of a purification process taking place continuously in the spiritual system of divine life. Whatever we fail to eliminate from our own spiritual systems, or convert into acceptable elements and energies for usage by the spirit of that life itself must necessarily be engulfed by the life spirit, then "digested and excreted." It *cannot avoid* returning to us a proportion of the past poisons and impurities which *we ourselves* have released into its system by our behavior as living beings. This is no form of punishment whatever, but only the fulfilment of a natural function on a spiritual scale. We are getting back no more than our own detritus to deal with again, possibly from a long while ago in addition to some of more recent manufacture. Don't blame deity for human dirt it has to get out of its system somehow.

We should know the normal fate of excrement well enough. In the course of nature it would return to the earth, break up into constituents, then get re-used to fertilize plant life which animals would eat and so on, indefinitely. This happens on a spiritual scale too. In early days we did not have our present problems because we were scattered in small quantities over the surface of the earth and our excremental proportions were relatively negligible. When humans began to multiply and concentrate in urban areas, excrement collected much faster than it could be fed back properly into circulation, so resultant diseases became inevitable.

It was the same with "spiritual sewage." Disseminated over an acceptable area, it could be absorbed and neutralized well enough. Produced past a certain point however, it could not do other than constitute a serious inner health hazard. The ecological pollution we have made by our faulty handling of chemical and radioactive waste is relatively slight compared to the contamination of our inner atmosphere by toxic collections of consciousness. Millions of people thinking thoughts that decompose into dung-like residues which keep mounting up without being cleared away can only produce two end-effects. One, they can poison our spiritual systems to dangerous degrees. Two, they can generate enough inner equivalents of sewer gas to explode violently. It is possible they might do both.

No excrement is dangerous *if properly disposed of.* Even excreta loaded with lethal bacteria can be disinfected and destroyed by applying knowledge and care plus proved methodology. It would only be hazardous if left lying around where other humans would come in contact with it. Everything depends on *how* it is dealt with. Again the same applies in a spiritual sense. Consciousness itself might be described as the food which keeps our minds alive. It is our thinking which converts a proportion of it to the making of what was once called a "mental body," and the remainder to a sort of excrement which should be voided harmlessly. Any possible damage to our inner systems comes from retention of what we have reduced to "dung" until reabsorption of its toxic nature causes illness sometimes capable of manifesting on physical levels. Most people these days realize that a mind can poison a body, but few know how or what might be done to prevent this. Conversely, a body in a state of chemical toxemia can affect the mind by damaging the brain so badly that the mind cannot work through it properly, so a vicious circle is set up, usually with serious results.

Do not fall into the simple trap of supposing there are "clean" thoughts and "dirty" ones and that we should think nothing but the former while we resist the latter. It is not the subject of any thought which is clean or dirty. Such designations result entirely from what you do with them in your own mind. You can think of anything you like, providing you put your thinking through an efficient process for distributing thoughts properly. The Tree of Life should show you how to do this. Whatever cannot be allocated to any of the Spheres through appropriate Paths should be decently excreted through the "other end of the Abyss" and thus effectively "earthed" so that it may be converted into other forms of consciousness in due course.

Jesus once put it that it was not what went into a mouth that defiled anyone, but what came out of it. He said: "Whatever goes in by the mouth passes into the stomach and so is discharged into the drain. But what comes out of the mouth has its origins in the heart, and that is what defiles a man. Wicked thoughts, murder, adultery, fornication, theft, perjury, slander—these all proceed from the heart and defile a man." In other words, do not allow out of your mouth whatever should exit by the anus. In terms of the Tree of Life, never regurgitate from the Abyss partly digested fragments of inner supplies. Keep pushing them along their proper line of descent until the "good" bits are placed through the Paths at suitable Spheres, and the "bad" bits emerge excrementally from your opposite "inner end" just before they materialize at Malkuth.

An old symbol of purity arising from putrescence was the lily on the dunghill metaphor. This was developed in Rosicrucian symbology from the fact that the best roses flowered from well-manured ground, and the unpleasant smell of the dung was transformed into the fragrance of the rose itself. So if you wanted your soul to be as sweet and beautiful as a rose, then you would have to bury the spiritual equivalent of your own dung around your roots and start the transformation from there. The symbology went into Alchemy also, where the miraculous Stone began to develop from the "filthy fluid" which eventually became the Elixir of Life after a prolonged series of elaborate purifications. In fact almost the whole concept of Alchemy depended on the theme of one purgation after another until perfection was reached, and a great deal of its processes were concerned with preparations being subjected to slow heating in flasks buried in dung-heaps which kept them warm by the chemical decomposition.

There was a famous occasion on which the great Paracelsus began a lecture at a German university by uncovering a dish on which was an odorous heap of excrement which he then began to brandish around amongst the disgusted and insulted audience, who protested vehemently. Roaring back at them, Paraceluss raged that if they could not comprehend the significance and value of what he held on that plate they would never be fit to call themselves doctors of men or anything else. Further, he declaimed in his usual style, until they did understand something of what he was speaking about, he was not prepared to continue the lecture, and forthwith left the room indignantly. We are not told whether he took the offensive dish with him or left it on the rostrum. He was some centuries before his time. Modern people would appreciate his point quickly enough, but how long has it taken to learn this? How long before we perfect a spiritual sewage system workable throughout our world?

As a practical start, it is suggested that you try combining a symbolic act of spiritual excretion with an actual performance of physical evacuation. This may be a startling or unusual idea for you to cope with, but it is quite a workable one. There is nothing particularly difficult about it. Its fundamental concept means that you have to combine your efforts of inner excretions with your outer ones. That is to say at the same time you use a physical toilet, concentrate on whatever you need to evacuate from your spiritual system and try to feel the two motions leaving your body and soul coincidentally. You will be surprised at the sense of relief this brings once you learn how to accomplish it.

What you have to learn, however, is to *separate actual ideas from their effects on yourself.* An idea by itself does neither good nor harm to you. What causes either of those effects is your absorption of and reactions with them. That is what you should be trying to control by means of this exercise. It is possible to have both from the same idea, and then you need to retain the good effect and reject the bad. So you have to distinguish between them consciously, absorb only the beneficial constituents into your system, then excrete the residue for conversion to useful inner fertilizer by powers beyond your ability to control. Just as you are sending your physical excrement along a sewer at the other end of which it will reach a sewage farm or similar facility which converts it back to valuable chemical products, so you should send your spiritual equivalent along an inner line which leads back to points where it may be treated appropriately for re-cycling through other channels of consciousness.

For example, say you have some particular item in your life which is causing you deep inner resentments, fears, or anything your commonsense alone should tell you is beginning to poison your spiritual system. What you need to excrete is the *results of this effect on you*. You should say something like: "I must get this harmful material out of my system as soon as I can, otherwise it will only poison me still more without altering the actuality in the least. So get out of my inner system and stop having such a bad effect on me." (Here you can identify and name whatever it may be while you make both mental and muscular efforts at expulsion.) "Out you go! Out! Out!"

Suppose it should be a person connected with your problems of inner elimination. You have to see at the start that it cannot be the person himself causing the difficulty, but your own reactions with whatever he may have said, done, or been, to result in that reaction on your part. Therefore you must reorganize your reactions. Those *are* within your control and it is better to alter them than to continue to direct resentments, hatreds, or other disruptive currents of consciousness against *your own ideas of that person* which do nothing except damage your spiritual system. So what you really have to eliminate are actually your own conceptions and feelings of how such a person's behavior or presentation of himself has affected you. More specifically, you need to eliminate the bad side and retain the good where this might be possible.

Therefore you might as well collect your thoughts in a reasonable manner concerning whatever it may be, and having run your mind round its perimeter, so to speak, reduce it to fundamentals this way: "If there is any good in so-and-so for me, I need to sustain it in me somewhere. Whatever may be bad I ought to be rid of before it does my system any harm. So here goes. Anything good—stay. Anything bad—out." Leave it to the "God-in-you" to know what should remain and what must be rejected with the refuse. If you cannot make any clear decisions for yourself, don't be too proud or independent to ask for inner help from any entity or essence willing to help you who stands above your spiritual station in life. That is what they are there for, to approach and ask when you have come to the end of your own resources.

You could ritualize this down to the last detail if you feel so inclined, but this might not help very greatly. What matters is the depth and sincerity of your efforts, plus the way you put everything into your own words, providing you mean them from the bottom of your soul. Perhaps you might notice that in any account of the miracles attributed to Jesus, he never went through any very elaborate rituals, but more less said: "Let such and such be the intention of God to happen here and now." That was all, and then the happening followed. We, being only very much lesser parts of God may not be able to make things happen quite so quickly, but at least we might learn something from the example set.

This is just a first step, yet an important one, in correlating body behaviors with the divine designer of that body. There are other methods of ritualizing evacuation activities, but this method of "beginning at the bottom" (literally) is a very practical one. If you are imaginatively literate, you could try to write down in the clearest possible language all the horrid things in yourself you would like to be rid of, check this over carefully, then burn it ceremonially, and finish by flushing the ashes down the toilet. Always remember, though, that any ritual without the fullest inclusion of consciousness allied to intent is no more than aimless antics.

Questions

1. Can you relate dung with divinity? If so, how?
2. Why was hanging once regarded as a most shameful death?
3. Why was death by bloodshed once considered a noble death?
4. How does the Abyss connect with an excretory function of divinity?
5. Describe the divine excretory cycle of action.
6. How should you dispose of mental and spiritual matter that is equivalent to physical excreta?
7. Work out and describe your own system for disposal of "spiritual sewage."
8. Describe the Rosicrucian analogy of the rose and the dung-heap.
9. Choose the eight most important sentence in this chapter.
10. Explain the necessity for corruption in creation.

·21·

Tree Thinking

Let us return to the Tree again. This time we shall try to think out some of the deeper purposes behind it, and what we are actually going to do with the thing once we get it deeply enough into our consciousness. In other words, let's consider its practical values and the solid reasons why we should spend a considerable proportion of our time and efforts in grasping its principles and applications. We already know a great deal about its symbolism and the ideology behind its construction, and we should be aware that it is a schematic layout of relationships between man and God. But can there be anything more to it?

Yes, there can. Plenty. But here we shall principally concern ourselves with the usage of the Tree as a systematic processor of consciousness, that is to say, as a kind of basic computer through which intelligent humans can process *all* their workings with consciousness in order to become more aligned with the Great Consciousness behind life itself. The design of the Tree does not merely suggest *what* we ought to think of but, maybe more importantly, *how* we should think and arrange the patterns of our perceptions in life.

As usual, start at the bottom, this time by considering the thought systems of animals and lesser evolved humans. It is doubtful if we could really call these systems at all, they are so random and haphazard in nature. The vast majority of their mental workings are connected with what might be called the economics of existence; security, sustenance, and sex. Their major aims of life are seldom much above maintaining a material standard of living as advantageously as possible. As William Booth of the Salvation Army once remarked: "It's no use talking about God to a starving man. Fill his stomach first and his soul later." Conversely, one might point at ascetics intentionally depriving themselves of food and acquisitions in order to *increase* their awareness of that deity. The main difference between the two instances is that the type of human Booth dealt with seldom had any particular system of thinking, and voluntary ascetics have usually constructed very complicated ones.

Unevolved humans do not so much think as react. All living matter reacts according to its inbuilt specifications. Actual thought, however, is a process of consciousness involving the individual attention of some creature which has developed the ability through evolution. Thought is not consciousness itself, but results from consciousness being *put through a process intentionally* by the originator of that intention. Therefore when Descartes made his famous "I think, therefore I am" axiom, he was fundamentally wrong. What he should have said was: "I am conscious, therefore I exist. I think, therefore I can use my consciousness." It is perfectly possible to be conscious without thoughts at all. To quote another famous saying by an anonymous farmer, "Sometimes Ah sets and thinks, an' other times Ah jest sets." By inference, he had outlined the process of thought as being an expenditure of effort and willpower.

Probably the majority of humans do not think according to any particular system other than whatever they have had to invent for themselves by experience. They process their consciousness by subjecting it to several familiar criteria, then drop it casually into the depths of their minds where it tends to associate more or less with others of its type depending on main characteristics. On the whole this seems to serve well enough for an average human to get through a commonplace life without too many complications. In more recent generations there has been an increasing need for civilized humans to develop a "specialized" section of their minds in which are stored all thinkings concerned with whatever skills or abilities they employ for making a living or earning a place in their section of human society. They have perforce had to organize this part of their mentality according to some system, quite often the sequence in which data was imparted, cross-referenced by a later learned "order of importance" list. Very often this only applies to the specialist, which explains how some academics may shine so brilliantly in their subjects or fields, yet be so disorganized otherwise. Their systems are not geared to cover wider areas of consciousness.

This happens because so comparatively few humans are trained to think and cope with their consciousness according to *any* kind of system. They may be supplied with information and data from a great variety of angles, but they are seldom shown how to sort it all out, classify it in relation to themselves and others, assess and put priorities in their proper places, then make everything into a connected pattern which will advance their purpose in life and help them realize this for themselves. This is precisely what the Tree system of thought processing is designed to do.

If you take a quick glance at any representative section of humans, you will have to admit that the most advanced among them are always those who are able to process their consciousness most effectively in some systematic manner, usually designed with specific aims in view. These may not be *good* aims at all, and are often deplorable, but the basic fact remains that it is system and order which ultimately conditions human consciousness in any particular direction. Be very careful here not to confuse system with "smartness" or "sharpness" in a social or business sense. It is possible to find people who may seem very unassuming and non-committal on the outside, who show very few external traces of the spiritual system they have built up to process their inner awareness. On the other hand, those with inadequate or barely existent thinking systems usually indicate this obviously enough after a minimum of casual contact.

How do people set up any sort of a thinking system in the first place? They begin by establishing at least a minimum number of standards connected with themselves against which to measure or gauge thoughts, concepts, or workings of consciousness engendered or encountered in the course of existence. For instance, an infant will set up a standard marked "Mummy-Good-Me" at one end, and "Mummy-Bad-Me" at the other. By experience that child will soon discover what use of consciousness will result in pleasure relationships with its female parent, and what is most likely to produce painful or unwanted ones. By the constant use of calculations against their self-set standards, humans learn the use and ultimately the control of consciousness resulting in rational thinking. This much should be built into the genetics of most humans.

From such a simple start all the magic our minds will ever encompass grows and develops. Whatever follows is but a matter of cultivation and patient attention. Our most adult frameworks of thought are only extensions and improvements on those we set up in early childhood. Any kind of thought-training system depends on the careful selection of criteria, and the use of those to correlate all the consciousness involved so as to achieve an intended end-effect. For example, in business training, the end-effect is profit, and all the criteria are set up with this in view. Trainees are instructed how to think and act in the most efficient and economical way *having regard to contemporary conditions in life* so as to manipulate men, women, and money for the purpose of producing profit which is then re-cycled through the national or world economy, leaving a handsome percentage with the manipulator. Again the basis of the entire affair is the arrangement, relationship, and usage of the criteria selected.

With religious training, exactly the same fundamentals are followed, except that the criteria are entirely different. Once more trainees are told to accept specific criteria of doctrines and dogmas, then limit their thinking within the layout set before them. What is so often uncertain in this field is the goal or purpose of the process. Many are so vague and unclear that they are scarcely understandable. A Christian would say "salvation," with its implications of inherent human wickedness and necessity for redeeming a debt to deity because of human disobedience to an originally divine command. A Buddhist would say "Nirvana" or release from reincarnation and imprisonment by personality. Other faiths would have their own ideas of ultimate heavens, hells, or spiritual destinations beyond limits of earth life.

In the case of the life Tree, its criteria are set up in the clearest possible way linking the highest and lowest of living creation through fundamental principles of a universal kind by means of a simple mathematical arrangement. It was never meant to be either difficult or abstruse. Any complications or concealments were caused by its commentators, not its designers. All that was needed to grasp the concept behind it was a belief in some kind of a Supreme Consciousness, and a connection between that state of being and ours through a chain of graduated consciousness, ten stages which can be counted on the fingers. Everything else arises out of that by the exercise of thought and ingenuity.

There are several ways of counting the Spheres on the ten fingers. The most general one is from right to left, starting with Kether on the right thumb, Chockmah on the index finger, and so on, continuing from the little finger of the left hand at Tiphereth, and concluding with the left thumb at Malkuth. There are other combinations, of course, such as attributing the Spheres to a musical notation and striking the notes up the scale. The little fingers would then sound Malkuth and Kether, while the thumbs would hit Geburah and Tiphereth. There are no hard and fast rules, so you can invent your own if you like.

The general idea of processing consciousness through the criteria of our Tree starts with the standpoint that consciousness is a force-flow through *you*. It flows into you from other sources, and out of you again with the modifications you may have made to it. If you are able to make those modifications in accordance with the Tree pattern, you will be doing so in about the best way yet discovered by human experience. All you have to do is *put that consciousness through the Tree plan while it is in yourself.* This may sound like a long and involved process at first, and so it might seem from reading the description and trying its initial stages, but it is actually a very brief one when you get the idea and it takes no more time than any other thinking process, maybe much less. So don't be put off by fancied difficulties, but just follow how it is supposed to work.

First of all, which way do you want to circulate your energies, outwards towards other humans, or inwards towards your

Figure 2.10. Simple electric cell

Figure 2.11. Self as cell with Tree connecting inner and outer awareness

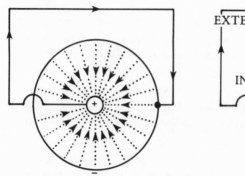

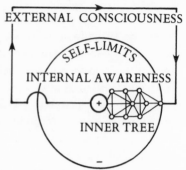

source of spirit? If you want to reach humans, *or the spirit intends to reach other humans through you,* then your consciousness has to be processed *down* the Tree from 0-10. If you mean to direct your attention towards the spirit-in-you, or others are trying to reach it through you, then you need to direct consciousness *up* the Tree from 10-0. You have to "switch" accordingly so that you mediate either towards God or Man.

Think of the simple electro-chemical battery cell you use for flashlights or small radios. It has a positive (plus) pole in its center, and its casing is negative (minus). When one is connected to the other via some conducting circuit, an electric current flows from plus to minus *outside* the cell, returning from minus to plus *inside* it (Figure 2.10) and so completing the cycle of energy. Now think of yourself as being a kind of cell like that with the "divine spark" at the center and your body as the outside casing. Figure this inner divinity as Kether, and the outer physical body as Malkuth (Figure 2.11). Instead of the conventional Spheres as a Tree, see them as ordered circular areas around your center as in Figure 2.12. Next, think of the Kether in yourself connecting with the Malkuth of the Trees of other living beings than yourself, and then through their Kethers back to your own Malkuth forming a circuit of consciousness (Figure 2.13). If you want to be very technical, you can think of the Spheres on your own inner Tree as being an ideal arrangement of molecules constituting your real spiritual nature.

Figure 2.12. Self-cell with Spheres considered as areas between Self-center and perimeter

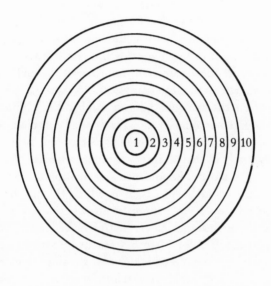

Figure 2.13. Self-cell connected to others through respective Trees

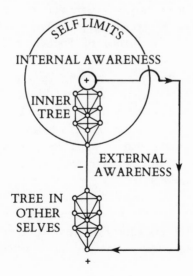

This of course would typify a fairly advanced sort of scheme by assuming that most other humans also have "Tree plans" in themselves for returning your consciousness to you, which we know quite well they don't. You generally get the stream back in a messy and mixed-up condition which you have to clarify as best you can by putting it through your own internal workings. If these are in good order, the stream will improve in the end, but if not, then it will emerge with more complications than when it went in. That is so often the way we confuse each other's thinking.

Say a given amount of thought-formed consciousness enters your area of awareness. Your immediate problem is how to cope with it analytically so that all its constituents are classified correctly in their orders of nature, importance and relation to your life Tree concepts. There could be pieces of it which fit any or all of the Spheres, and whatever you cannot fit elsewhere, you will have to dispose of via your internal Abyss. Let us make a color analogy by supposing that a full-color plate has reached your Malkuth. From there it is passed back to Yesod which absorbs all the silvery-yellow moon shades before going to Hod which takes out the orange, and Netzach which removes the green. Yellow vanishes at Tiphereth, red at Geburah, and blue at Chesed. This does not leave much, but whatever does not drop down the drain while crossing the Abyss goes to Binah which removes the dark shades, and Chockmah where the light shades vanish. So what is left? Only clarified consciousness represented by the brilliance of Kether, and this is "pushed through" into the unmanifest for re-issue elsewhere.

Now do you see something of the scheme? You let previously processed consciousness flow through your self-structure so that it encounters the Spheres of the Tree in their proper sequence. Each Sphere should extract whatever belongs to it, or the Abyss should engulf what is alien to your system for future excretion. Then, finally, the cleared and conditioned stream of consciousness should be released for re-use in Cosmos. You have been enriched by your stored supplies of mental material, and you have processed the consciousness which brought you these, so that it can be re-cycled beneficially. The active Spheres of your Tree have become criteria or selective standards of assessment which you have set up by means of hard meditative work, or ritual symbolism of psychodramatic art. Unless you have so built up the Sphres in your psyche and authorized them to act as you intend, they cannot possibly mean anything more than somebody else's words on paper or tape.

Remember that you presumably have *some* criteria already acting within you which you will have established before you ever heard of the Tree system. This means you have to persuade them to align with the Spheres as far as they can, or pass them on to the more efficient Sephirotic selection scheme as it takes up their work. This will happen naturally enough in most cases, but you may have a bit of trouble converting some of the "lower" sorts of criteria. For instance, the "What's in this for me?" selector which most humans set up rather early in life at the Hod position could take a lot of convincing before it will alter to: "How may I live honorably?" with its implication that probity is better than profit. You cannot reasonably expect your inner Tree to work perfectly the moment you make out its bare outlines in yourself, but as you carry out the needed construction through your mind and soul, you will find yourself relying more and more on the clarifying effect it has on your consciousness.

As an experiment, read this small piece of prose from an adventure story, and see if you can find all the Spheres in it. As you discover them, locate each on the Tree. They are not in order, and some may occur more than once.

"The blazing sun shone pitilessly on the crown of his bare head as he plodded painfully along. His whole world seemed empty of compassion. Nevertheless he determined to win through everything and emerge with at least the rags of his self-respect around him. If only he could see why this had befallen him, he vowed then and there he would never be caught in the same trap again. Staggering slightly with exhaustion, he steadied himself with an effort and tried to believe firmly in what he was thinking."

A solution will be given at the end of this lesson. See how closely it compares with yours. Try picking up a storybook or any literature you please, then read a chapter or so identifying words or whole ideas with Spheres, Paths, or anything else to do with the

Tree. It does not matter if you cannot find all the Spheres, just pick what you can out of the script and associate them as you are best able. This exercise can be quite a lot of fun.

By this time you should see the whole idea with complete clarity. Take the Tree concept as a complete set of criteria through which to process the whole of your consciousnsess whether incoming or outgoing. You could think of the Spheres as being ten specifications for a factory inspector to check the finished product against. If it passes those tests then it is worth sending on, but if not, then it must either return for further processing or be condemned as scrap for re-cycling. That is a normal part of modern manufacturing to prevent people from finding nothing but rubbish in the shops. If a firm has adopted good standards and adheres to them, then its products gain a favorable reputation among consumers and future sales are more or less assured. Once any firm gets a reputation for poor quality and substandard stuff, its sales fall off to an eventual point where it may be forced into bankruptcy. Everything depends on adopted standards and integrity.

The Tree concepts are not really stiff or forbidding standards at all, no more than any ordinary decent human being should have already accepted in principle if not in practice. All that may be peculiar to anyone is their sequence and relationship with each other. Let us take a quick run-through again while we consider them as test-selectors of incoming consciousness:

10. What is purely material about this and belongs entirely to the physical world? Deduct that quality and pass the rest back.

9. What is dreamlike or imaginative about it? Deduct that and pass the remainder back.

8. What is splendidly intellectual about it? Retain this here and pass the rest back.

7. What is triumphantly emotional about it? Retain this here and pass the rest back.

6. What is well-balanced and beautifully harmonious about it? Keep that quality here and pass the remainder along.

5. What is restrictive, defensive, disciplinary or severe about it? Retain that here and pass the rest back.

4. What is releasing, compassionate, permissive, kind or beneficial about this? Let this stay here and pass the rest on.

X. This is where anything unwanted or alien to you should be disposed of down the Abyss for reduction to excreta and subsequent expulsion from your system. Nothing but consciousness so purified should pass on.

3. What is understandable and clearly comprehensible about it? Keep that here and pass what is left on.

2. What is Wise about it in the sense that it should become part of your eternal experience? Let that residue stay here, and you should have left only:

1. A clarified and absolutely pure stream of consciousness fit to conceive anything in Cosmos, yet ready to pass into:

0. *Perfect Peace Profound.*

Of course you will find quite a lot of material with only a few alignments to the Spheres. Consciousness comes in all conditions, which again will depend a lot on your personal opinions and predilections. Some would classify a particular thing with one Sphere or Path, and another person would totally disagree and place it firmly elsewhere. Neither would be right or wrong, because both have a responsibility to locate whatever it was on the Tree wherever they firmly believe it should go. So don't worry if you can't place everything you encounter exactly on some Sphere or Path of your Tree. Bits of it will go one way, and other bits elsewhere until most of it aligns somewhere, and what you can't place anywhere else you could always shove down the Abyss, though it is a pity to void perfectly good material which might have been useful if you took the trouble to look properly.

A clever little "gimmick" you might find helpful while practicing selective exercises is to make or obtain a small Tree-glyph about an inch and a half in size (3.5 cm) in cardboard or metal, and stick it in the center of your forehead, or secure it there like a Hebrew phylactery with cord ties at the back of your head. Then you have to imagine your physical brain as a life Tree with Malkuth at the front taking in consciousness and processing it from one compartment to another until it comes out clear at the top of your

Figure 2.14. Spheres as a brain pyramid

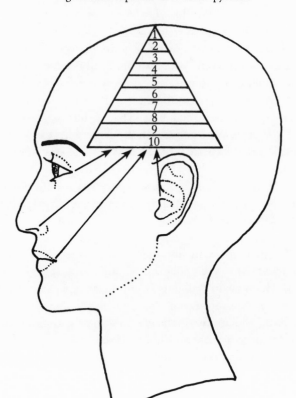

head. You could see your brain as pyramid-shaped inside your skull if you like, as in Figure 2.14. Here the Spheres are "layers" or steps one above the other. You may include the Abyss inlet and outlet if you want to, or simply take them for granted. A very nice meditation symbol can be made by constructing a twelve stepped pyramid with the Sphere-layers painted in proper colors, and the Abyss spaces separated from them by five wires at the top and three at the bottom as in Figure 2.15. These wires of course represent the Paths crossing the Abyss and its exit.

To reverse consciousness and project it towards others, or simply to "get a thought for yourself from God," start thinking from zero and begin fitting components from each Sphere as you work down towards Malkuth, something like this:

0. From *nil* with *will*
1. Be clear consciousness
2. Worked wisely
3. With Understanding (here cross the Abyss) and experience
4. Compassionately and generously
5. Yet with strict economy
6. So that all will balance beautifully
7. Let there be emotion and artistry to this
8. As well as intellectual Splendor
9. Be there a firm Foundation and basis for these beliefs
10. I express everything as an outcome of my origination.

What wonderful people we should be if all our expressed thoughts were preceded by such processing! We have often been told to think before speaking, and this is surely the best way of *how* to think. Relatively few humans go back nearly so far as Kether to

Figure 2.15. Spheres as a twelve-stepped pyramid, inclusive of Abyss inlet and outlet

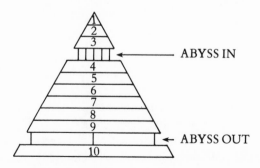

collect their thoughts. An enormous amount comes from no further than Yesod at its dream-fantasy level, or the next stage of prestige and power at the lowest levels of Hod-Netzach. Fortunately for the world, a fair number of humans have reached a point where they start thinking from Tiphereth with a sense of balance and proportion, but not quite so many can begin by combining Severity and Mercy equitably and practically. Fewer still are able to cross the Abyss by Knowledge of life and commence by drawing directly from the fund of Wisdom and Understanding which has accumulated behind human awareness ever since it began evolving from our genetic stock of subconscious collective experience resulting from every thought and conclusion which has passed through the mind of each human ever born on this earth. Maybe only the barest minority of mortals are able to make close contact with the source of pure consciousness at Kether and mediate this right through themselves down to an end-output, but this need not deter you from symbolizing the process on your own account by the principles suggested here.

We have been considering consciousness as being connected directly with the Spheres, but of course it extends from Sphere to Sphere via the Paths, and each Path has its particular type of thinking to associate with. This depends on the relationship between the end-Spheres involved. Such typification is very much a matter of opinion and decision on the part of the humans themselves. Some will accept arbitrary attributions regardless of inaccuracy, largely because this is easier than figuring things out for themselves. Others will make up their own without any adequate research or rationalization, then refuse to alter them when fresh illumination indicates that this should be done. There are many attitudes among orthodox occultists. Perhaps the best is to follow whichever Path system seems most reasonable and adaptive, but always be prepared to expand or exchange ideology if good and sufficient cause comes along. Inflexibility in mental and spiritual affairs is a sad fault, but so is inconsistency and demanding change for the sake of change alone. A balance must be struck between the two extremities of attitude and standpoints taken from there accordingly.

It is suggested that the pursuit of Paths should not be fixed with too much firmness until you are reasonably satisfied that laid down specifications suit your special type of mentality adequately. Once you are fairly positive about this, then firm them up and do not alter your concept of their essential natures without very sound reasons indeed which you are able to express with the utmost clarity. This does not mean that you should not add or subtract anything from a Path concept, or improve your ideas about it by changing the format of them without altering the fundamentals. Even here there must always be some very good reason to account for changes. For instance, if they are for experimental purposes, you should specify why or what you hope to learn from this before putting anything in action. *Never* do something "just for fun" or "to see what happens" in *any* realm of consciousness. That would be totally irresponsible, and against all the Tree stands for.

When you learn to treat the life-force of consciousness with as much (if nor more) respect and responsibility as an artist treats the media of his or her ability, plus regard all the symbols you have been entrusted with as the tools and instruments with which such media are shaped, then you will have learned the most magical of all lessons. Only life itself can teach you more from that point on, but the Tree is a great help in learning. If, by any chance you believe that the best criteria in life are the old Ten Commandments, these connect with the Tree very solidly, and you can attach them to the Spheres as follows:

1. Thou shalt have no other Gods before me.
2. Thou shalt not make to thyself any graven image.
3. Thou shalt not take the name of thy God in vain.
4. Honor thy father and thy mother.
5. Thou shalt not murder.
6. Keep holy the Sabbath.
7. Thou shalt not commit adultery.
8. Thou shalt not steal.
9. Thou shalt not bear false witness.
10. Thou shalt not covet thy neighbor's goods.

As you continue working with the Tree and taking it with you into every corner of your life, you will find more and more that it is controlling the course of your consciousness and leading you very quietly, though sometimes dramatically, towards increasingly higher levels of inner awareness. Meantime, the thing to do is go on patiently plodding the Paths and searching the Spheres along all the aspect of life you encounter. You will discover bits of the Tree everywhere you look. What did you find in the commonplace paragraph from an adventure tale a few pages back? Here is one solution:

"The blazing sun (6)/shone pitilessly (5)/on the crown (1)/of his bare head as he plodded painfully (5)/along. His whole world (10)/seemed empty (0)/of compassion (4)./Nevertheless he determined to win (7)/through everything and emerge with at least the rags of his self-respect (8)/around him. If only he could see why this should have befallen him (3)./He vowed then and there he would never be caught in the same trap again (2)./Staggering slightly with exhaustion, he steadied himself (6)/with an effort and tried to believe firmly (9)/in what he was thinking."

If you managed to work this out, try getting a set of colored pencils to match the Spheres and then underlining words or passages in any literature which suggest particular Spheres or Paths with the appropriate color. This is a very helpful exercise indeed because it encourages your mind to accept the workings of the Tree through every area of awareness. The more you realize that the Tree is not just a pretty picture to hang on your Temple wall, but a blueprint with which to structure your life, the better sort of life you can make for yourself on this Earth or anywhere else.

Questions

1. Distinguish between thinking and non-thinking awareness.
2. Trace the development of consciousness through the Spheres of the Tree of Life.
3. Relate your "internal Tree" to your "external Tree."
4. Make a diagram showing how your consciousness "filters" through the Tree from one level to another.

5. Write a brief descriptive paragraph covering the fundamental ideas of the Spheres from the top to the bottom of the Tree.

6. Write another paragraph reversing the process using different allusions from the bottom to the top of the Tree.

7. Read through anything you like aligning Tree connections with each separate idea encountered.

8. Show the Tree plan as a multi-productive assembly line.

9. Choose the ten most important sentences in this chapter.

10. What meaning does "Tree thinking" have for you?

· 22 ·

Rites and Rituals

The late Dion Fortune (Mrs. Pendry-Evans) once remarked: "All that remains to us of Ceremonial in the West is in the hands of the Church, the Masons, and the producers of cabaret. The Church evokes love of God, the Masons love of Man, and cabaret the love of Women." Presumably she was referring to public ceremonials, being forbidden by her initiation oath to speak of occult ones. In which case, she had forgotten or overlooked military ceremony which inculcates admiration for the qualities of alertness and coordination by the action of many men as one. She also ignored legal ceremony which arouses respect for the power and purpose behind the laws of any country, and plain social ceremony which aims at making life more pleasant for people who observe it among themselves as a common means of communication. Had she said that civilized conduct by human beings East or West depends on their ceremonies in any field of action, she might have been nearer the mark.

Most people seem to suppose that ceremony is a behavior of its own which requires robes, regalia, or some unusual accessories, possibly accompanied by appropriate music or elaborate gestures. This is not strictly true at all, and would only indicate the type of ceremony in progress. Ceremony in itself is an inner attitude which demands disciplined behavior of soul, mind and body for the sake of some particular purpose. Take the simplest ceremony, that of shaking hands. Mind and soul have to agree that there is reason to make the body assume a pleasant expression on its face, extend its right hand towards another human, and utter some stock phrase from the automatic supply of words stored in its brain. The whole action may be meaningless beyond the fact that the owner of such a body sees some need for putting it through these ceremonial procedures. Without ceremonialized methods of associating with each other, our lives in this world (or any other) would be most uncomfortable, to say the least.

So what makes a ceremony or ritual an "occult" one? Absolutely nothing whatever except its motivating intentions combined with its nature. For instance, some specific dance movement might not be "occult" at all if carried out by youngsters in a public hall, yet highly "occult" if performed by trained mystical workers in "temple" conditions of consciousness. *Any* form of ceremony may be considered "occult" when done by those with an ability to infuse magical meanings into it, and there is *no* form of ceremony which is automatically "occult" or magical in itself and would work regardless of who performed it and no matter how badly. *All* "magic" derives from the consciousness and the inner abilities of its practitioners linked with co-operators living in life-states other than the physical limits of this universe. Humans by themselves have not yet evolved to a point where they are able to mediate the tremendous energies of existence directly. We can only adapt attenuated proportions of them according to our individual or collective capacities, and many a fatal mistake has been made by overestimating competence and underestimating possibilities.

Almost every occult-minded person has sometimes felt irritated or amused by well meaning people who warn solemnly against having anything to do with magical ceremonial practices of which they themselves have no actual experience, nor even the least knowledge apart from lurid fiction and ecclesiastical exhortations against "dealing with the Devil." Asked to produce evidence of dangers from occultism, they either become vague and quote the Bible, refer to psychiatric cases mentioned in the popular press, or mention historical instances of very uncertain significance. Their irrational fears of the "unknown" may well be motivated by sexual or other problems, lurking in the depths of their psyches, but the unpalatable fact remains that these are not absolutely and entirely groundless.

Whether by ceremonial or different means, you can make contact with inner influences which might damage your mind and soul quite seriously if you are unable to cope with them properly. If you want to know what might happen, you have only to visit a mental hospital. Very few of those you will see there may have had anything to do with occult practices, but that is the sort of trouble you might expect. Nevertheless you have to understand this. If the possibility of such breakdowns was not already in those people they would not have succumbed to whatever induced them. Put another way, the "seeds of madness" were present in the first place, and all they needed was encouragement to grow and mature.

Ceremonials designed to awaken inner awareness and the arousal of "occult" abilities in human beings are particularly liable to stir up and bring out a lot of latent possibilities from minds and souls subjected to them. This is especially the case in effective initiation ceremonies. If these have really "hit the mark" with candidates, the normally hidden side of their nature is likely to confront them with considerable force and present problems which have to be tackled according to need. In competent circles of the Mysteries, a new initiate should be able to rely on his companions for help and guidance through difficult periods, even though they cannot take him safely through inner areas where he must rely entirely on his own "Light" for clarification of consciousness.

That is why such a heavy emphasis is laid on acquisition of *stability* and *balance* before practical magical ceremonies are normally advised or permitted. Again and again students and candidates are told to concentrate on these qualities until they are able to achieve at least a reasonable percentage of them with reliable accuracy. This may sound somewhat severe, but no reputable association of occultists *dare* include among their number of intimate initiates anyone who is spiritually unstable and therefore untrustworthy in character. That is why so much preparatory work is demanded over a prolonged period. The final test is usually by initiation itself. This will soon call out any inherent weaknesses or fault-liabilities which may then be rectified, or else the candidate is classified by result and placed where he or she may be of greatest value to all concerned, including themselves.

It is a frequent complaint of students who follow courses of instruction such as this one that "They never tell us anything practical, but just waffle on about the philosophy and ethics of the system until we get sick and tired of hearing it over and over again." There could perhaps be some degree of justification for this, though we have tried our best to avoid moralization or preaching so far as possible, while keeping to the strict basics of Western esoteric beliefs and practices. At the same time there has to be a code of ethics observed between any reasonable source of instruction and those applying to it for guidance. On the one hand, it has to be assumed that nothing will be advised or promulgated which is likely to injure the psyche of an average human, and on the other, that no use of any knowledge gained through following recommended practices will be intentionally applied against other souls. That is to say, we have to trust each other all we dare, and such is the limit within which we may work.

If you are operating by yourself and are determined to use ceremonial means of altering your consciousness so as to make contact with other than human sources of intelligence, you may well be wondering what is the best method of beginning, or how you could improve on your technique so as to get better results. There is only one sensible thing to do. Systemize ceremonial practices into their proper categories as we have been doing with the Tree of Life, and then carry out each by itself like a drill until it becomes natural, effective, and you achieve as much fluency with ritual procedures as you may have with reading, writing, or speaking. In other words, familiarize yourself with ceremony as you would with any other art or skill. Start with the simple things and keep working until the complicated ones become almost second nature.

Suppose we make an original start by allocating some definite type of ceremonial behavior to the Spheres of the Tree and then tackle each in turn methodically so that proficiency is gained

Figure 2.16. Ceremonial procedures associated with the Spheres of the Tree

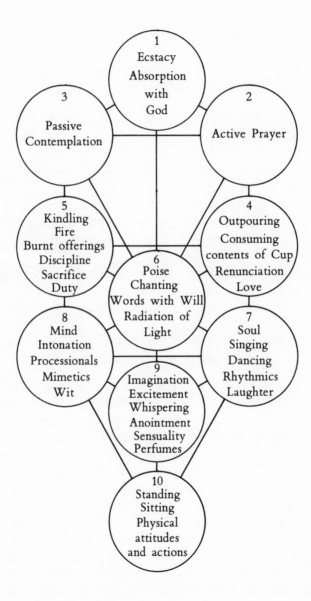

over a wide range of action. Our Tree could appear as Figure 2.16 (see page 329) and a brief glance should tell you why.

    10. Begins with purely bodily movements and positions, such as sitting, standing, relaxing, tensing, and kneeling.

    9. Brings in imagination and excitement on sensual levels. Whispering, anointing with perfumed oils, arranging symbols, and so forth.

    8. Involves mind, intonation of words with sense of their significance, processive movements and expressive mime. Also humor.

    7. Involves soul, singing, dancing, rhythmics, gaiety, laughter and improvisation.

    6. Poise and harmony, full chanting and "radiating light." Spiritual stability and directing action to deity with word and will.

    5. Kindling fire and burning offerings. Incense. Involves sense of strict discipline and duty.

    4. Pouring libations. Consuming contents of Cup. Outpouring of Love. Renunciation of lower nature.

    3. Contemplation. Approach to deity by acceptive consciousness.

    2. Prayer. Approach to deity by active consciousness.

    1. Ecstasy. Sense of union with deity.

    0. *Nil.*

There are a great many other details of ceremonial practice to consider than these, but this broad range of ritual practices should take you considerably further than a great many people who have been attempting the art without much guidance or encouragement from any source except their own uninstructed enthusiasm. Naturally, not every ritual will require the use of all possible ceremonial practices, and a few will demand only a minimum of them, but it is a good thing to have a working knowledge of and some practice with a reasonable number of the procedures you might expect to find in an average Temple or Lodge concerned with perpetuating the esoteric, psychodramatic symbolism of the Western Inner Tradition. Thus, even if you are outwardly a silent and physically motionless participator at a ritual gathering, you will be able to function in yourself as if you were acting in the full capacity of any officiant. In fact, that is precisely what you *should* do.

Regard ritual practice in the same light as a soldier sees drill, an athlete consider exercises, or a ballet dancer accepts daily rehearsals. It is necessary discipline for coordination of body-mind-soul consciousness with the objective of gaining skill and eventual expertise in the art. No one can ever hope to achieve any degree of proficiency with any art without devoting much time and effort to the practice of its elementary principles. This is true of ceremony as much as any other ability, and yet it is extraordinary how many people are unwilling or unprepared to offer more than minutes for learning the practice of ritual behavior. Somehow they expect to put on a robe, pick up a symbol, and sail to the top of the Tree in one swift swoop. It never seems to strike them how unreasonable or absurd their attitude might be. Few indeed are they who are willing to begin from the bottom and work steadily up the Tree like the Serpent of Wisdom, but they will arrive there a lot sooner than those who fall off the first branches and walk away in annoyance resolved never to return.

It is obviously impossible in the short space of these pages to teach every single salient point concerning ritual practice, but at least some valuable ideas about essentials might be imparted. For instance, if you were being shown the principles of military drill, the first thing you would have to learn is how to stand still in one place without fidgeting for increasingly prolonged periods. That is exactly how you should start. It sounds so easy until you try, if you are not accustomed to the action. Yes, the *action*. Keeping still is an act, for it means maintaining a constant stream of conscious command to all nerves and muscles in your body, and this has to come from your *active* mind which concentrates on the concept of obedient stillness and alertness. In military terms this is called being at *attention,* and that is a very good description of the state. It means holding body, mind and soul in a coordinated condition of attention and readiness for whatever may be coming next.

Your hands, however, are not normally held rigidly at your sides like a soldier, nor are your feet together at the heels with the toes pointing at an angle of forty-five degrees. Your feet are in line with each other but at a comfortable distance apart with your weight distributed evenly between both. Your hands should be held close to your breast, palm facing palm, finger and thumb tips pressing lightly together pointing upwards and slightly forwards. The hands are thus ready to be moved at any moment without catching in robes. When the right hand is in use by itself for any reason, the left is simply held flat to the breast pointing generally to the right shoulder. This keeps sleeves out of the way as much as possible. Make sure you always observe that rule.

There are two main inner attitudes to adopt when in the position of attention; full alert or just normal attentiveness. As you might realize, holding a standing body at maximum alertness for any prolonged period would constitute a strain beyond what might be termed "reasonable needs." So you should normally remain in a comfortable state of attention without an undue sense of strain or muscular tension, yet prepared to increase and sharpen this condition at a moment's notice to a point which is only short of activity by the smallest fraction. Try this. Bring yourself to the position of attention and concentrate your gaze on any small nearby object. Presently you are going to pick this up quickly, but not until you give yourself the order. Get ready to shoot your hand out on command. Hold yourself back with one part of your mind and keep preparing yourself with another. Eventually give the "Go" sharply and clearly either in your mind or audibly. Grab your objective and bring your hand back to the breast position. Did you feel how the mental mechanism worked? If so, then you know how to control your consciousness during ritual attention. In passing, it may be said that sudden moves like that are very rarely made during esoteric practice, but it is a good way to demonstrate the degree of attention called for during an average ceremony.

Practice switching from attention to alert until you can distinguish between both and call either into consciousness at your command. There should be no actual physical movement involved, except perhaps that you may experience a tensing and relaxation of muscles and nerves. When you have some idea of how this feels, you can go on to the "standing rest" position. There are many occasions when this is called for during periods when you are actually on your

feet, but may relax physically to some extent, maybe while listening
to music or someone speaking outside the context of the rite. It
amounts to the military "stand at ease" where both feet are apart
and hands clasped behind the back. Robed or gowned ceremonialists
do no more than make their stance comfortable and push their hands
into opposite sleeves across their bodies so that the meeting sleeves
hide their hands altogether. Hands are either clasped or holding
opposite forearms. Whether robed or not, get used to adopting this
position when standing in semi-attentive style. One special point in
connection with standing should be emphasized: *do not put all the
weight of your body on your heels.* If you continue doing this for any
length of time you are liable to faint. If anything, keep your body
forward, mostly balanced on the balls of your feet, and if you are
conscious of too much weight on your heels shift balance very
slightly away from them.

From standing, we come to sitting. In many temples, the
seating is deliberately made firm and unyielding so as to ensure an
alert and upright posture among participants and discourage
dreaminess or laxity of attention. For the same reason, normal
dining chairs usually have hard seats and no elbow rest. They are
specially designed for people with good table manners in the same
way that benches or similar seating is designed for those with good
temple manners. So if you do have a private temple, you might as
well install the same type of seating in case you are called on one
day to work with other esotericists and find it difficult to adjust
with their conditions. Ordinary dining chairs will serve admirably.
So would anything with a straight back or simply a stool. You are
supposed to sit upright on a seat so that your back does not touch
that of the chair and you are held by the support of your spinal
column alone.

When sitting, go straight to the front of your chair and
stand facing it with legs almost touching the seat, then turn on your
own axis deosil and sit by folding your body at the knees, at the
same time arranging your hands as required. When sitting in the
alert position ready to rise as needed, your hands should be flat on
your knees, palms down and fingers extended, arms close to sides. If
you are relaxing from strict attention you may sit with clasped

hands in your lap or just leave them there loose, but always before rising bring them back to the alert position on the knees. One point in particular: *do not fidget*. If you must move for some good reason (such as to blow your nose) then do so with an economy of movement and cease as soon as possible. Learn how to *sit still* unless you have to alter position, in which case, move in a ceremonial manner, that is, with precision and purpose. Few behaviors are worse than constant fidgeting. It indicates an undisciplined nature and a restless mind, neither of which are very welcome in well-conducted Western Mystery gatherings. Again if you have a temple of your own you may as well learn to behave in it as if it were filled with companions who were very conscious of all your actions therein.

Movements will vary a lot depending whether your temple is practicing Hermetic or Orphic rites. The former are a lot more restrained and disciplined than the latter, which includes dancing and music of a liberating nature. Since the Sangreal system leans more to the Hermetic and mystical side of the Tree than the Orphic, we will therefore consider movement from that angle. It needs to avoid any extravagant, unnecessary, or purposeless gestures. Every single move should have a maximum of meaning in a minimum (yet adequate) amount of motion. That is the criterion to aim for. Each move should be clear-cut, precise, neat, and entirely expressive of intention and motive behind it. There should be no doubt in the mind of an average intelligent observer why such a move was made in preference to staying still. Everything must point to some reason why the move had to be made because nothing else would serve to symbolize the spiritual action taking place. All movements have to be symbols in themselves which express exactly what is happening in inner dimensions of life which cannot be seen with physical sight. Thus they are mimetic signals visible to human eyes which may be followed by appropriate action of the soul or mind. That is their purpose, and without it they are entirely meaningless.

For instance, the circumambulatory movements of ritualists symbolize the circulation of consciousness forming into a focus of force from which to draw the dynamic energy needed to accomplish the purpose of the ceremony in progress. Besides pushing their bodies around a perimeter, participants should be moving their minds and souls in an equivalent fashion so that they become conscious of a stirring mobile current of inner energy which is beginning to gather up momentum and power that may later be diverted to drives connected with the reason or reasons behind that particular ritual. It might almost be thought of as a vast fly-wheel set in motion by the efforts of the participants, but it is really more like the initial formation of a nebula which will later condense in Cosmos and become a whole universe of its own. In any case it symbolizes the conversion of potential energy to kinetic for the performance of some purpose, and that is the way ritualists interpret it.

You should already have practiced putting some meaning into magical movements, but this is something which can scarcely be done too often. You can do it at any time at all in your ordinary work by making even your commonest movements mean something magical in your own mind. That should greatly facilitate any ritualized movements you make in your temple. Had you realized, for instance, that you might have to adjust the speed of your movements to allow for changes of consciousness connected with them? This is not a case of the-quickness-of-the-hand-deceiving-the-eye; it is the movement of the hand not exceeding the speed at which a following mind can think. That is an important considera-tion. There are also times when the mind is tempted to skip ahead of motion-meaning with some very familiar ritual, and this is where you have to enforce "magical discipline" and bring that mind firmly back to the pace of the symbolism being enacted. If you intend to control consciousness, this is a very necessary procedure. *Always keep to the rate and rhythm of the spiritual symbolism within any esoteric ritual.* To get "out of tune" with it would be like some member of an orchestra forgetfully playing a passage several pages ahead or from another work altogether.

Another stage up the Tree at concept 9, we enter the world of imagination and excitement which stimulates anticipation. Purists are apt to play this down, or otherwise belittle it as belonging to a state of "false glamor." One occult organization proudly announced that at last it had succeeded in getting rid of all glamor attached to its rituals, and henceforth it would guarantee completely glamorless ceremonies. Forthwith its membership declined to a few "old faithfuls" and masochistic mystics. Now the word "glamor" is a corruption of the old French *grammarie*, signifying a spell or enchantment usually to make someone or something appear more attractive than it might otherwise. Nevertheless a semblance or appearance of appeal to sensual feelings is something many people want and need in magic, and if they do not find it in any form they will seek elsewhere for satisfaction.

Magical and religious ritualism depends very greatly upon its appeal and charm over the physical senses in order to captivate the consciousness bound to mortal bodies and persuade this to serve the spiritual ends of higher and holier purposes. Magic does not deny or degrade sensuality or suppose it shameful in any way. Spirituality and sensuality are far more closely connected than any puritan would care to admit. Intelligent mystics have long understood the commonsense of using the thrills of bodily sensuality to induce an appreciation of spiritual life-spheres. Hence the so-called "glamor" of occult ritualism and allied religious practices. The fascinating smells, sounds, sights, touches, and tastes of physical things which focus attention on inner activities—where would magic be without them? What would esoteric ceremonialism be like if totally deprived of color, rustling robes, secretive whispers, thrilling music, stimulating scents and arousing contacts, all combined in the right proportions and atmosphere? Those are the stepping stones from which we rise to more advanced levels of life, but it would be foolish and futile to pretend they are needless or claim superiority over their sphere of influence unless we are indeed so evolved that we are beyond spiritual ceremonialism of any sort.

The study of sensual arousal in magical ritualism is a very special subject on its own, and has psychological ramifications running in all directions. Try this small experiment of whispering something into your own ear. Cup the left hand round your left ear close to the face, put the tips of the right hand fingers into the edge of the left palm and bring the slightly cupped palm of the right hand close to your lips. Then start whispering anything you like, especially something very intimate and personal to yourself. Do you not feel some kind of a strange thrill thereby?

In old times, a candidate was sometimes left alone in a room or chamber with marked echo-effects, and from concealed speaking-tubes or apertures he would be subjected to whispers from all angles which probed into the depths of his mind and soul arousing him to all kinds of reactions. He was expected to remain still throughout the barrage. It was an unforgettable experience of a character-altering nature, which was the objective of the exercise in the first place. Whispers are likely to have more effects on human beings than the most strident screams, and if loaded with magical meanings are apt to be potent almost beyond expectations.

Anointment with perfumed oil, especially by another person, is another way of arousing awareness. The combination of touch and scent strikes very deep and ancient chords from a human soul. It is perhaps strange how the sensation of contact or hovering hands seems to persist long after physical application has ceased. Somehow this particular ritual action conveys an experience of being someone very special and marked out for a privileged purpose. We have to remember that Sacred Kings were so anointed in former days, and there is bound to be genetic recognition in whoever has a single trace or contact with the Blood in themselves today. They may not know this consciously, but the "Blood-in-them" will remember and react to some extent. If this is being applied as a test, make sure the anointing oil is prepared according to the old biblical formula as specified in an earlier chapter. If not, it will not smell right or arouse the appropriate reactions.

This sensuous sphere in magical practice is usually the one where all the fears, forebodings and warnings are liable to claim justification. The influences here are extremely powerful, especially in the cases of very emotional people or those with strong sex drives. If these can be held in some kind of control by the overruling Will of an individual, there is no particular danger of overbalancing. But there can be a severe threat to sanity here among those unable to cope with the stimuli encountered at this point of progress. In our times, however, it is only fair to say that such a threat is no greater, and possibly a lot less than those presented by modern electronic discotheques plus those of drug abuse and similar dubious diversions offered to young folk for the sake of their money.

It is probable that the deadliest danger presented by magical practices is the encouragement of megalomania or delusions of personal power to a point where those so afflicted become a menace to themselves and all others around them. This is because they are totally unable to distinguish between the "I-Self" which belongs with deity alone, and the personal projection of it into this world which results in an ordinary human being. This can be a very fatal mistake—for the human end of the combination. An "overdose of God" is liable to be the most lethal of injections. Provided this is known, understood, and fully realized by the human concerned who is prepared to take all reasonable precautions against it, there is no very great danger, but otherwise there may be disastrous results. This was the reason why Roman emperors at their triumphal processions, when they were dressed as gods in their chariots, with the acclamations of multitudes reaching them from all around, were supposed to have a slave standing close behind them whose duty it was to whisper at intervals in their ears: "Remember man, thou art but mortal."

In our days, we may have to rely on relatives or friends cutting us down to size when megalomania threatens, but there is no absolute guarantee this would work if it were encouraged by the influences encountered in magical practices. Most of the risk, however, arises from remaining deliberately at this sensual level and refusing to rise above it towards more rational spheres of action. All dangers from one type of inner influence can usually be equated or balanced out by another of an opposite nature. Nevertheless it would be most unwise to underestimate the possibilities of character-distortion by those influences encountered through occult ceremonials. Megalomania on a minor scale can still make life very unpleasant, mostly for those affected by it from others. On the other hand, it is impossible to handle any type of energy in existence without some kind of hazard to life or health, as witness our energy supplies of electricity, gas, or nuclear power. The inner energies with which esoteric ceremonialism is designed to deal have their peculiar hazards mostly to mind and soul, but sometimes to bodies as well. Yet our spiritual civilization needs those energies quite as much as our material one in this world needs physical energy. So we may as well learn how to handle them as safely as we can.

Questions

1. How would you define an occult or esoteric ceremony?
2. What makes *any* human behavior ceremonious?
3. Analyze ritual activities into categories suitable for each Sphere on the Tree of Life.
4. What do you think is most essential for any ritual practice?
5. What sort of person do you think makes for a good ritualist?
6. What type of ritual feels most comfortable for you?
7. What sort of person should *not* practice ritual work?
8. Discuss, in general terms, the symbology of ritualism.
9. Choose the eight most important sentences in this chapter.
10. Argue both the pros and cons of ritual practice in a written paper of less than 500 words.

·23·

Rationale of Ritual

Here we have progressed up the Tree to the eighth Sphere where ritual magic is mostly concerned with the mind and its conceptual abilities. The accent in modern Western esoteric practice lies principally on mental workings and appeals to rationality, hence this Sphere deals with the wording of ritual scripts and the interpretations of symbols intended to process consciousness beyond the range of words altogether. Yet it must not be supposed that any ritual has to be confined to a single Sphere. Most rituals have elements that are drawn from many or all the Spheres. It is only a question of proportions and preponderances. Specific sections of ritual practice are only classified with definite Spheres for the sake of study and approach by those who take the Tree as a method of magical working with consciousness.

A prized possession of every serious Western occultist should be a good etymological dictionary which clearly defines the meanings of words, their origins and applications. A word by itself is no more than a noise or a scribble. To make any magic with it there has to be a compression of consciousness packed into its pronounciation, and the greater the compression or amount of meaning concentrated behind such a focal point, the more magical that word will become. There is no magic in any word per se, no matter how peculiar or arcane. There are simply words which make better containers of specialized consciousness than others, possibly in one human language only. The art of creating ritual scripts depends on knowledge of such words and combining them so as to create a format which will process and pattern the energy of any consciousness using them.

For this reason an effective ritual script commonly has an element of poetry in it, not so much in the sence of rhyme as of rhythm and an association of ideologies with their enlivening inner energies. Anyone following the script with attention and comprehension would have to push their consciousness through a pre-set series of stages calculated to produce specific effects not only with the thinker but also with whatever inner intelligences his or her mind might be linked with in consequence of such thoughts activating it. In other words, esoteric rituals should be so worded that correct thought-codes are evoked in the minds of performers for making contact with the class of spiritual consciousness sought. Unless those vital overtones of thought are actually aroused and allowed to circulate through the consciousness of a ritualist, no effective release of causative energy will be possible.

As you are probably aware, we think on several levels simultaneously, but for the purposes of simplification these can be considered as the Four Worlds of origination, creation, formation, and expression, or the process by which Deity creates Cosmos out of Its consciousness. In the case of a properly presented ritual script we encounter an expression of formed ideas directly. What we are expected to do with them is *experience* them so that we can reach the creative level behind their forms, and then the originative level behind that. This means using the words as metaphorical rungs for climbing to a heightened state of consciousness which is capable of originating fresh currents of conscious energy in whatever direction we will. First take the wording at face value and be aware *of* it. Then enter its meaning and be aware *with* it, after which convert that meaning back to the terms of its original awareness and be conscious *as* it. Put as simply as possible, if God thinks down to your level through the Four World process, then think back at Him, It, or

Her the other way and send your thought by return of the circuit via the expressive, formative, creative, and originative states of consciousness. That is the only logical and reasonable way of working.

This does not mean reducing thoughts to *nil*. It means returning them to origins, from which point they can be re-expressed in a multitude of ways but only in accordance with that particular origin. For example, the obvious origin of a Shield-idea lies in the principle of *protection*. That could apply in perhaps thousands of ways from insurance coverage to the shell of a beetle. The expression of any idea depends on the creative and formative stages behind it, and those can be altered at will, but the basic fundamental has to remain a constant. It has been a major concern of occult philosophy since it commenced to find the minimum combination of original ideas responsible for the whole of cosmic creation. Hence the Tree concept and the chief magical symbols, also the Masonic "Lost Word" legend and the "Unutterable Name of God." All are attempts to make contact with the basics of being by human consciousness.

So in the case of symbology with words arranged to constitute the mental working of any esoteric ritual procedure, these are not supposed to be taken at their literal value, but used as forms from which to extract the force of their meanings at original levels. This can scarcely be done unless each word and combination of words is properly comprehended and grasped. Hence the value of an etymological dictionary in the event of encountering dubious words. Never be in doubt of what words are intended to mean. Find out as certainly as you can and then run this back to its root-origins as far as you are able. Then you will be aiming your attention in the direction of the creative consciousness behind the concepts which make up our intelligent lives.

Working with words in this fashion is more of a cultivated art than a natural ability. It is very much akin to a sense of poetry appreciation in which words *and the way they are spoken* are only employed for the sake of the inner experiences they should invoke by impinging on the imagination of the listener. Poetry is not primarily meant to be read as words on paper, but spoken, heard, and reacted with. It is the same with ritual scripts. They are intended to be not only read, but *resonated with* at the same time. This is only possible if the reader has a good voice and is able to sing, chant, or intone the wording in an adequate way for raising the right responses both in himself and others present. It is scarcely possible in written material to illustrate this point, but it may be understood that intonation is a style of vocalizing one stage beyond that of ordinary speech much as a poem is generally declaimed, and full chanting is intonation at a stage nearer to singing than speech. Here at the Hod position we are concerned with the intonation style of uttering ritual scripts. No such script is read in an ordinary conversational tone except for purposes of practice or rehearsal, or to comment on passages.

Actual vocalization of rituals can really be learned only from those capable of the art themselves, and from listening to examples of recorded elocution and dramatic readings. It is granted that would-be ritualists may never achieve anything like the abilities of professional platform people, but at least they could improve on some of the sadly substandard performances afforded by many practitioners at present. It is not a pleasant experience in the least to sit through ill-pronounced prose and verse in harsh or irritating accents uttered with no feeling for significance or comprehension of nuance. You may argue that if no one but yourself is going to hear the words what would it matter, but this is not valid, firstly, because of pure principle which points out that you should take the trouble to do a thing properly for its own sake, and secondly, because there should be "inner ears" trying to recognize the ritual you are working. This might not be heard in the sense of a physical sound, but would certainly be "received" as a structured pattern of frequencies codified in accordance with recognized procedures of Western esoteric ritual. There is a "correct" pattern of working within a certain limit of standards which, though fairly broad, do have extremities. One should remain between these boundaries if recognition is sought at reasonable inner levels.

What this means in practical terms is that if you work rituals badly, clumsily, and with very poor performance, nothing of very great importance is likely to occur to you. This does not mean that a sincere cry for help in genuine need would ever be unheard despite how poorly it might be made from a technical viewpoint. It does mean, however, that a crude, uncultured, unstructured, and inefficient ritual production is no more likely to attract a very good class of inner intelligence than an equivalently bad show would bring in a cultured type of audience at a commerical theater. It all depends on the sort of audience you are aiming for, whether you are putting on a stage or a spiritual production. If whatever you are doing sends out signals into "inner space" which indicate that you are indeed trying to work a ritual production with care, effort, and as much skill as you can manage, then be assured that this will arouse some kind of response, even if you are unaware of this consciously. So take all the care you can to perfect your practices.

There is so much magic in words and their usage that it is virtually impossible to calculate its effect on human history alone. Words have evoked reactions from humans which have altered the destiny of nations in a matter of moments. A few words may wreck the final chances of humanity on this planet. If anyone doubts the power of words, let them consider those attributed to two people only: Karl Marx, and Jesus of Nazareth. Both left legacies of words which have changed the history of humanity *forever*. So too have others, of course. *You* must have uttered words at some time which have altered your life and fate somehow, even to very small degrees. We all do. This Hod concept of the Tree is where to learn control of words through ritual practice.

It is possible to raise consciousness a great deal higher than normal levels by the use of words in the right way. They are stimulative or depressive, healing or hurtful exactly like drugs or chemical alterants of body and mind. The entire science of word use (which may genuinely be called magical) has to be learned here, or at least the bare rudiments must be grasped. It is quite obviously impossible to impart all techniques in a "cover-all" course such as this one, but if it helps draw attention to the import and placement of words with ritual usage related to the Tree, that is of sufficient value at the moment.

Words are the song of the mind as song makes the words of the soul. Both are bodies of consciousness for the spirit which is behind life itself. All have to make harmony together in order for any magic made with them to work. There is so much to *do* with words, even if their field is not unlimited and there are higher forms of expression. Realizing their limitations and learning how to live and work with them is all part of the Tree-climbing process to encounter here. This is an art of its own with a mastery accomplished by relatively few people, but a level of proficiency is possible to all who tackle the task with care and commonsense.

Of first importance is knowing to the fullest sense what words really mean. Explore, examine, and *experience* the depths and implications of ritual words and phrases. Learn how to *ride* words as if they were carrying you somewhere important. Then learn how to *fly* them as if they were lifting you ever higher towards spheres where no words were needed. They are only *vehicles* for such a purpose. Utilities you have to employ in pursuit of inner realities. Until you can handle them properly, avoid those long, apparently meaningless "magic" words derived from ancient sources. For example, the so called "Barbarous Names of evocation." They are not words in the true sense at all, but pure sonic carriers of consciousness for which there *are* no proper words in *any* language used by humanity. One might call them cries, wails, noises, or anything else to indicate the "pre-speech" sounds made by babies to gain attention from their mothers or guardians for any primitive reason.

Those "Barbarous Names" were derived mostly from very early human attempts to gain attention from their Gods before literate and intelligent speech and writing was possible among humanity. Would you expect a grown, educated, and cultured human to continue uttering "baby-talk" all their adult lives? Of course not. So why go on addressing a presumably intelligent God in the equivalent thereof if you hope to attract Its attention? Yet again it has to be remembered that not *all* our sonic communication consists of intelligible words. We do make meaningful noises at each other in various ways. There are nice noises like the ones that lovers and friend utter, nasty noises like shouts and curses, warning sounds intended to help at a distance, and all kinds of wordless calls understood by most humans because of their tone or pitch. Ritual sonics have the same significance sometimes, and all have to be considered in their proper place as adjuncts of communicative intentions.

It might be supposed that if words should be transcended altogether in approaches to infinite intelligence, why should they be bothered with in the first place? This is purely because they are an integral part of human awareness at our present position in evolution, and must be taken into account whenever we attempt to direct our consciousness towards Divinity. Our Earth-entities are symbolized *expressively* by our bodies and their movements, *formatively* by our minds and their meanings which are conveyed by words, *creatively* by our souls and their significance shown here as music and allied arts, *originatively* as our Spirits, indicated as intentions and intelligence. None of these are here to be ignored or avoided. We are in this world to work through them and rise above them eventually. When we master movements we can afford to be still. When we have willed through words we can afford to be silent. It is the control-process itself which counts at every level of life. Usage of words through the disciplines of ritual practice is an essential part of Western esoteric training.

This starts, as might be expected, by listening to skilled ritualists reciting verbalized scripts and empathizing with them in silent response as closely as possible. The mind must not be allowed to wander away, but must follow the word-meaning into its depths as far as you can. Remember this is no more than you would do if you were glued to a TV set. If you cannot attend to the action and performance of an esoteric ritual somewhat more closely than you would be captivated by electronic entertainment, then you do not deserve to earn a claim as a member of the Western Mysteries. Your whole attention has to be focused into the meaning of the words and then pushed back through that meaning into perception of the purpose and "Will within" them. You must not only *listen* to them, but *live* them at the same time by making your active mind think in conformity with their purpose and pattern.

When you are intoning the words for yourself, you have to do the same thing in your mind while this is enhanced by the sonic vibrations of the utterances setting up a natural resonance in your nerves and sensory systems which should bring in your soul as well to much greater degree than if it reached you via your external ears. Practice listening to your intoned words with the *inside* of your ears if you can. This takes the "knack" of opening the Eustachian tubes connecting ears and throat by a muscular semi-swallowing contraction of the throat, and then humming slightly so that a slight hum becomes an absolute roar in the ears. Sometimes it helps to pinch the nostrils and try (gently) to expel breath through it while the lips are shut too. Clearing the ears in this way greatly increases the sensitivity of hearing afterwards, and it is an old hunter's trick while listening intently for the approach of quarry. If you are not familiar with it, this may take you some time to acquire, but it is an ability which could be very useful in time of need.

Now comes the vexing question of whether to learn ritual scripts by heart or not. There are two distinct schools of thought, each with a valid viewpoint. One says "yes" because of an inconvenience of working from ritual books all the time and relying so much on the written word. The other says "no," because things learned by rote tend to become automatic and do not captivate the mind which wanders away from over-familiar areas. With complicated rituals which have to be followed from the written script, there is a possibility of encountering something quite fresh and revealing on every occasion, whereas with well-known words often repeated, there are seldom many reactions of real interest. It is a case of familiarity breeding contempt. No hard and fast rules can be made here, and it must remain entirely a matter of personal choice which individuals or groups must decide from their own experience.

Crossing to the next Sphere of Netzach as considered from a ritualistic viewpoint, we encounter mostly "mood" music, singing, dancing, emotional contents and rhythmics. The singing does not have to have words which mean anything in particular, but must be evocative of definite feelings from the depths of despair or grief to the heights of joy and gladness. Color comes into play more than usual here and responses may be very sensual. The interpretation of this in ritualized terms is age-old in practice, but there is no reason why there should not be perfectly valid modern equivalents *providing* these really do evoke the right responses from those involved. If up-to-date rhythms and sonics only arouse feelings of antagonism or irritation among any participants, it is best to stay with the older, simpler, and more traditional frequencies.

Again, all rhythmics here must be in accordance with purpose. Most rhythms are natural and quite obvious to both practitioners and observers. For instance, one jumps for joy, laughs and claps hands. For sorrow, one assumes a bent position, weeps and wrings hands or hides face with hands. There should not be great difficulty ritualizing the contents of this Sphere, but a knowledge of choreography would help. Most of the old Temples had their special types of dancing, little enough of which is left to us now except maybe the dances of Bali Temples and the unique whirling Dervishes of Egypt and Lebanon. Our "sacred dances" of the West have descended to folk dancing, so there could be a lot of justification for work on reconstituting religious and magical dance methods as applied to modern practice.

The reasons for dancing in ritual procedures, of course, was to work up the appropriate emotional moods and enthusiasms for applying energies to whatever purpose the rite was consecrated. Dancing and singing evoked energies of the soul which could not possibly be expressed in words, yet which complemented the implications of whatever such words may have hinted at. Dancing is only gesture of a whole body to express perhaps more than could be conveyed by moving a part of that body such as a hand or feature. It also causes a greater flow of adrenaline, and other glandular stimulants around the sensitive systems of the body, and it increases breath and heart actions, metabolic functions, and every allied cause of body-soul partnership. To dance is to be conscious not *of* meaningful motion but *as* that motion. Or at least that is what it *should* be when rightly related with ritual.

There is an entire language of body movements in combination with matched music which is capable of expressing the gamut of human motives and intentions from one end to the other. Any confirmed balletomane would agree with this, yet how many esoteric ritualists have made a careful study of the subject and built their findings into their rites? Not nearly enough. So many seem to think it sufficient if they strip off all clothing and prance around with gay abandon. That may be amusing or just exhibitionistic, but it is *not* expressive of disciplined and purposeful behavior if it has neither structure nor evident intention in its performance. All these factors are necessary before mime and music has any magical meaning. This has to be as clear in this Sphere as words were in the last, and also transcended in the same way by consciousness cleared back to the level of origins.

Energetic dancing is obviously an activity belonging to the younger members of the tradition, but older ones need not feel deprived while they are able to watch, empathize, and sway their souls in keeping with the music. It is always consciousness that counts in the end. Dancing itself is not an end in any esoteric ritual, but a means thereto by inducing specific states of awareness calculated to assist production of such a purpose. That must never be forgotten, and the same is true of singing. Co-ordinated combinations of song and dance for definite ritual purposes is a very highly skilled art demanding an enormous amount of experience and knowledge to apply successfully. All amateurs of the art would be well advised to remain with very simple procedures.

Rising another Sphere, we come to Tiphereth, where poise, harmony, beauty and balance are all concentrated. This is the "normal" position of a working priest mediating God and man for a single spiritual reason. The main method here is a focused collection of previously described procedures, characterized and condensed into fine points of practice. The body posture is usually upright with stylized raised forearms. Ceremonial bows are made from the waist, and all movements tend to be economical and neat. Those close enough to notice might observe that a very slight vibratory tremor occurs in the hands and perhaps throughout the whole body as though the priestly person were "shimmering." In a way, this is true, because the mediation usually results in a distinct radiation of energy throughout the immediate atmosphere. Clairvoyants can perceive this plainly enough as the aura seems to expand and pulse with power.

Here the vocalization is by chanting. There are many modes of this, and probably the richest in Western practice is the Gregorian with organ accompaniment. Many recordings of this are easily available. To get the best effects, the script should be written to harmonize with the chant-rhythm. The general principles of chanting are based on rhythmic passages of measured monotone punctuated by rises and falls of pitch at intervals between them. To some degree this may be compared with the sonics of any motor when power demands are applied or removed from it. Its normal note drops when it slows due to extra demands, or rises when the load lessens.

That is precisely what chanting symbolizes in ritual practice. The regular running of the Spheres supplying spiritual energy to our state of existence varied by the demands our consciousness place on them. There is supposed to be a sort of sonic produced by the "motion of the Spheres" which amounts to the "keynote of the universe." Anyone able to attune themselves thereto would theoretically communicate directly with the consciousness of the Creator which thought everything and everyone in our Cosmos into existence. The East symbolizes this sonic as OM, and the West as AMEN (OMN). Either way it makes a chant-note to regulate ritual procedures with, and it is at this point of the Tree where the skill of chanting has to be learned.

Another stage up we come to Geburah, the fifth Sphere, where all ritual procedures have to do with Fire. In old times, burnt offerings were common, and customarily the uneatable parts of animal sacrifices such as the entrails and fat, were generally burned as the Gods share of the ceremonial feast. The rest was roasted and eaten by the offerers and their guests. In very early days the sacrificed Sacred King's body would have been cooked before being consumed at a communal meal held in his honor by those on whose behalf he had died. The baking of modern communion bread is the last link with this once Holy Fire.

Today our ritual fire practices are generally limited to offerings of incense and burnings of petitions on paper, plus lighting of candles and lamps dedicated to particular purposes. Quite a few folk customs connected with fire are kept up here and there in some countryside areas to this day, rolling a fire-wheel downhill at Midsummer, for instance, or the kindling of "need fire" with friction of flint and steel. This once had to be done by twins, then the fire was separated in two and the local cattle herds driven between them. There is a host of fascinating fire details which would amply repay research. Such study is possible in any good public library. The use of fire in modern times for Temple purposes, however, is mostly restricted to easily controllable forms such as candles, censers, and heavy pottery fire-pots. A fire extinguisher is a necessity and should be in easy reach despite careful concealment. Naked flames of some kind are essentials as symbols in Temples. Electric lights are no substitute for real fire, even if it is no more than a votive lamp or memorial candle. The genuine living flame remains our only possible link with an esoteric tradition connecting both past and future through our present consciousness.

In the far past when fire was vital to the survival of small tribes, it was realized that so long as a single glowing ember existed among them fires could always be kindled from it and their attempts at civilization would prosper. Should that last ember be fully extinguished, the tribe might perish also of cold and lack of protection against wild beasts. That is what fire meant for them. Now we see this as the Divine Spark within ourselves which is our immortality, and if we ever let it go out from lack of care that would be the end of us as individual beings also. The finest fuel to feed that flame with is faith. Every time you light a votive candle or lamp, think of that light within you which may only amount to the smallest spark, but so long as it is held within your secret heart, it will be sufficient to lead you through any life you will experience anywhere. With it, you will always live. Without it, you die forever. In fact it *is* you. So, take good care of yourself!

This is where you have to learn the value of discipline, duty, and sacrifice. Sometimes these are ritually represented by the symbol of a scourge which stood for the retribution you might expect if you deliberately broke the laws of life or dictates of divinity. Misuse of this symbol became a very wrong practice and something to be greatly deprecated. If an actual physical scourge is ever produced, there is no need to do more than touch it ceremonially while saying or thinking something to the effect that you acknowledge you may deserve corrective chastisement (not punishment) from God or Fate because of your wrong conduct and you hope this will reach you in some way you are able to bear with honor and a sense of fulfilment. It should surely be obvious to any rational mind that no amount of beating a human body could possibly correct the errors of a human soul. Never forget that man is never punished *for* his sins but *by* them. That makes all the difference.

From the fire sphere at Geburah, we go to the fluid Sphere at Chesed. This where all rituals with water or wine are worked. That includes consummation of the Cup's contents and the renunciation of attachments to Earth life. Renunciation is not exactly the same as sacrifice. The root of the word comes from *nuncius,* an envoy, and it signifies to send such an envoy back where he came from. There is an implication of "Returned with thanks and compliments," the polite and courteous refusal of an offered favor in such a way as not to cause offence. This roughly means that having advanced to this level of life at Chesed, a human could be entitled to other rounds of incarnation under quite good conditions and prospects. If that opportunity were accepted it would only be a matter of fair pay for fair work, but there is no *obligation* to accept it. Such an advanced soul has the option of *renouncing* it in favor of crossing the Abyss and reaching the supernals, but no one can renounce anything that they are not entitled to, so the word has to be used very carefully here. It is utterly meaningless renouncing any spiritual opportunity which has not yet been earned.

Most of the rituals here are concerned with libation (pouring an offering of wine or water to the earth), lavation (ceremonial washing of hands, face or feet), aspersion (casting of lustral water over the heads of the congregation), or potation (drinking consecrated contents of the Cup). Since oil is a fluid, anointment could also be considered in addition to filling of lamps. It is interesting to note that before lamps can be lit at the fire Sphere they must first be filled at the fluid Sphere. Mercy before Might, always.

The most precious fluid of all was (and still should be) blood. Its significance goes deeper and deeper into the psyche until it absorbs into the Absolute of All Itself. Though we symbolize it nowadays with wine, such a consecrated wine should be treated as if it really were the "Blessed Blood" within us. If we partake of sacramental wine purely as a memorial of Sacred Kings who died on our behalf in old times, it will be nothing more than a toast to their memories. If on the other hand we sip the same wine while believing in the "Blessed Blood" we hope to hold within us, that is what it must become for us. *Symbols are for us whatever we make of them for ourselves.* In the Christian version of the Mass, the wine is mentioned as the "Mystery of Faith," and that exactly describes it, but it is the faith of the partaker which makes it whatever he receives.

On the way down the Tree, this Sphere is ritually symbolized by baptism, a ceremonial entrance into Earth life from the waters of the unmanifest. One might say that humans swim into this world from an ocean of amniotic fluid. On the way back there is a ceremonial washing of the corpse before disposal which has now lost its meaning but was once said to wash away the stains of sin. Dirt has been a symbol of sin for a very long time now, and only the properly purified can hope to cross the Abyss safely and live peacefully with the Supernals.

Many are the ceremonies devised to symbolize crossing the Abyss. Legend said that it was like trying to walk along the edge of a sword, hence the Sword-Bridge concept, and the "strait and narrow" path. In a sense, the entrance to life in this world *is* a narrow passage, the seminal canal, and if we take the exit route of the "silver cord" connecting our physical bodies with their psychic equivalents, there is a "narrow way" again. If you have a physical Sword symbol, arrange it suitably somehow and align its point with the closest focus of your eyes, then shift your gaze *slowly* down the edge of the blade towards the hilt. If you feel your glance shifting towards either right or left, think to yourself: "That's me down the Abyss," go back to the point and start again. You would have to concentrate much more closely than that if this were the real thing, but it makes a bit of practice in advance, so to speak. If you can get a companion to focus a fine spotlight on the tip of the sword, and then draw it back along the edge of the blade while your attention follows it, that would not only make the exercise easier but give you some good symbology to work out as well.

The moment you cross the Abyss however, you will find yourself in a totally different world of consciousness. Although Sephirotic images and ideas have been attached to these Supernal Spheres, as they are called, they should really be without forms at all, and considered as forces—or energies—alone. Strictly speaking, they cannot be ritualized by any of the regular methods applying to the other Spheres below the Abyss since these are pure polarizations of consciousness by themselves; positive at Wisdom, Sphere 2, negative at Understanding, Sphere 3, and neutral at the Crown-Summit, Sphere 1. From a spiritual viewpoint this translates as Prayer at Sphere 2, Contemplation at Sphere 3, and Ultimate Union at Sphere 1.

You can only ritualize them by reaching and holding in yourself semblances of those specific states of consciousness. In the case of most humans, this may only be momentary conditions of simulated self-awareness suggestive of the actual condition aimed at, but even that will be of considerable help and should certainly be attempted again and again, because here we are dealing with the fount and origin of consciousness itself. Whatever happens here will be reflected right down the rest of the Tree and automatically affect your thinking with all the other Spheres. Once you get the Supernals into correct perspective, the rest will follow quite naturally. So do be prepared to do a lot of inner work with the Supernals.

It is suggested that when you want to try ritualizing this level of the Tree, you do so with an absolute minimum of externalizations. This can be done seated by slight changes of body posture alone. For Sphere 3 (Understanding) simply fold hands loosely on lap and bend head. For Sphere 2 (Wisdom) raise head level and bring up forearms with palms of hands to front level with shoulders (altar attitude). At Sphere 1 (Crown-Summit) hands crossed on breast and face upturned. Eyes kept closed throughout, of course.

When you are tackling Sphere 3, remember you will adopt the negative attitude of conscious awareness. Forget all the rubbish you may have heard about the need to avoid negative thoughts and how you should always "think positive." How could any positive exist without a corresponding negative to produce it? That would be like the famous Zen koan of one hand clapping, or trying to describe a rod with only one end. Negative thinking is no more evil or harmful than positive is good and beneficial. It is no more than another way of looking at the same thing, as it is said that an optimist sees a half full glass while a pessimist sees a half empty one. If negative sees the worst that can happen, and positive only the best while neutral transcends either and balances both, the results are usually a fair indication of what actually happens in the end. All three aspects of awareness in balance with each other are an absolute necessity for effective consciousness.

So you should never work onesidedly with any of the three Supernal Spheres or concentrate on one alone without considering the others. If you are going to start a negative stream going at Sphere 3, always proceed to 2 and then neutralize at 1 subsequently. Eventually you ought to use all three currents of consciousness simultaneously. To stay "thinking positively" is just as wrong as continuously invoking a negative aspect. Reality is always a right relationship between extremes on any level of existence. This means a properly balanced mediation of complementary opposites from the top of the Tree downwards.

What you should be looking for here is a perfect relationship between the masculine side of yourself and its feminine counterpart whichever physical sex you happen to be. Both of these have to be mediated by your central self which is neither and both combined as your identity. Symbolically, you locate your feminine portion at Sphere 3, its masculine partner at Sphere 2, while your pure Self-Spirit directs them together from Sphere 1. If there were such a thing as a perfect human being, it would be a completely balanced and poised combination of masculinity and feminity in the same individual with only the best characteristics of both. Try to imagine such a being if you can, produced from a combination of Spheres 1, 2, and 3, blending and projecting their power past the Abyss on the Tree of Life. Identify with the idea as much as you are able, while ritualizing through awareness alone.

Try it this way for a start. Disregarding your physical sex, consider yourself as female attempting to understand the meaning of life in relation to yourself. First, ask why there should be so much sorrow and suffering if not to enlarge and enhance experience leading to growth of soul and increase of Spirit among humanity. Think of the necessity for all the difficult and bitter things happening to humans which prove to be the only factors likely to make them improve themselves or drive them closer to Divinity because of desperation. Think on those lines for a little while, and above all try your utmost to Understand why anything of such a nature should occur in Cosmic circumstances.

Next switch to a masculine attitude. This time you are looking at life from a Wisdom angle. Realize that Wisdom alone will show you how to make the most of your life and convert its apparent failures into vital spiritual successes which will bring only the very best to everyone involved. So it is the inherent factor which helps any human being turn the adverse events of existence into any kind of advantage. Think of Wisdom as being a condensation of everything experienced by all your ancestors, implanted in your individual DNA if you like, but see it as that within yourself which is constantly trying to make the best out of the very worst. Though you may not call it so, this is your Sangreal.

Treat this quality as something enabling you to make sense and spiritual meaning out of life for your own good, and also for helping those other souls bound to you by Love in its largest interpretation.

Having got so far, go to the ultimate Sphere of 1, the Crown-Summit of existence. Here you see the whole of Life purely as an experience of everything it has to offer. Nothing is exclusively good or evil, because those are the only human points of view, but everything is necessary to create conditions causing changes of consciousness resulting in re-alignments of awareness which come closer and closer to an ultimate and intended state of Perfection throughout Creation. This experience is not inflicted on individuals in order to punish or reward them, but solely because it may be the one factor influencing them to alter themselves, bringing them nearer to whatever they were designed to be by Deity in the first place.

Realize from this that your life in particular is only what is likely to bring the best or worst out of you on your own responsibility, and in the end its credit or debit will be yours alone to bear towards another birth. You yourself are neither man nor woman but a human being struggling to transcend and balance both polarities and eventually become free from either as a better type of being altogether in a state of spiritual existence far beyond material boundaries.

From this loftiest point of the Tree, look downwards towards your physical projection and metaphorically say something like: "I am as I will be because I need to become my True Self as Deity decreed at my origin. Whether I have to be male or female matters not providing it is for that purpose. Although I may be rich, poor, healthy or sick, I realize this must be entirely dependent on how I react therewith for the sake of my soul-state. Each episode of a human lifetime is but a single stage in my total development and another step towards the Ultimate of Perfect Peace Profound." Try to see Life from an entirely dispassionate and detached viewpoint regarding everything in terms of a direct relationship between your highest possible level of Self and an All-inclusive Deity. Whatever enhances that relationship is of utmost importance, and whatever alienates or disturbs it is to be avoided or negated. Nothing else matters in the slightest. That, and that alone is the decisive factor of Life for the Real You.

If you can manage to process yourself through those attitudes with any sort of success, you should work them in combination with each other as well as consecutively. Descend the Tree by starting at Sphere 1, followed by 2 and 3. Go back to Sphere 1, then try splitting simultaneously into 2 and 3 while still keeping 1 as the balance between them. All this with no more than changes of conscious attitudes signified by the minimal ritualization of suggested physical postures. On the other side of the Abyss you are not supposed to possess a physical body at all, and it only comes into the picture as a concession to human nature.

Now we have reached the top of the Tree for the final time in these studies, and so here we hand over to you this entire contribution towards your further enlightenment through your own efforts at using it. Remember it is only a single strand of our tradition, though an extremely valuable and essential part of our esoteric integrity. It was earlier said that our Creator constructed Cosmos by means of numbers, letters, and sounds. Our past studies have shown how to create a rational Cosmos in your consciousness with numbers, so we still have letters, or the literary legacy of our tradition to deal with, and later sounds, or the purely spiritual and aspirational component of it. Like the Supernals, they all fit together and should be considered as a unity. If you are looking for a trinitarian comparison, numbers might be thought of as the Father, letters as the Son, and sounds as the Holy Spirit or Paraclete combining them into a Single Spirit of Deity.

So it would be a bad mistake to assume that Qabalah alone contains the answers to every question a human consciousness might demand of any Deity believed in with sincere faith backed up by rationality. There are other ways of approaching the problems of human existence and trying to solve those vital queries of spiritual survival as souls of this earth—and elsewhere. It seems unlikely that we shall ever solve them to the entire satisfaction of everyone forevermore, but at least we can make many meaningful steps ahead in such a direction. Shall we attempt some with the companion works of this present Sangreal Series? Do you remember that the very top of every Tree concludes with the Eternal Question—Eh na? Why not? Where do we go from here? So that is exactly what we shall say now. Not goodbye, but just—Eh na?

Questions

1. What are the essentials of a good ritual script?
2. Discuss the "magic of words."
3. How are words the "song of the mind?"
4. What is your favorite method of chanting and how do you practice it?
5. In what way (give examples) can you ritualize with the life-elements?
6. What do you understand by the term "Barbarous Names of evocation?"
7. Devise a different type of dance for each sphere on the Tree.
8. Design a mime-rite for any particular Path.
9. Choose the ten most important sentences in this chapter.
10. Do you feel there is a place for religious ritual practice in modern times? Discuss pros and cons of this in less than 1000 words. In this, set down your thoughts on the importance of ritual.

Valedictory

If you now suppose you know "all about Qabalah" that shows you have learned *nothing!* You have received enough of it to figure out its further developments for yourself, presuming you are willing to spend the time and effort. Providing you have its seeds deeply enough in your mind (not your brain), your Tree will continue to grow by itself. That is what Qabalah is all about. The original plan was not just to push a load of pre-formed, inflexible and unchanging doctrines into anyone's mind, but to impart ideas which would of themselves awaken that dormant awareness lying in the depths of a sincere soul awaiting a call to consciousness from other levels of life.

Remember that Qabalah deals with the Tree of *Life*, not death, which is merely considered as non-life. So long as you exist anywhere, you *live*, whether or not you have a physical body connecting you to this world. You can only die by totally ceasing to *be*. That is why it was said: "Our God is the God of the living, not the dead." Existence and life are synonymous to a Qabalist. Life moves, changes. Life develops, is never static even though it may *seem* motionless to our very limited senses. So, of course, Qabalah changes as human intelligence increases and extends its range into recondite areas of investigation. It is a presentation from the past that hopefully you will awaken *now* and reshape for passing on to the future. No one expects you to sit down and write learned books for the rest of your life. The fact that you absorbed what you received is enough to influence everything you communicate to other people who in turn will absorb something useful even if they are totally unconscious of it. That is how Qabalah propagates and is a *living* tradition.

You do not need to go around telling everyone about Qabalah, preaching or lecturing on the subject (you would probably bore them to tears in any case). The less you discuss it, except with those as interested as yourself, the better. Qabalah is something you should receive in one form yet give out in quite another form. At one time, among very strictly religious people, Qabalah was considered impious, and possibly blasphemous! This was because it dared to question the mysterious ways of God and the workings of His will. To these ascetics, God was to be worshipped and respected, or more to the point, feared. He was definitely not to be questioned nor His affairs investigated by impertinently curious humans. Yet, it is that very spirit of inquiry which has led to our present position as creatures of consciousness. Cynical suspicions apart, there need be no doubt of the debt we owe to the minds which questioned everything and quested everywhere in the search of Knowledge (Daath) needed to perfect our Tree of Life.

The principal value of Qabalah is that it serves as a training system which coordinates the higher faculties of man—mind, soul and spirit—into an effective focus for the force of creation itself. One might as well ask what is the value of teaching arithmetic or mathematics in school. The obvious answer is because it helps a young mind into those patterns which are best able to cope with the complex structures of human civilization built on a numerate basis. It would be very difficult to live in a modern, materialistic world without an understanding of numerical relationships. The same is true of a civilized spiritual world. Hence, Qabalah.

Qabalah, per se, is something much larger than any sectarian specialization. It is an innate and inherited faculty in many (but not all) human beings which enables them to make balanced and properly proportioned relationships with the spiritual fundamentals underlying the construction of our conscious universe. We in the West generally accept the formalized concept of it as arranged by Semitic scholars for the same reason that many accept scriptural doctrine and codes of conduct found in the Bible. Namely, it is definable, appeals to the mind and soul alike, is well organized, reliable in essence when comprehended, and most of all—inspiring!

Granted that a great deal of bad human behavior may be loosely blamed on the Bible, but upon careful examination it could be equally claimed that it was human misinterpretation of the biblical metaphors and allusions which was at the core of the problem. Qabalah pointed toward inner perceptions which the scriptwriters of the Bible dared not put down on parchment. Hence its confinement to oral transmission for so many centuries. The collective consciousness of mankind needed to evolve up to a point where it became able to accept something of what Qabalah had been camouflaging for so long. Even now, we are only just approaching that mark.

This "occult secrecy" and concealment concerning Qabalah was never practiced for its own sake by its initiates. Apart from the problems of human prejudice and persecution of an educated minority by barbaric masses of mankind, it was soon realized that trying to force cultured consciousness into unready, resentful, and incapable minds was not only stupid, but also unkind. In fact, it was positively cruel to those souls that actually suffered when confronted with such mentality. In a way, it would be like punishing a dog because it would not learn algebra. Before anything of the Qabalah could be imparted, it was necessary to insure that the ability to receive it existed. Early schools of Qabalah would not accept students before they were forty years old, and they had strict selection rules, sometimes depending on facial proportions and body-markings which were thought to indicate suitability.

Today, for example, the facts of radio and television are available even to idiot children. A picture with sounds appears on the screen of a big box and is controlled by simple movements of knobs. How such entertainment gets there is unimportant to viewers only concerned with their own reactions. Suppose an intelligent child asks to be told the whys and hows of the process? An explanation can be offered only in terms comprehensible to the child's current state of consciousness. An expert adult knows quite well that a specific level of education must be reached before the average mind is capable of grasping all the technicalities and intricacies of electronics. So he gives the child some encouragement by explaining what may be possible in elementary ways, while making it clear that there is much more to come later when the child grows old enough to understand.

That is exactly what took place with Qabalah. It is not "for the masses" nor, in its essence, was it ever so meant. At the same time, it is always useful to have an approximate working knowledge of its general principles. This much you should certainly have if you have sincerely applied yourself to these studies. Whether you want to go any further is entirely up to you. The tools have been placed in your hands, you have been told how to use them, building material lies freely all around you and how you combine them together with your consciousness must remain a matter for your own decision. Qabalah by itself is only a part, albeit an important one, of your "esoteric education," just as much as arithmetic and mathematics were once items of your early schooling. Look on it in that light.

The best education is a well-balanced one, and the complement to mathematics is literature in its widest sense. Those who excel at either are seldom equally good at both. If Qabalah is the math of esotericism, then legend and lore are its literature. Between them is built up that pure mysticism which constitutes the Spirit enlivening everything to do with either form of cultured consciousness. That is how the Western Inner Tradition should be cultivated and kept going from one generation to another, each adding its own contribution to the continuity of a heritage belonging to all of us who care to claim it.

That is probably why it was chiefly Western and non-Semitic Qabalists who stressed the major importance of the Tree of Life and connected up all other concepts to it in subsidiary fashion. Original Semitic specialists were much more concerned with complicated combinations of alphabetical letters, their shapes and configurations, nuances of interpretation, and all the rest of those procedures. Most of them had become so hypnotized by methodology for its own sake that they lost sight of once pure aims and intentions. They were convinced they were firmly on the track of the code by which the creator put Cosmos together with consciousness, and if ever they discovered how to use this for themselves, they too would "be as the Gods," determining their destiny according to their own wills.

This might be an all too familiar pattern with many of our modern scientists and technologists who are so busy taking life to pieces for the sake of their studies that none of them know or care enough about putting it together in order to live it with worthwhile aims. They become so deeply committed to the acceptance of a purely material universe as the be-all and end-all of existence, that they incapacitate themselves from any wider vision of human purpose or ultimation. In the past, we have suffered from so-called "spiritual" teachings which denigrated human bodies, reduced all their functions to "vile appetites of the flesh," twisted and warped ordinary instincts into "sinful urges" and all the rest of it, while advocating regimes of living as if we had no bodies to distract us from Divinity alone. In our present, we have exactly the opposite trends which encourage us to live as if we were nothing but intelligent animals entirely without surviving souls. Perhaps in the future we might find a balanced combination of both standpoints, showing us how to evolve sensibly from one state to the other so that we may eventually exist beyond bodily boundaries in altogether better conditions of living than our physical world has to offer.

It could be that our contemporary patterns of life in Western cultures have come about partly because we have reduced the science of mathematics and our sense of valuations to entirely materialistic levels and generally see no spiritual purpose behind them whatsoever. To us, they are only essential utilities in the fields of commerce, science, sport, and virtually every human activity except our struggle in the spheres of Spirit. Orthodox Christianity and most other faiths would consider it ridiculous, if not implicitly blasphemous, to worship by means of reciting a multiplication table, yet they will accept numbered recitations of prayers such as rosaries, litanies, psalms, and verses of hymns. A sincere Qabalist, however, would take an ordinary "Twice-times" table to signify:

Once WISDOM makes Wisdom $(2 \times 1 = 2)$
Twice WISDOM makes Mercy $(2 \times 2 = 4)$
Thrice WISDOM makes Harmony $(2 \times 3 = 6)$
Four WISDOMS make Glory $(2 \times 4 = 8)$
Five WISDOMS make The Kingdom $(2 \times 5 = 10)$
Six WISDOMS make Understanding $(2 \times 6 = 12)$ $(1 + 2 = 3)$
Seven WISDOMS make Severity $(2 \times 7 = 14)$ $(1 + 4 = 5)$
Eight WISDOMS make Victory $(2 \times 8 = 16)$ $(1 + 6 = 7)$
Nine WISDOMS make Foundation $(2 \times 9 = 18)$ $(1 + 8 = 9)$
Ten WISDOMS make Wisdom Plus $(2 \times 10 = 20)$ $(2 + 0 = 2)$

Once we accept that numerical symbols are a valid form of spiritual expression, they can be used for any type of religious reason imaginable. That is a very good use of Qabalistic principles.

Index

Sangreal Sodality

The word "Sangreal" may mean either "Royal Blood" (sang-real), or "Holy Grail" (san-greal). "Sodality" simply means "companionship." Within the Western Mystery Tradition the Holy Grail is not a "what," but a "who," and specifically it relates to anyone who willingly dedicates to Divinity his or her life energy in some way on behalf of humankind.

William G. Gray was passionately interested in the Western Mystery Tradition—he studied the mystical qabalah, the secrets of the Golden Dawn, and the western magical tradition. He was probably the best known qabalist in the world. Because he wanted to help people gather information and experience, he founded the Sangreal Sodality. People who share in his belief in the efficacy of the mystical traditions of the West gather here to share in their individual and collective Quest for an intimate working relationship with Divinity.

For more information about joining a Sangreal Sodality group in your area, send a self-addressed, stamped envelope to any of the following groups:

Sangreal Sodality
Holy Grail Chapel
(Warden: Marcia Pickands)
3 Burhans Place
Elsmere, NY 12054

Sangreal Sodality
(Warden: Marcus Claridge)
Awen
28 All Saints Rd.
Cheltenham
GLOS GL52 2EZ
Great Britain

Sangreal Sodality
Emerald Temple
(Warden: Marcia Pickands)
61 Central Ave.
Albany, NY 12206

Sangreal Sodality
(Warden: Bruce Cole)
P.O. Box 370181
Miami, FL 33137

Irmandade Cabalistica
(Warden: Pedro M. Braile)
Do Santo Graal
Rua Do Rosario 33
CEP 27500, Resende, RJ
Brasil

Sangreal Sodality
(Warden: Jacobus Swart)
P.O. Box 7762
Johannesburg 2000
Republic of South Africa

Wm. G. Gray was born in Middlesex, United Kingdom, at 2:10 P.M. on the 25th of March, 1913. Astrologically this gave him Sun in Aries, Moon in Scorpio, and Leo rising.

On his father's side, Bill Gray comes from a long line of churchmen. His grandfather was an Anglican rector and his heritage extended back to Archbishop Walter de Gray of York, England. His mother was Scottish-American and in midlife became a prominent astrologer. This was young Bill's first introduction to the occult, and through his mother he was able to meet many members of the Golden Dawn and other esoteric groups in England.

He joined the British Army as a communications technician and served several years in Egypt where he came into contact with additional material relevant to the *Inner Tradition*.

Shortly after his return home, England became involved in World War II and Bill's military outfit was immediately transferred to France, where he was in action until he was evacuated during the Dunkirk disaster. It was at this time that he swore to devote the remainder of his life to the Western spiritual way of life. After the holocaust, his health broke and he was discharged from the British forces.

For a short period, Wm. G. Gray was a member of the Society of the Inner Light. This organization was founded by Dion Fortune, the author of many books on the Western Tradition, and who had been of great help to him in his early occult studies. Bill Gray's own especial mentor was a Rosicrucian associate of "Papus," Dr. Gerami Encausse. Gray attributes his own psycho-spiritual development to this advanced initiate.

Wm. G. Gray did not begin writing until the late 1960s, when he wrote an essay on Qabalah purely for the benefit of a few close associates. They were so enthusiastic about the article that he was encouraged to expand it into what is now one of the classics of Qabalistic literature, *The Ladder of Lights*. When Israel Regardie was asked to read the manuscript, he was full of praise, and acclaimed it both unique and original. Since that time Wm. G. Gray has written many more books about Qabalah and the Western Tradition.

Wm. G. Gray was married to an ex-service woman who, like his mother, was a professional astrologer. He established himself as a chiropodist in the West Country of England and there devoted his free time to the study and advancement of the Western Inner Tradition. He died in 1992 on All Soul's Day and was followed two weeks later by his devoted wife, Bobbie.